MOVING FORWARD

MOVING FORWARD

A STORY OF HOPE, HARD WORK, AND THE PROMISE OF AMERICA

KARINE JEAN-PIERRE

HANOVER
SQUARE
PRESS

HANOVER
SQUARE
PRESS

Recycling programs
for this product may
not exist in your area.

ISBN-13: 978-1-335-91783-6

Moving Forward

Library of Congress Cataloging-in-Publication Data has been applied for.

HanoverSqPress.com
BookClubbish.com

Printed in U.S.A.

I dedicate this book to all of the people who have been told "no." I hope my story inspires and motivates you.

MOVING FORWARD

AUTHOR NOTE

I have changed many of the names of my family and friends as well as some details to protect their privacy.

TABLE OF CONTENTS

INTRODUCTION

Coming to America

I carry something special in my wallet. My cousin Jeannot Pierre gave it to me before my first day working for President Barack Obama in the White House. "Remember this?" he asked as he handed me an old snapshot, the corners creased, the colors washed-out.

I gasped. I had forgotten the trip our extended family—me and my cousins—had taken to Washington, DC, in the summer of 1982, just before I turned eight. There we were, seated on the base of the railing in front of the South Lawn of the White House, with the Truman Balcony in the far background. Jeannot gave me the photo to remind me of the pride my family takes in my success, of all of the people in the Haitian American community I carry on my shoulders.

I kept that photo with me from then on. Every day when I got money out of that wallet for a cup of tea or a bagel at the cafeteria in the Eisenhower Executive Office Building (EEOB) in Washington, DC, I couldn't help but glance at the image of that timid, skinny young girl sandwiched between my much older cousins. Back then, I was so shy that the nuns who taught kindergarten at my Catholic school called my mother in to say they were worried about me. "She doesn't play with other children," one said. "She just keeps to herself."

Over the years, I worked hard to overcome that. "You've made us ALL proud," Jeannot told me; code for how unlikely it was—inconceivable, really—that anyone from our family could get to the White House. My Haitian American father and mother, a New York City taxi driver and a home health care aide, didn't closely follow American politics. They were more likely to discuss the viciously oppressive dictator dynasty of François "Papa Doc" Duvalier and his son, Jean-Claude "Baby Doc" Duvalier, who ruled Haiti from 1957 to 1986, than any American president. Like many immigrants, they came here to find a better life for their children. I was proof that their struggle had been worth it.

As an openly gay woman of color, I have also had my own struggles entering the world of politics, which, even now, can feel like a boys' club. Despite the record number of women who ran (and won!) in the 2018 US midterm elections, women occupy less than 23 percent of the seats in Congress even though more than half of the population is women.

But when I was at the White House, I was usually too busy to think about how I had gone from being that meek schoolgirl with braids to the confident woman in a crisp tailored pantsuit who worked as Obama's regional political director in the Office of Political Affairs. I was the eyes and ears of the president of the United States in twelve northeastern states, from Maryland to Maine.

The Political Affairs wing has three offices in a corner on the first floor of the EEOB. The Eisenhower Executive Office Building is a beautiful historic building close to the White House's West Wing. (The West Wing is home to the Oval Office, where the US president works.) The first time I flashed my security-clearance badge to the sharply dressed marine standing guard at the double-door entrance and walked into the West Wing, I remember looking around and thinking, *This is so small. It looks so much bigger on TV.* (As a campaign operative for Senator John Edwards in 2007 and 2008, I binge-watched the NBC 1999 to 2006 TV series starring Martin Sheen as a fictional American president named Josiah Bartlet.) Still, it's hard not to be awed. I also felt a constant sense of responsibility, because I was a black woman working for the first black American president.

When you work at the White House, whether it's for a Democrat or a Republican, you have to put in twelve- to fifteen-hour workdays—or more. There's a reason why most people don't last a whole four-year term (and under President Donald Trump, turnover among his staff has occurred at a historically high rate). It's an absolute joy, but it is also a heavy lift. I liked to get there between 7:00 a.m. and 7:30 a.m. to prepare for our first meeting at nine o'clock, and I rarely left before 9:00 p.m. I would go home to my furnished basement apartment in a semi-sketchy part of town in northeast Washington. (I had taken a pay cut to work at the White House.) My place was cold, dark, and dreary, but I knew I didn't need more than a place to crash. A good night's sleep was never a given. There were plenty of times that my boss emailed me at 1:00 or 2:00 a.m. expecting me to get back to him ASAP. And I did.

In those days, I walked around with a BlackBerry phone (the preferred device for politicos) for White House work in one hand and, in the other hand, another BlackBerry, issued by the Democratic National Committee (DNC), for political work. Tax-payers did not pay for President Obama to do fundraisers or other political events, so having different phones for different pur-poses kept us honest and out of trouble. Because I was so intent on doing things the right way, I even carried a third phone—a personal one—in my pants pocket for calls and emails from my family and friends. This was not a requirement. I just wanted to be extra mindful. The stakes were too big to make a mistake.

The pressure was high, but I was proud of my role and wouldn't hide it. When phone number three rang and I would tell the person on the other end that I had just gotten off Air Force One with the president or I was about to make a trip with Vice President Joe Biden on Air Force Two, they would say, "Karine, listen to you. You don't even realize how cool your job is."

Getting involved in politics can be intimidating. If you weren't participating in debate club, or Young Democrats of America, or Model United Nations by the time you finished high school, I know it can feel like you have no chance in politics. That's why I'm writing this book. I am proof that that's not true. I was a late bloomer. You hear stories about folks whose passions and talents were already obvious by the time they were in kindergarten. I am not like that. I wasn't drawn to a career in politics until after graduate school.

Just how little did my family discuss American politics growing up? Meet Michael Dukakis. The first time I encountered politics was late on a Thursday night in July 1988. I was thirteen years old. My sister, Edwine, was six; and my brother Chris, four.

My siblings and I were curled up on my parents' queen-size bed watching the television that sat on the corner of my mother's wooden vanity dresser. When we lay back against the pillows, the TV was exactly at eye level. We were hoping to catch a rerun of the popular sitcom *A Different World* on NBC. The show was a cultural phenomenon, focusing on black students attending an HBCU (Historically Black Colleges and Universities). It was the first time I had learned about HBCUs. They made college look fun, and also normalized the black American college experience and traditions of black colleges. In addition, the show served as a

PSA on many hot-button issues at the time; for example, a young black woman dealing with AIDS. As a young black person, I was able to turn on the TV once a week and watch a group of black college students deal with life changes and also pursue their professional dreams. Alas, that night *A Different World* had been preempted for special coverage. That was okay with us. TV was a rare treat. *Any* show was better than no show at all.

As we settled in with my mother, I turned up the volume. Olympia Dukakis—the Oscar-winning, helmet-haired actress—appeared on the screen speaking emotionally and purposefully. "We all know that many Americans have come to this country with nothing, nothing but hope," she said. "Well, today, one of their sons stands before you with the opportunity to become president of the United States. Ladies and gentlemen, it is with honor, pride, and with love that I give you Michael S. Dukakis."

Before she could finish saying her first cousin's name, music that sounded like a symphony began blaring. The camera panned to what must have been thousands of people waving blue-and-white placards that read Dukakis/Bentsen in the air. I noticed that the chyron read "Democratic National Convention." From the back of the convention hall, a handsome dark-haired man surrounded by hordes of security started for the stage where Olympia Dukakis had just been standing. As he walked, he stopped to wave and shake hands, a big smile on his kind face. The pop song "America" by Neil Diamond was pounding with the lyrics "They're coming to America."

We were not usually still up past 10:00 p.m. on weekdays, but because it was summer, the rules were a bit more relaxed. We all jumped out of my parents' bed and danced with my mom until the song ended. We were so worked up we missed Michael Dukakis's entry onto the stage and then his speech. But it really didn't matter what Dukakis said as he accepted the Democratic nomination. The song—its lyrics a celebration of immigrants coming to America to start anew—had already sold us on him.

Dukakis himself was the child of Greek immigrants who settled in Massachusetts before the first World War. His father, Panos, went to Harvard Medical School and became a successful obstetrician. His son Michael Dukakis would go on to become the longest-serving governor of Massachusetts. Michael Dukakis was talking to us! Just like Olympia Dukakis said, he represented those of us who came to this country looking for opportunity.

For the three months until the general election in November, my siblings and I sang that song every time we saw him on TV. It was the first time that politics had hit me in a personal way. It was also then that I realized I was a Democrat. My mom would say, "I love Dukaka." No matter how many times I said, "Mummy, his name is 'Dukakis,'" she still called him "Dukaka." After a while, I gave up correcting her. She translated it the best way she could.

I will never forget the lead-up to the general presidential election in 1988 singing Neil Diamond's "America" and feeling hopeful about the future.

I still feel hopeful about the future and America. That is why I am writing this book.

Everyone's path into politics is different. Perhaps ever since turning off the TV in the early-morning hours of Wednesday, November 9, 2016—stunned that Donald Trump won enough electoral votes to become president—you have been filled with fear and anger and want to channel those emotions into change. Perhaps you are among the millions of people who have taken to the streets, called their senators and congressmen (and congresswomen), and voted in state and local elections since the bleak day in January 2017 when Donald Trump stood on the west front of the US Capitol, placed his hand on two Bibles—his own and Abraham Lincoln's—and uttered the thirty-five-word oath of office to become our forty-fifth president. I know how depressed I was listening to his inaugural address. Instead of a message of hope and a spirit of unity, which is what presidents usually try to do in these first moments when they have the nation's attention, Trump painted a dark picture, using words like *carnage* and *depletion* and *decay*.

Maybe you're worried about losing your health care. You're a Dreamer—or love one. You are frightened by the growing economic chasm between the billionaire class and the rest of us. You have family members who are disabled. Or maybe it just frosts your last nerve that President Trump has never released his taxes (bucking a norm followed voluntarily by every president after Richard Nixon).

Perhaps you are a parent like I am—my darling Soleil is the light of my life. I am raising her with my partner, longtime CNN national correspondent and anchor Suzanne Malveaux. You are terrified about the nation's direction and its new climate of cruelty. President Trump's January 27, 2017, executive order, the Muslim travel ban, led to protests at airports across the country. Lawyers and paralegals rushed to help stranded Muslim travelers—many who were professionals and students working and going to school in this country—pro bono. You feel sickened by reports of babies as young as three months old being separated from their parents at the Mexican border and of children being housed in fenced cages with no one to comfort them. You grieve when you think of Jakelin Caal Maquin, the seven-year-old Guatemalan girl who died on December 8, 2018, in the custody of the US Border Patrol. Or Felipe Alonzo-Gomez, the eight-year-old Guatemalan boy who died on Christmas Eve, 2018. Maybe you caught Brett Kavanaugh's unhinged and utterly partisan performance before the Senate Judiciary Committee on TV and didn't like what you saw but felt powerless when he became the newest justice to take the bench on the Supreme Court. Or you are tired of hearing President Trump bash the media, intentionally undermining one of this country's most important freedoms: the freedom of the press,

one of the six essential rights guaranteed to US citizens in the
first amendment to the Constitution.

You have all this pent-up anger, but politics is terra incognita
for you. Perhaps you've never voted and need friendly encouragement. Perhaps you are embarrassed to admit you don't know
how to register to vote. Maybe you keep up with the news but
don't understand the core differences between Democrats and
Republicans. Maybe you have a yearning to run for office yourself but need guidance.

I'm here to help. Everyone, regardless of their age, their socio-
economic status, their location, their education, has something
unique to offer. My goal in writing this book is not just to tell
my story, but to show that politics can be accessible to anyone
who wants to take part, no matter how or where they grew up
or how young or old they might be. In these pages, I will look
back on my life as a first-generation Haitian American and also
share with you what I have learned about politics. I want this to
be a handbook for people who may know nothing about politics.

I am different from a lot of the political operatives I know. Born
in Martinique to Haitian parents, I am a naturalized American
citizen, the legal process by which people who were not born in
the United States acquire full US citizenship. As I mentioned,
I never ran for student council in high school. I wasn't a Young
Democrat in college.

I am not like David Axelrod, who was the brains behind
Barack Obama's two successful presidential campaigns. Today he
is the founding director of the University of Chicago Institute
of Politics and a CNN senior political commentator. (He also
hosts a podcast called *The Axe Files*.) Nor is my background like
that of Donna Brazile, who managed Al Gore's 2000 presidential
campaign and twice stepped in to chair the DNC. I don't think
David or Donna had a donkey—the symbol of the Democratic
Party—stamped on their diapers as babies. But they were going

door-to-door canvassing by the time they were in elementary school and high school.

No, I am not from a connected family like the Kennedys. John F. Kennedy was the thirty-fifth US president. One brother, Robert F. Kennedy, served as US attorney general and as a senator from New York. Another brother, Ted, was a senator from Massachusetts. Their children and their children's children have been in Congress for decades. Look at one of the Democrats' rising stars: Massachusetts representative Joseph Patrick Kennedy III—the one with the red hair! It is a true political dynasty.

Today, as the chief public affairs officer for MoveOn.org; an MSNBC political analyst; a frequent op-ed contributor; and a lecturer at the School of International and Public Affairs (SIPA) at Columbia University, my alma mater, I work for the American people by speaking out for ordinary folks—people like my parents, who have struggled for every single dollar and who still lost the house they had paid for. Every time I see the red eye of the TV camera or grip the sides of a podium at a rally, I calm my nerves by reminding myself that I speak for the millions of people who do not have a voice in our society.

In this book, I will offer step-by-step advice for getting involved in progressive causes. Going beyond the usual tips— "Join a campaign! Find an issue!"—I will offer practical, specific advice. For instance: keep a political Rolodex. I have meticulously maintained mine since my first job in local New York City politics in 2004. I like to say that it is my most valuable possession—and I am not joking. Networking is *the* essential skill in politics. Almost every job I have gotten came from a contact I had from an earlier job. It's like my own version of the game Six Degrees of Kevin Bacon.

I will also explain the difference between policy and politics and how engagement in making society more just and fair doesn't always mean working with a politician. And every experience, including, in my case, being called upon to be a last-minute bridesmaid in the wedding of my then boss, can teach you something.

There has been a sea change in this country, making millions of people want to engage in politics as never before. In the age of Donald Trump, the need for all of us to participate has never been more crucial. Those who care for America should be—and are—filled with a historic sense of urgency. I want to harness this energy by offering a powerful tool to help people overcome their fears of jumping in and helping out. Together we will create positive change.

CHAPTER ONE

My Story

In the mid-1980s, when my mother had been in this country for a little less than a decade, she became fixated on winning the million-dollar sweepstakes from American Family Publishers. When we got the mailer announcing it, she couldn't stop talking about how Ed McMahon, Johnny Carson's sidekick on *The Tonight Show*, would be coming to our front door to give us our prize, like he did in the commercial she had seen on TV. My mother was so excited that even the responsible, serious-minded, mature kid in me believed that he would ring the doorbell one day soon. A preteen, I was in charge not only of holding on to the gold-colored envelope but also of making sure we filled out the form correctly so we were positioned to win.

At the time, my mother, a home health care aide for senior citizens in Far Rockaway, Queens, New York, was working for a friendly elderly woman in her nineties whom she called

"Mrs. M." We became close to her family. One Saturday afternoon, when we were visiting them at their posh Long Island home in Nassau County, my mother brought up the subject of the envelope. Mrs. M's grown son and daughter-in-law, both in their fifties at the time, gently told her not to get our hopes up about winning. The news crushed our get-rich-quick dream and left us feeling ashamed that we had been so naive.

The golden envelope was never spoken of again. I thought of this incident from time to time when I worked on the presidential campaigns of Barack Obama, John Edwards, and Martin O'Malley. Each gig brought me face-to-face with extraordinary people—smart, passionate, absolutely devoted to the progressive agenda for helping underserved communities. They were sympathetic and good-hearted. But I imagine that they came from families who would never have been so gullible and easy to exploit.

I always knew that I'm a bit different. I'm not sympathetic—I'm empathetic. I know firsthand the struggles of millions of Americans who work several jobs but somehow at the end of the month, always come up short. I know people who end up exploited because their English is too limited to grasp government forms, multipage legal contracts, mortgage applications, tax liens, medical bills, or even, yes, sweepstakes. The United States is a country of opportunities, but for many those opportunities are hard to come by. It can be a cold place where the odds are stacked a mile high against you, no matter how hard or at how many jobs you work.

I know what it's like for folks like that, because these are the folks I come from.

Let me start at the beginning of my family's story. I am a proud Haitian American, but I wasn't born in Haiti, nor, alas, do I speak much Haitian Creole, the language spoken in Haiti—a blend of French, Portuguese, Spanish, English, and West African languages. (Although my parents always spoke Creole to each other, they spoke English to their children.) Several years before I was born, my mother and father left Haiti and moved to another Caribbean island, Martinique, which is officially an overseas region of France. As a kid I would hear stories about how cool my father had been when he was younger—how he rode a motorcycle and courted my mother, nine years his junior. But those lighthearted days were already behind them when they moved to Martinique for better paying jobs.

They were trying to raise themselves out of poverty, but this move came at a cost. My mother and my father left my older brother, Donald, just seven months old, in the care of my grandmother in Haiti. Donald died a month or two later. My parents did not get the unbearable news that he had died for several months. They never shared the cause of Donald's death when I was growing up in their belief that secrecy is the best policy. When writing this book, I asked my mother again. She said that officially Donald died of a severe stomach virus. But she believes that it was because he was deliberately neglected.

About a year later, on August 13, 1974, I was born in Fort-de-France in Martinique.

This was not what my mother had in mind. My official due date was August 23. My mother had applied for a Canadian visa, and she planned to give birth in Canada—with the ultimate goal of getting to the United States. She had the crazy idea that she would hide her belly so immigration authorities wouldn't notice that she was pregnant. It's an indication of how desperate my parents were to improve their children's lots that she would have flown at that late stage in her pregnancy and risked trying to conceal it. But all that had to be scuttled when I arrived ten days early.

Another part of my mom's plan: a baby boy. After she lost Donald, it never occurred to her that she might have a girl. With money so tight, the scant prenatal care she could pay for did not include a sonogram. "What are you going to name her?" the hospital nurse asked as she handed newly swaddled me to my mom.

"I don't know," my mother answered. "I didn't think of any girl names."

"How about 'Karine'?" the nurse suggested, seizing on a popular name in Martinique at the time.

That's how I came to have my name. ("'Karine' is a blessed name," my mom used to say whenever she told this story. "It fits you.")

Scrapping the idea of Canada, my mother went back to her nanny job in Martinique almost immediately. She worked from 7:00 a.m. to 7:00 p.m. six days a week, leaving me in the care of a woman who lived three apartments down from my parents, on the same floor. One afternoon when I was four months old, my dad came to pick me up from the babysitter and saw that I was completely listless. He called my mom and my godmother and rushed me to the hospital emergency room, where the doctor checked me out and sent me home. This happened three separate times. The last time my dad took me home, I started having seizures. Terrified and not knowing what to do, he carried me to the babysitter's apartment, believing that was the safest place for me, and called my mother again. When she arrived, my mother found me slumped in a corner wearing nothing but a diaper soaked in diarrhea and urine. My mom snatched me up and ran back to the hospital. "I'm not leaving until you figure out what's wrong with my baby," she screamed. Finally, the doctor ran tests, which showed that I was dehydrated. I ended up staying in the hospital on an IV for a week and a half.

My mom has always said that if she hadn't been firm with the doctor, I would have died. It was a heartbreaking reminder of what had happened to Donald. I'm sure she thought that maybe if she had been in Haiti, she could have saved him, too.

After I got well, she quit her nanny job and stayed home to take care of me. Then, in their ongoing effort to advance themselves, my parents, who were dreamers, survivors, travelers, and risk takers, moved to Paris, France, when I was a year old. My mother got a job as a nanny and house cleaner to a family with a little boy. She was the main breadwinner as my father couldn't find a regular job. He worked sporadically as a handyman.

I learned to speak French, hung around with my mother, and later attended a Catholic school. I was too shy to make friends—at one point the nuns called my mother in to tell her how much of a loner I was—so my parents were my buddies. But it was a precarious life for the three of us. My mother and I would leave our apartment at 6:30 a.m. and not get home until 10:00 p.m., spending up to four hours a day commuting. Also, racism was omnipresent. Parisians groused to my mother right to her face about how the country was overrun with immigrants. The upside is that she was able to stockpile $10,000 to start a new life. When I was five, we left France to join older relatives who lived in the thriving Haitian community in Queens Village in New York City.

My first memories of America center on our home on 212th Street in Queens Village, a duplex with green-and-white aluminum siding that belonged to my aunt Mimose and my uncle Frantz, one of my mother's adopted sisters and her husband. My aunt was a tall dark-skinned woman with tiny dark moles around her eyes who peered out at the world from behind eyeglasses that sat at the tip of her nose and made her seem stern. But in fact, she was very affectionate. A registered nurse, she was married to Uncle Frantz. He was a dignified man who had been a lawyer in Haiti and who now worked as a Realtor. Older than my parents, they lived downstairs and rented the one-bedroom apartment upstairs to us. For years, I slept in the breakfast nook. The small doorless space was just big enough for my twin bed. Our tight quarters were even more confining for a kid, because I—and later my sister and brother—was never allowed in the living room. That was saved for company, and the furniture was laminated in plastic to protect it when the rare guest sat down. The only time I was allowed in the living room when there were no guests was to practice on our brown upright piano—which I despised.

At first, I spoke only French. While my aunts and uncles loved what they saw as my European flair and treated me as a special little girl, my cousins teased me for being different. I felt like an outsider even in my own family.

Even though we lived within earshot of Jamaica Avenue, a vibrant shopping street lined with an eclectic mix of mom-and-pop stores reflecting cultures from around the world, my childhood was 100 percent Haitian. Strict. Conservative. Roman Catholic. Crucifixes on the walls. Radio tuned to a Christian station. No TV. No sleepovers with school friends. No backchat. Out of respect, we would keep our eyes downcast when speaking with our parents or any adult. When we misbehaved, we were sent to kneel in the corner.

I had to take piano lessons with Uncle Frantz, who taught neighborhood kids in order to make extra money. Usually sweet and soft-spoken, my uncle called me Gâchette, French for *trigger*. My aunt actually came up with the nickname, which spoke of my inexhaustible energy. But he was a real taskmaster when it came to teaching me. Day and night, he would call upstairs to me, "I don't hear you practicing."

Besides a TV, reserved in those days for my parents' entertainment, our piano was our only luxury. My parents didn't care about whether or not we had the best clothes or shoes. I wore the same Strawberry Shortcake Halloween costume and carried the same orange Snoopy lunch box year after year. They cared only about making sure we were going to the best schools they could afford—certain that Catholic schools were superior to public. The first school I attended in Queens was a local parochial school called Saints Joachim and Anne, founded in 1924 and run by nuns. Our classes were held in a well-kept low-rise building made of blond brick. The school had a majority of African American and Afro-Caribbean students, with a smattering of white and Latinx students.

Afford was a relative term. There were those awkward hours, and sometimes days, that I spent in the principal's office waiting for my parents to scrounge up the money to pay my tuition.

As a child, I often felt different from the other students. Even though my uniform was just as tidy and my white shirt bleached and so stiff with starch it practically stood up on its own, I sensed that the other Haitian American and Caribbean students came from better-off, more middle-class families. My parents were often gone days, nights, and weekends, working two or three jobs at a time. We were working-class, always feeling that we were dancing on an economic tightwire. An unexpected expense—a visit to the emergency room, a smashed car bumper—could send the whole family plummeting into an abyss of possible homelessness and no food in the fridge. As it was, there were often times when the utilities could not be paid, leaving us without lights and heat sometimes for days.

There were other embarrassments. My lunches were one source of humiliation. My mother would give me leftover fried chicken, rice, and steamed vegetables—typical Haitian food—packaged in recycled aluminum foil from the week before. By the time I got to school everything would be soggy, and the other children at my lunch table would make faces to show their revulsion. Every day I would pray for peanut butter and jelly. I finally decided to take charge of the situation. In my family, we didn't throw food away, so I hid it. After days of piling up uneaten lunches under my bed, I woke up to a mouse skittering beneath my bed.

The mouse was a revelation for my mom. She bent over and looked under my bed. There was a mountain of crumpled aluminum foil packets. She thought I had liked my lunches, because I presented her with an empty Snoopy lunchbox every night. She was furious at first, and I expected a spanking. But she calmed down almost immediately. I was just six years old. She realized that an older child would have simply tossed the packets of food in the school's lunchroom garbage can every day. I remember her talking to me in a gentle tone. *"Karese,"* she said—Creole for *pet*. "If you don't like what I make you for lunch, you should tell me so I can make something different. You can't pay attention to your teacher with a grumbly tummy."

After that, I got the dreamed-of all-American lunch: PB&Js made with white Wonder Bread, Welch's grape jelly, and Skippy creamy peanut butter. Plus cookies. It helped me feel like I belonged. She later told me that she felt horrible for not realizing sooner that I had been so unhappy. She had been too busy working to notice.

My mother made up for the nutrition at dinner that I missed out on at lunch. Every night, she would give us a "potage." It was a soup-like mixture of vegetables—carrots, potatoes, string beans, spinach, and collard greens. She would boil it in a big pot overnight, then add fish, beef, or chicken on alternating weeks. Refrigerated, it would last for several days. Fruit was also on the menu. She would also make big jars of juice—a combination of pulverized carrots, pineapples, beets, and oranges—that we drank three times a week.

Another of her health obsessions that I felt as an indignity was what my mother called "the weekend cleansing." One Friday night a month, starting when I was young and going all the way through high school, she would give me (and when they got old enough, my younger sister, Edwine, and my younger brother, Chris) a laxative concoction that she believed kept us from getting sick. It was a thick white liquid, and to say that it smelled and tasted nasty does not begin to cover it. It was a Haitian tradition "to make sure your system is kept clean," my mother always said.

Once the potion kicked in, which was almost immediately,

it was pretty much over for us for the rest of the weekend. My siblings and I would find ourselves glued to a toilet for three straight days. This didn't matter when I was young. I wasn't allowed to go outside and play with friends anyway. But as I grew older, it limited my social life. So much for trying to explain to prospective friends why I couldn't kick a soccer ball around with them on a Saturday afternoon or hang out at the mall.

I didn't learn to read until the third grade. I was behind on every level—the English language, math skills, general knowledge. My parents, working multiple jobs, were not in a position to help me with my daily schoolwork. They believed that school would teach me, and they often talked about how I would one day become a doctor.

There was also the stigma that all Haitian Americans in our community felt, especially those like me who weren't born in the United States. In the 1970s and '80s, Haitians were considered dirty—even disgusting. First, the country's pigs were diagnosed with Asian Swine Flu and had to be completely eradicated. Far worse, Americans held Haitians responsible for the spread of AIDS. Decades later on January 10, 2018, when the president of the United States was reported to have called Haiti a shithole country, it was a kick in the gut. As soon as I heard it, I immediately became a little girl of ten again. My stomach hurt, and I felt an overwhelming sense of undeserved shame. I wanted to hang my head.

Trump has said so many horrible things about different groups of people before and after he announced his campaign on June 16, 2015. He falsely claimed President Barack Obama wasn't born in the United States. He called Mexicans rapists and drug dealers. He insulted a disabled reporter. He derided a Muslim Gold Star family. I'm sure that every one of those people felt the way I did. That this was personal. That those were fighting words. The adult me felt an urgency to defend my people, my community. I remembered the powerful words of Martin Luther

King, Jr.: "A time comes when silence is betrayal." I have used the power of my TV pulpit to speak out against this wounding smear.

I knew my parents loved me and wanted the best for me. But mine was not a carefree childhood. My father worked in a factory and later got his New York City taxi license to drive a yellow cab. My mother, a kind and conscientious caregiver to the elderly, would be gone twelve to fifteen hours a day. She made up in hard work and hustle what she lacked in education. Because my parents were always working—or it felt that way—I would take care of my siblings. I would feed my sister, who was born in 1982 when I was seven, from the reheated food my mother prepared every morning. My brother was born in 1984 when I was nine. It was often my job not just to give him his bottle and change his diaper but to make his appointments to see the pediatrician. When they got older, I was the one who walked them to school every morning, took them to the library, made sure they did their homework every afternoon, and was in charge of their school projects. I bought a pair of clippers so I could cut Chris's hair every two weeks. After dinner, it was early to bed. One of the best things about summer was that we got to stay up late enough to see our mother when she came home, usually around 9:30 p.m.

I don't remember what age it started or ended—sometime between ages seven and ten—but when my parents were at work, an older male cousin, Eduardo, would check in on my siblings and me. In my memory, he was a tall, well-built man. Although Eduardo was in his late twenties, he always struck me as kid-like—even childish. What I remember best was his distinct, off-putting odor. He always smelled like mildewed towels.

Eduardo repeatedly sexually abused me. "Karine, are you here?" he'd call out on his way up the stairs to our apartment on the second floor. Above our apartment there was a tiny attic with two mattresses leaning against the slanted wall. This created a crawl space where I used to hide from him. I'd scrunch into a ball and stay still—praying over and over in my head he wouldn't find me. Sometimes I'd stay there for hours to elude him. This is the reason that tight small spaces give me intense anxiety today. Even now, the smell of musty clothing is a trigger for me.

I don't know why I didn't tell my parents. Perhaps I feared that Eduardo would lash out at me, my siblings, or my parents. Or perhaps I had absorbed in the way that children do that this was shameful and somehow my fault. And that, as with Donald's death, my parents preferred to keep hard things secret. But eventually an older female cousin saw how I flinched and clung to her when Eduardo walked into the room at a family gathering at my auntie's house and understood that something was horribly off base. She told my parents, and I never saw him again.

Childhood sexual abuse is so common in America. Experts estimate that up to 25 percent of girls have suffered some form of this crime and up to 16 percent of boys. I urge other people to seek help, no matter how long ago it occurred.

Even in elementary school, I was already starting to handle the bills because my reading was better than my parents'. Trained as an engineer who had worked teaching high school, my father could read some English. My mother, who never finished grade school, could not read. I knew how much or how little money was in their checking account and which bills needed to be paid first. I was my parents' lieutenant, shouldering a lot of responsibility. Soon I was able to read not just paper but people—to tell who was good and who was out to rip us off. There was a constant wave of no-good hustlers who preyed on those they saw as weak. Living in New York is always a hustle. You have to hustle and someone is always hustling you. I would come with my parents when they bought used cars and, eventually, I sat in on meetings with Realtors when it came time to move out of

Aunt Mimose and Uncle Frantz's house to make room for their adult daughter and her growing family.

I was ten when my parents found their dream house, a red-brick Colonial with a bedroom for each child and a yard to play in, at 19 Garfield Place in Hempstead, on Long Island, outside New York City.

My parents were so thrilled with the accomplishment of buying a house, they couldn't see that this was not a well-thought-out decision. It was a tough African American neighborhood. At that time, there were no Haitian Americans in Hempstead except us. The street was directly across from Lincoln Park, where there was a thriving drug market. Empty crack vials lay on the grassy patches of sidewalk a few feet from our front yard.

I never felt safe.

I was also unhappy. My parents decided to put me in the local public school. I was scared by how rough the kids were in my fifth-grade class at Franklin Elementary School. It was only a six-minute walk to school from our house, on the other end of the park. But as scary as the park was, the school, at times, seemed worse. A low-slung, redbrick building, it didn't appear to be menacing. A few years later when the movie *Lean on Me*, about a decaying, underperforming high school in New Jersey was released, though, I automatically thought back to Franklin Elementary. I had been sheltered in Queens, and I found it jarring to be with a teacher who couldn't control her class. I was also desperately lonely. Edwine was only a kindergartener and Chris was three years old—hardly playmate material. I was so relieved when I made one friend, a girl named Tysha, whose mother was the crossing guard.

Within a year my parents discovered how terrible the nearby public schools were—among the worst in Nassau County—and transferred Edwine and me to the local Catholic school, Our Lady of Loretto, connected to a church by the same name. I was much happier at this school, which I attended from sixth

through eighth grade. The other parents were similar to mine—
very motivated about their children's education.

I was terrified of one of the nuns, who had salt-and-pepper
hair and was rumored to carry a ruler that she used on kids'
palms whenever they misbehaved. Our school day was steeped
in Catholicism. We regularly attended Mass and took Com-
munion. In seventh grade we were preparing for confirmation
(my confirmation name was Elizabeth), and we were drilled on
church history and the sacraments, including the scary sacrament
of penance and reconciliation. I hated having to sit in the small
dark confession box. Besides feeling claustrophobic, I didn't like
having to admit my "sins" to a priest. I never knew what to say,
so I made things up. "Forgive me, Father, for I have sinned," I
would begin. "I didn't eat all of my dinner last night."

One thing that amused me was that even classes that seemingly
had nothing to do with religion—geography, say—somehow
wound their way around to it. For instance, we concentrated on
countries with large Catholic populations. We learned a lot about
Spain and Italy but not so much about Canada next door except
for the province of Quebec with its large French Canadian and
very Catholic population.

I didn't mind attending Mass—it was only an hour long. But
with a Catholic father and a Pentecostal mother, I was confused
on the whole question of religion. My mother had been raised
as a Baptist. This was unusual in heavily Roman Catholic Haiti.
She joined the Pentecostal church before her marriage. I thought
if I remained Catholic, I would be disloyal to my mother, and
if I converted to Pentecostalism, I would be unfair to my father. I can't remember a minute when I wasn't racked with guilt
over *something*.

My mother loved her Pentecostal church in Jamaica, Queens,
and found a real community of close, supportive friends there.
Today, she is head usher, which is a big honor. She is in charge
of the other twenty-four ushers, whose job it is to welcome

congregants, hand out the programs and envelopes to collect money, and keep unruly children in check. They all wear the same color every Sunday—the hue varies depending on the month or season—but my mother always wears a special gold badge that proclaims Sister Elaine, the Head Usher.

Sundays were a huge event when I was growing up. Women and girls had to wear dresses and stockings, their arms covered. The Sunday services lasted three or four hours in the morning and then again in the evening. And they were even more intense than they were long. Getting the spirit of God involved an emotional outpouring—fainting, dancing in the aisles, and speaking in tongues (which upset and disturbed me).

It took until high school—I went to a large Catholic school in Uniondale, Long Island, called Kellenberg Memorial High School—for me to feel at home on Long Island. Kellenberg was a distant second choice for me in 1988, when I was applying to high schools. I had my heart set on Friends Academy, a co-educational Quaker prep school, in the tony enclave of Locust Valley in Nassau County. It was more prestigious than Kellenberg, with smaller classes. Plus, I wanted a break from Catholic teachings. I was devastated when I didn't get in, though looking back, I have no idea how I would have gotten back and forth to Friends Academy from Hempstead, since my parents could never have spent the hours required to drive me. I also wonder how I would have fit in at Friends Academy, which, back then, was overwhelmingly white and wealthy.

Three miles from our house, Kellenberg, with its beautiful, tree-filled campus, quickly became an oasis for me. While the school was primarily white, I liked it for its mix of whites, Latinos, and blacks. I reconnected with other Caribbean kids for the first time since I left Queens.

Sports changed my life. My middle-school classmate and friend Maddie from Our Lady of Loretto and her brother, Maurice, who was a year ahead of us and a star on the boys' cross-country team at Kellenberg, nagged me good-naturedly for months to persuade me to try out. Until then, I had never considered cross-country. My parents stressed academics, because they were convinced that would help us get ahead. And with my petite frame—I am five feet two inches—I thought the only sport I might possibly be good at was gymnastics, which I had zero interest in. The closest I'd ever gotten to a track was watching Florence Griffith Joyner (Flo Jo), Jackie Joyner-Kersee and Carl Lewis in the 1988 Summer Olympics on TV. But once I tried out, I was pretty surprised to find out that I was fast.

Our coach, Mr. Martin, was also an unlikely mentor—the human equivalent of that old adage not to judge a book by its cover. Probably in his midthirties in 1989, he was skinny and short—about five foot five—and he never wore anything but a gray T-shirt and gray sweats with his wallet jammed in the front pocket. A soft-spoken white guy with closely cropped red hair, he predominantly coached girls of color, managing a bunch of cranky teenagers. He looked utterly forgettable and low-key. But he got our respect. He had the energy of six people, and he expended it all on us. He left nothing on the field, and he showed us how to do the same. To give our all.

Running cross-country in the fall and track in the winter and spring opened up my world. I ran 400-meter intermediate hurdles, the 800-meter, and was a standout cross-country runner, setting records on Long Island. I was proud to be a Kellenberg Firebird, to wear the school's royal blue and gold colors as I competed in invitationals against other students in parks across New York State. Our toughest competitors were the New York City public schools, which usually clobbered us. But we cared far more about our long-standing rivalries with the Catholic St. Anthony's High School in South Huntington, Long Island, and Sacred Heart Academy, an all-girls school in Hempstead. My name and my track results would be read over the PA system in class the next morning. I was popular for the first time. It was very exciting to run in famous events like the Penn Relays. First held in 1895 at the University of Pennsylvania, the Penn Relays is the largest track-and-field event in the country. Our team was no competition for the big public high schools, but I loved the experience of being part of something bigger than me; of being part of something with such a long history.

Two parks, where our most challenging meets were held, have remained fresh in my memory. Sunken Meadow State Park on the North Shore of Long Island is a legend among cross-country runners because the five-kilometer course features "Cardiac Hill," one of the toughest—and aptly named—courses in the United States. Van Cortlandt Park in the Bronx, the third-largest park in New York City, is gorgeous with hard cinder trails and punishing hills. We would compete mostly on the weekends, and because the cross-country season went deep into November, a lot of the meets were held in cold, rainy weather. For me, at fifteen, they were the ultimate mind and body challenge. Before every competition, I would test myself by asking, "Do I have the strength, endurance, and speed to win?" The question became my mantra. I'd ask the question over and over again while listening to my favorite prerace hip-hop song on my Walkman— "Mama Said Knock You Out," by LL Cool J.

Competing in cross-country and track and field played a significant role in giving me a sense of belonging at Kellenberg. I gained the self-confidence I had always lacked. Even though I still stood at just five feet two inches, I'm sure I walked a little taller. Sports also enhanced my ability to see myself as a team player. At practices we competed hard against each other, but on meet day we were all together, rooting for the good of the team. This was another experience that has proved invaluable in politics.

I had spent my life as a city kid, but I found that I enjoyed running long distances, whether it was tackling steep hills, navigating soft sand at the beach, or just breathing in the sweet smell of grass on the track. Flying over the ground, I experienced that sense of euphoria and intense well-being known as a "runner's high." Even today, I love to relax by running, which has irritated more than one nonathletic friend. To me, it is never a chore.

Although I had found my place at Kellenberg, I still felt different from other kids. While my teammates' parents shuttled them to practices and track meets, my parents never came to see me compete. Ever. Other parents sometimes gave me rides, but I had to figure out how to get back and forth to school on my own, walking the three miles if I missed the bus.

Looking back, there were so many times in my life where I felt that I was going it alone. I felt that I was trying to be an American, someone who attempted new things, who went different places, who risked failure. I never expected to see my parents as I competed in track-and-field events up and down the East Coast, but I still felt a pang when I happened to glance up into the bleachers, where other Kellenberg families were cheering. I had friends whose mothers, fathers, siblings, and even grandparents had gotten up at 4:00 a.m. just to get to the track. I had noticed this in graduate school as well. I had friends whose parents read their papers and talked every night with their grown children. They encouraged their kids to attend office hours and to make themselves known to professors. Now that I teach grad students at Columbia, I know how important it is to do these things. But at the time I would notice that often my friends would balk when their parents tried to micromanage their lives in graduate school. These parents had the right idea and the best intentions, but they didn't realize that it was time to let their little chicks go.

It was a letdown to win a big race and then wait for the Hempstead bus, medal hanging around my neck with a ribbon. I wondered: Are you a star if no one sees you shine? Sometimes when I was at the bus stop, my teammates' mothers and fathers would pause as they drove by, roll down the window, and yell

out, "Great job out there, Karine!" My parents just didn't engage. It wasn't a case of sports being my thing and not theirs. If I
had been inducted into the National Honor Society, they would
not have come to that ceremony, either. As with my lunches, it
took my mother weeks to notice what we were doing in school
at a granular level. They were too busy; too consumed with
keeping their fragile toehold on the middle-class life they desperately craved for me and my siblings.

It sounds hard, and it was. But there was a certain freedom.
Some of my friends' parents were almost too invested in their
children's activities. As loving as that "support" might seem, I
noticed that it brought an awful lot of emotional pressure. It's a
lot easier to handle not qualifying for a track event if it's just you.

Another thing that set me apart from my family is that around
this time I decided to become a vegetarian. I have remained
one ever since. My mother claims I'm shorter than my siblings
because of my refusal to eat animal protein, but I don't like the
taste or effect of meat. I urge everyone to consider becoming
a vegetarian because of the huge benefits to the planet. I also
credit my excellent health to this decision.

I didn't find academics as easy as sports. In ninth grade, my
English teacher, Sister Grace, refused to read my papers, because she said my handwriting was "atrocious." She gave me an
ultimatum: spend my study breaks taking penmanship lessons
with the retired nuns who lived in the convent at the school, or
fail her class. For hours it seemed, I would sit with these elderly
sisters in their nineties and trace the loops for each upper- and
lowercase letter. I suppose that today I would simply have been
given a laptop.

I felt different for another reason, too. Being the eldest of three
in a Caribbean immigrant family, I was expected to set the bar
high, to be a perfect child. No trouble at school. No drinking.
No drugs. No sex. You must be better than that. When I was
sixteen, all I wanted was to be a regular teenager, to do what the

American kids did, so I went to a house party in Queens with friends. I didn't do anything on my parents' forbidden list. But I had so much fun being cool for once and hanging out that I lost track of time and got home in the hours before dawn. My parents were so strict that we did not have a curfew—we were always expected to be at home, not out, period. It was okay, I reasoned, because I'd had a blast. I wasn't really all that scared to face my parents.

I should have known better.

When I gingerly shut the front door so as not to make a sound and tiptoed inside close to 4:00 a.m., my mother was waiting up for me, sitting rigidly on the edge of the laminated couch, still in her flowered health aide scrubs. Livid, she accused me of doing drugs and of being a whore.

"I'm not drinking or doing drugs," I yelled. "And I am *definitely* not having sex with boys. I'm a lesbian!"

I had never said those words before in my entire life. Not even to myself. Maybe because it was so late at night. Maybe it was because I was tired of not facing the truth about myself and the feelings I had suppressed for years.

Suddenly, everything got pin-drop quiet. She looked confused. "What's a lesbian?" she asked.

"Mummy, it's when a girl likes another girl romantically instead of a boy."

My mother didn't say a word. She didn't have to. I could see the revulsion on her face. For this she had worked two jobs for decades? For this she had sacrificed everything? My sexual orientation, I realized, had the power to destroy the person I loved most in the world and to whom I felt the deepest gratitude. You must be the child of an immigrant family to grasp how making your parents' sacrifice worthwhile colors everything, including whom you can love.

She stood up, smoothed the wrinkles out of her pants as if they were the most important thing in the world to her, walked to her bedroom, and shut the door. Literally and figuratively. We didn't speak of my being a lesbian again for decades.

That early-morning encounter left me so angry and hurt. It was years before I had another conversation with anyone about being gay. Although I had somehow known I was gay when I was five years old—don't ask me how—I didn't face my sexuality again until I was in graduate school in my twenties and had my first girlfriend.

To this day, my mom has never mentioned that night to me. But a few years ago, my cousin Jeannot told me that she had called him the night that I came out to her. My mother was frantic and wanted his opinion on what to do. I don't know what advice he offered or whether she took it. I do know that when I found out about the call almost twenty years later, it felt like validation that the conversation with my mother had really occurred.

I regret that I gave up on my mother so easily and didn't try to help her understand me better. But mostly I regret that something so significant in my life became yet another family secret.

But being silent on the subject was not the same as putting it out of my head. I still had to deal with who I truly was—and with the fact that the students I had crushes on were not boys but girls. I had my heart trounced by a lean, lithe Haitian American relay runner two years ahead of me named Fabienne. She was straight, and I think she thought of me as an annoying little sister if she thought of me at all. Being at a Catholic school added to the guilt I felt. My friends pined over boys incessantly, and I had to pretend to share their enthusiasm for Topic A at lunch in the cafeteria, in the locker room, and on the bus to cross-country and track meets. I listened to them describe what it was like to lose their virginities, revealing nothing of the heartache I suffered over my girl crushes. I wasn't ready for physical intimacy. But I was so confused by my feelings that during my junior year in high school, I thought intensely about becoming a nun as an easy way to bury my sexuality. No longer would I feel guilty about it, I reasoned, because it would be off the table. On my long-distance runs, I would daydream about how freeing that would be.

Becoming a nun would also give me a way to make a difference in the world, I thought. At Kellenberg there was an emphasis on helping the underserved and socially marginalized. I wanted to do good, and so I told a few of the brothers and sisters at Kellenberg about my plan. "I feel that I have a calling," I remember telling a sweet-faced nun one afternoon while we were sitting in the library. I don't know what these wise men and women who had taken their own vows saw—or didn't see—in me, but they urged me to go out into the world before making such a life-defining commitment. For this, I am profoundly grateful.

So I went back to trying to be the all-American—heterosexual—girl. My senior prom in the spring of 1992 was the SAT test on whether I had succeeded. The truth is, I had not. There wasn't a boy at school who wanted to take me to the prom. My track-star status had not parlayed into being a girl who the boys wanted to date. Undeterred, I concocted a plan to get myself to the prom. This was a long time before prom-posals were a thing, so I like to joke that I was ahead of my time!

My neighborhood friend Bethany Golding had a handsome brother a couple of years older than us who had already graduated from high school. Adhering to the strict codes that govern big brothers and baby sisters and their friends, Brendan and I had never said anything but a mumbled hi to each other—without raising our eyes from the floor. But one afternoon in early May, I dropped by their house when I knew that Bethany's mom would be home—and Bethany and Brendan would be out. Mrs. Golding was an awesome lady who looked out for all of the kids on the block. "Can I ask you a funny question?" I said when she came to the front door. "Do you think Brendan would take me to the prom if you asked him to?" She got so excited she clapped her hands together and flashed me a huge grin.

"Come inside and have some iced tea," she said. "Let's make a plan."

He was the perfect date. He opened the car door for me, brought me punch, and spent a ton of time with me on the dance floor. He had purchased a wrist corsage with pink blush rose buds to match my chiffon halter dress. He looked even handsomer than usual in his tuxedo. My mother—thrilled—had devoted hours to creating the perfect updo for my hair. Everyone at school was shocked that I was there with a date and whispered to each other trying to guess who he was. The night was a huge coup for me. I had passed the test, despite my angst about my sexuality and my popularity.

It was a happy ending to high school.

I believed that I had my future all figured out. I would make my parents proud and become a medical doctor. This was my dream even when I was a little girl in my plaid uniform with my hair tied up in big red ribbons like all the nice Haitian girls walking to Saints Joachim and Anne School back in Queens Village. You see, in my Haitian American household, becoming a professional was the key to success. My parents believed that there were only three paths to reach the American dream: become a doctor, become an engineer, or become a lawyer.

My parents decided early on that becoming a doctor was my calling. I'm sure they got the idea from one of my mother's adopted relatives who was a doctor in North Carolina. Dr. Chantal was smart, admired, and financially comfortable. She also had a wonderful warmth that enveloped us when she visited. I'm sure her bedside manner with patients was amazing. She devoted every vacation to volunteering in clinics in Haiti. Dr. Chantal's commitment to giving back to others inspired me. It makes sense that my mother would want her eldest daughter to become a caring, financially established professional like this impressive woman.

But my Kellenberg guidance counselor saw things differently and tried to puncture my dream with a dose of reality. We were meeting in her office in the fall of my senior year. Looking up from a copy of my transcript and SATs, she took off her glasses and cleared her throat. "Karine," she said. "I really think your talents would be better served as a nurse. You know it's not nearly as heavy a lift as becoming a doctor."

For a few days, I felt so awful I couldn't eat. I practically had to remind myself to breathe. I didn't have anyone to confide in, and I didn't know what to do. But I was walking to the bus stop one morning when an idea popped into my head. I didn't have to listen to her. I could pursue my dream no matter what she thought I was capable of. "Do I have the strength, endurance, and speed to win?" I asked myself. "YES!" came my resounding reply!

Although there were some track scholarships offered for college, I chose to focus on academics. I lived at home and enrolled at New York Institute of Technology, a private research university in Old Westbury, Long Island, less than a half hour from our house. The campus, with its redbrick, marble, and columned buildings, was cobbled together from former baronial estates owned by the Rockefeller, DuPont, and Whitney families. My parents didn't care that it was mainly a commuter school. They were thrilled that I was attending college and taking premed classes. I fiercely focused on biology, chemistry, and all the required science courses to the exclusion of anything that took away from studying. I didn't even try to make friends, settling instead for a few casual acquaintances I'd sit next to in class or say hi to in the library. In retrospect, I must have been lonely, but at the time, I didn't think about it.

Instead, I basked in my parents' and my other relatives' enormous pride. Karine Jean-Pierre, MD.

I failed.

My scores on my MCATs—the Medical College Admissions Test you take for medical school—weren't good enough to get me in. I studied, enrolled in a prep class, and retook them—and did no better. When I got the envelope with my scores in the mail and realized my aspiration had reached a dead end, I was not only devastated but also lost.

I still remember my father standing at the kitchen counter, the windowsill overflowing with my mother's carefully tended aloe plants, and my mother seated at the small kitchen table in her scrubs after I got my second-round MCAT scores. Both of them were utterly bewildered. They didn't understand the concept of standardized entrance exams, and they didn't even know to ask me about how I'd done. What they grasped was how hard I had studied. There was always a disconnect—with me having to walk them through applying to college and now medical school. So they didn't get that these scores were my undoing. When I told them I had done badly, they didn't understand why I didn't try again. I couldn't get the point across that for me, medical school was unattainable.

I felt like an idiot. Thanks in large part to my inability to confront my sexuality, I was so afraid of who I *really* was that I invested absolutely everything into who my parents and siblings thought I was and wanted me to be. Becoming a doctor was to be my saving grace. I had always clung to it as if it were my life raft. So when I failed at this one thing, my entire world crumbled. I wanted to die.

I almost got my wish.

I know I wasn't thinking straight. How could I have imagined it was a good idea to devastate my family, to destroy my parents, who I knew loved me deeply. How could I think that my parents cared more about medical school than they cared about me? But at the time I was positive about my decision. For weeks, I thought about nothing else. Killing myself would help everyone. I would remove myself and my shame from the world. The only question was which method I would choose.

When I was in college I had the habit of dozing off in my car. I was so exhausted from studying all night that I would drive to my parents' house, pull into the garage, and fall asleep the nanosecond I was safely parked. It's crazy that I couldn't make it the few steps inside to get to bed. Many times, my mother would come into the garage to get me.

But one day, it was different. It was still light out when I drove home. I parked my old white BMW two-door convertible in the garage. I parked on the right-hand side, clicked on the automatic door opener of the two-door garage (my father used the left-hand side of the garage to park his yellow cab), and locked the wooden door leading into the kitchen. I climbed back into the driver's seat and made sure all the windows were open. I turned the key in the ignition, cranked up Mary J. Blige singing "Everlasting Love" on the car radio to blaring, and left the motor running. Feeling relaxed and happy for the first time in weeks, I lay back and closed my eyes. *I am doing this. This is best for everyone. Everyone will be happier when I'm gone.*

The next thing I remember was my sister, Edwine, screaming my name and shaking me. Hard. "Karine! Karine! Wake up!"

The light from the open garage door hurt my eyes, and my khaki pants were soaked in urine.

I don't know how long I was unconscious. Nor what would have happened had my sister not found me.

I said nothing to Edwine, turned off the car, and walked woozily into the house. I got straight into the shower. Later, I threw the pants away in the garbage can behind the house.

To this day, no one in my family has ever talked to me about my suicide attempt. The fact that I actually tried to take my own life is so shameful and agonizing to me that I have never had the nerve to broach the subject with Edwine. It is locked away, just like my brother Donald's death.

I am so lucky to have survived. I never again contemplated killing myself. But I still feel terrible about what I put Edwine through that day. I'm almost certain that this experience must have deeply traumatized her. Had I found Edwine unconscious, I would have been haunted for the rest of my life, always wondering if she was okay.

I beg anyone to get help if they have suicidal thoughts, sometimes called suicidal ideation. The National Suicide Prevention Lifeline is available twenty-four hours a day at 1-800-SUICIDE (or 1-800-273-8255), and its website offers services, including a live chat.

Should I have taken my high school guidance counselor's advice? Why didn't I just decide to become a nurse? Well, the plan was to wear a doctor's white coat, not a nurse's uniform. I had several relatives who were registered nurses or licensed practical nurses, and it seemed as though nurses did most of the work for far fewer financial rewards and a whole lot less respect. And look at my mother, the home health care aide. She earned a meager living. While some of the elderly people she cared for appreciated her kindness, her employers looked down on her, seeing just another uneducated black woman. Plus, the idea was for me to push forward, to be like Dr. Chantal, traveling back and forth to Haiti, helping in a medical clinic. I have never regretted my perseverance, and I have had to draw on it many times since then.

The hard truth: if I had wanted to go into medicine for the right reasons, I probably would have become a nurse or a physician's assistant, but the dream was about validating my parents' sacrifices and hard work, not mine.

One positive thing came of wanting to become a medical doctor: in one of my freshman classes at New York Institute of Technology, a fellow student who was a paramedic told me I should become a volunteer firefighter. So I headed over to the local volunteer firehouse (House 2) and started hanging out with a bunch of old white guys who took me under their wing. It was my only extracurricular activity. To my surprise, I loved chatting with these aging Vietnam vets who were more than twice my age. They were honest and funny, and I liked connecting across gender and racial lines.

I found that I was good at being a volunteer firefighter. And I loved having a firefighter scanner in my car, a bumper sticker-size orange-and-black firefighter sign that I would put on my windshield, and a blue light at the ready to plug into my car's cigarette charger. Boom! I would hear about a fire (mostly car fires), pop the blue light onto my dashboard, and head to the scene. Being a member of the team gave me a sense of purpose, importance, and agency.

I also found that being a volunteer firefighter helped me to understand the problems that a poor community like Hempstead faced, to see the reality of poverty and how it affected people. Once thriving, Hempstead had fallen on hard times. Today, with a graduation rate of only 37 percent, Hempstead High School on Long Island is one of the worst-performing schools in the nation. I found that going out on ambulance calls revealed people's struggles to me. I remember an older gentleman who gently reminded us to use gloves while helping him because he had AIDS.

There were also profoundly hard experiences. The first time I ever witnessed death up close happened when I was a first-semester college freshman. I was on the scene on Saturday night, December 3, 1994, when a family of five brothers and sisters ranging in age from seven months to five years—all babies, really—died in a house fire in Hempstead. I knew the house—it was a two-story, wooden-frame house on Liberty Court, just a few minutes from the downtown area of Hempstead Village. A pan of pork chops on the kitchen stove apparently caught fire and the blaze instantaneously spread up the stairs where the children were. The mother and father escaped along with the grandparents, but four of the five children were declared dead at the scene. The fifth child—a two-year-old named James—was transported to the hospital but died. Four firefighters were treated for minor injuries. The ramshackle wooden house was a tinderbox. It was Hempstead's deadliest fire in twenty years.

I still remember standing at the curb, the smoke burning my nostrils. In the December cold, the water from the fire hoses was turning to ice at my feet. The early darkness of the winter dusk enveloped me. I couldn't believe it. All of those young lives gone. How would their parents and grandparents go on? Could anyone?

The experience scarred me. It often comes back to me all these years later—particularly in the month of December—especially now that I am a mother. I am meticulous about never leaving the dryer running unattended, and on the rare times I use a match, I run it under cold water to make sure it is fully extinguished (and even so leave it sitting in the stainless-steel sink for several days before I dare to drop it in the trash).

Even though failing to achieve my childhood aspiration almost destroyed me, I eventually got past my crushing disappointment. To be honest, I'm not sure that my parents ever have. Since I was five years old, they had told *everyone* that I was going to be a doctor. It was like a gut punch. In their heart of hearts, I know they believed that if I had only kept trying, I would have "passed" my MCATs. What they could not grasp was that it wasn't a question of my working harder. I didn't have the scientific aptitude to score high enough on the MCATs. They felt that my career and life were over before they had scarcely started.

Having left one dream behind, I needed the answer to the bigger question of what I was going to do with my life.

This would entail working at a makeup company, contracting out as a temp; a lot of soul-searching; long, lonely runs on the beach; and stints as a counselor to young girls of color. And it would take four years.

CHAPTER TWO

Karine Jean-Pierre: Environmentalist

I can never erase the memory of my second day of graduate school at Columbia University in New York City. I couldn't reach my father. Over and over I kept calling him on his cell phone, my stomach roiling, a cold sweat beading on my forehead despite the glorious Indian summer sunshine. I was living with my parents on Long Island, and I was getting myself ready for my late-morning class. At 8:46 a.m., the first plane hit the North Tower, and I had no idea where my father was.

I did know where he had been that morning and what his schedule was. Like clockwork, every day at 5:30 a.m., he would be in his yellow cab at John F. Kennedy International Airport (JFK) in Queens, waiting for the first flights to land. At that hour, the passengers he picked up were almost always business-people heading into Manhattan. A cabbie like my father would drop off their first customer in the early morning and then drive around looking for the next fare. This meant my father could be literally *anywhere* in the city. Including lower Manhattan, now encased in the dust and debris from the collapsed towers.

As my fear took over, I immediately assumed the worst. Making everything even more terrible, there was no cell phone signal. The networks had suffered from infrastructure damage, and the enormous surge in cell phone traffic made it impossible to connect. The only people who could make and receive phone calls had BlackBerries. I thought it was just my father's cell phone that wasn't working.

On that gorgeous sunny day, I called my father over and over again for something like eight hours from my parents' house on Long Island. Each time, I became more frantic, imagining him crushed in his yellow cab, injured, crying out to rescuers who never came.

At least I knew that my mother was safe. I knew she was putting in an early-morning shift at the nursing home in Far Rockaway, miles away from the collapsing Twin Towers. My sister and my brother were also nowhere near Manhattan so I didn't worry about them.

I couldn't wrap my mind around what was happening. A terrorist attack on American soil? Airplanes flying into the towering skyscrapers of my beloved Manhattan, the place where I envisioned all my dreams and hopes for the future? I always thought of New York in September, when the summer heat broke, as a place filled with promise and possibility. Going back to my running days at Kellenberg, fall is my favorite season. I love the way the leaves change from a lively green to fiery reds, oranges, and yellows and then to brown before they dry up and crumble. The process settles me. I think most people see spring as a time of renewal, but I like the peaceful transition that takes place in fall—saying goodbye to what was once new and welcoming what takes its place.

But this cloudless blue-sky day could not have been more the opposite of renewal and possibility. A nightmare that extended beyond New York to Virginia and Pennsylvania. The Pentagon attacked? A jet crashed into a field? We didn't know what to expect next. I still get chills when I think back to it all.

I remember a photograph from that day taken by Agence France Presse photographer Stan Honda. It was of this slim, stylish black woman named Marcy Borders who had worked in one of the collapsed buildings and escaped. I will never forget that visual. They called her the Dust Lady. The image of her face, her hair, her suit, and her boots utterly coated in mustard-yellow dust. She later died of stomach cancer at age forty-two on August 24, 2015.

It looked like a photo from a war zone—which it was.

At last my father got to a pay phone and called our house landline. Thank God he was okay. I remember hearing his quiet calm voice and crying out to my brother, "Papi is alive!" But for him to drive from the city to our house on Long Island took hours. I remember waking up in the early dawn and going into the hall to hug him—a rare moment with my very reserved father. As he walked down the hallway to his bedroom, he said sadly, "I'm not going to earn much money this week, Ka."

My heart still breaks when I remember his words. My father—always worrying about making enough money for his family. Even on 9/11.

On Wednesday, September 12, the day after the attacks, I got back on the Long Island Rail Road train into Manhattan to recommence my first week at SIPA, where I was getting my master's degree in public administration and focusing on environmental studies. Columbia University had decided to continue with regularly scheduled classes. I couldn't decide if this was a good idea or a bad one, but I went anyway. My train ride to Penn Station was eerily silent. The country had been catapulted into a place of fear, mourning, and death in just twenty-four hours. I picked up a copy of the *New York Times* lying on the seat next to mine. The lead editorial captured some of what I felt: "We look back at sunrise yesterday through pillars of smoke and dust, down streets snowed under with the atomized debris of the skyline, and we understand that everything has changed."

Being on the train felt like I was traveling through an alternative universe where everyone had come to the realization that the end days were upon us. The morning hustle and bustle had been replaced by a hush. It felt like being at a funeral.

Usually the trains in the morning were standing room only with office workers heading into Manhattan. On September 12, however, the train car I sat in was nearly uninhabited. The hour-long ride took an eternity. The train pulled slowly into the tunnel that led us to Penn Station. As I had done hundreds of times before, I got off the train onto the concrete platform, passing through the subterranean dinginess of the railroad and quickly walking up the stairs to the main area of the station.

It was desolate. The majority of the stores were closed. I managed to find a newsstand with a ripped copy of the *Daily News* that read "Day of Terror, Special Edition." The headline, in large caps, was "IT'S WAR," with an unnerving picture of the top of the North Tower on fire and the second plane flying toward its twin. In smaller print at the bottom right of the front page, it read "Just an instant before the second jetliner hit the south tower of the World Trade Center."

Vehicles were banned from going downtown, and the attacks had precipitated flooding and damage to parts of the subway system south of 14th Street. The perpetually chaotic and boisterous New York City subway was suddenly a silent, subterranean ghost town instead of a functioning form of transportation. I decided that the best approach for me with all of the confusion was to walk the five miles to 116th Street and Broadway.

When I reached the exit at 34th Street and 7th Avenue, I looked up. The sky was blue and clear, just like it had been the day before. My internal gyroscope turned east on 34th Street to where the Macy's flagship store still stood. I could not help but think of the movie *Miracle on 34th Street* whenever I walked past. With our parents, my siblings and I had made a family tradition of watching that 1947 classic about the Macy's Santa Claus who really was Kris Kringle. (Later as an adult I was startled to realize that the little girl played by Natalie Wood in the film also shared my parents' dream of buying a house on Long Island.)

That day I wondered, would there be a Macy's parade on Thanksgiving ever again? Would they have those huge floats I had loved as a small girl just arrived from Paris who spoke no English? Would we ever be happy again? Would I ever feel safe again? Would anyone?

I have never been anywhere near a combat zone. But the streets felt the way I imagine a war-torn country must feel. The people who ordinarily occupied virtually every inch of the sidewalk were missing. Some streets were blocked off and there was a military and police presence at every turn. Everywhere I looked, there were massive guns held at the ready by stone-faced soldiers and policemen. With a weighed-down heart and a slight shakiness in my knees, I started my trek up 7th Avenue.

The hour-plus walk from 34th Street to the 116th Street campus was an out-of-body experience. I walked along Broadway like a shadow dragging behind the day. The few souls that I saw either looked like zombies or were weeping alongside the shuttered storefronts. Already there were those desperate, homemade posters and flyers with poignant photos of missing people dancing at weddings and blowing out birthday cakes.

That morning I was headed to my American Politics class held at Barnard College. Barnard, founded as a women's liberal arts college in the late nineteenth century, was a quiet, beautiful, safe haven with its brick walkways and manicured green spaces.

The class was taught by Professor Ester Fuchs, who chaired the Urban Studies Program at Barnard and Columbia and founded the Columbia University Center for Urban Research and Policy (CURP). Professor Fuchs was formidable—a feminist with a fiery, unapologetic approach to everything and everyone. She made it her business to elevate and support young women and women of color in her field. She was constantly coming up with ideas and taking on projects. It seemed like she had her hand in a million issues.

In class that day, I learned that she was a senior advisor to Michael Bloomberg's New York City mayoral campaign. She told us that the primary originally scheduled for 9/11 had been postponed. I was surprised, because I hadn't even realized that there was supposed to be an election on 9/11. I made a note to myself: pay more attention to politics and the world around me. September 12 is the day I began reading the newspaper every single day. I cannot stress how important and helpful this habit will be to anyone who wants to understand politics. Just one aside: the reason it's good to read the physical newspaper instead of just the digital version is that there are smaller stories that don't grab the headlines on the front page that we tend to overlook online. These are not the stories about what the president or Congress is doing—or presidents and prime ministers of other countries. These stories are the crux of local politics—about water and land issues, education, and development.

Professor Fuchs's class included undergraduate and graduate students who ranged in age from under twenty to thirty. We had students who looked like they belonged in junior high and students who looked like they could be their parents. The room itself looked like a high school classroom—from the 1950s. The walls were painted light yellow. The rest of the room was dark wood: the floor, the door, the wainscoting that took up the bottom third of each wall. At the front of the room where Professor Fuchs stood, there were three old-fashioned blackboards. The desks were arranged in neat rows.

I was amazed that the class was practically full. Then I realized that most of the students lived either on campus or nearby.

I was one of the few who had to commute a long distance to get to school.

Of all my classes that day, September 12, 2001, Professor Fuchs was the only professor I had who talked about the 9/11 attacks. She offered us a safe space to open up about what had happened twenty-four hours ago in our city and in the country. The course was called American Politics, so it made sense. But it didn't make the discussion any less fraught. Most of the students were crying. A few people asked how America had gotten into this position.

People began arguing—the mood was tense and combative. One student quoted Malcolm X's biting response to a question about President John F. Kennedy's assassination in 1963. Kennedy "never foresaw that the chickens would come home to roost so soon," Malcolm X said, adding, "Being an old farm boy myself, chickens coming home to roost never made me sad; they always made me glad." He meant that what goes around comes around.

September 11 made me think long and hard about the Middle East and the Arab/Israeli conflict. We had thought America was untouchable. Now, we had to see our place and our actions in the world with a different perspective. In my lifetime, Fortress America had never been breached. We were not impregnable, and we now had to have these difficult conversations.

After Professor Fuchs's class, I headed east, walking through Columbia's main gates at 116th Street and Broadway and then to the other side of campus at 116th Street and Amsterdam Avenue. At Amsterdam, I crossed the street, passing the law school and SIPA. In front of me lay Morningside Park.

Morningside Park sits in the heart of northern Manhattan, neighboring Morningside Heights and Harlem. Through the years, it has witnessed a lot of violence. But that day in 2001, I found solace just sitting on a park bench, surrounded by old, welcoming trees.

September 11 changed the world, the country, the city for-ever. It also changed me in a profound way. Like most young Americans, I had always lived with a sense of unlimited time spooling out ahead of me. There would be enough days for me to get to all the things I wanted to do. But the missing-person flyers and posters that became part of the cityscape in the com-ing months forced me to realize that my life could end in a sec-ond. This sense of mortality—this recognition of how fragile life is—has remained with me ever since. In a positive way, it has motivated me to grab hard at opportunities and run fast to get where I want to be. But it was a painful lesson to learn.

When I started at Columbia, politics was not on my radar. I wanted to study environmental policy. I credit my love of nature and desire to protect it to the long cross-country runs I took in high school along the sandy beaches of Long Island, the only sounds my breathing and the caw of a passing bird.

After not getting into medical school, I spent almost half a decade trying to figure out a path forward. I had embraced my parents' dream as my own for so long that I had no idea where *my* passions lay. I registered with a temp agency, and at one point I worked at Estée Lauder, the cosmetics company. Founded in 1946, the company had a manufacturing plant in Melville, New York, on Long Island, which was close to my parents' house. I assisted the scientists but early on I realized that this was not a career path for me. I didn't even wear makeup at the time. My mother and sister, however, adored the free samples I brought home—night creams, perfumes, antiaging serums. The works!

So often loving parents and kind teachers unconsciously im-pose their dreams on young people they care about. A book I have found very helpful is *Designing Your Life* by two Stanford profes-sors, Bill Burnett and Dave Evans. The authors urge you to try as many different things as possible. Too often, we become paralyzed by trying to think our way through what our passion might be rather than going out into the world and discovering it organically. For example, before you decide to get a master's in political science with the attendant massive student loans, go observe your state legislature in session or a town council meeting. Actually witnessing what passing laws involves is invaluable.

Here's a case in point: My environmental work started by complete chance. I got a summer gig as a phone canvasser at an organization called Citizens Campaign for the Environment (CCE) on Long Island.

I wasn't good at phone canvassing. In fact, I was terrible. I was a shy nineteen-year-old college student. I wanted to do a good job, but I detested asking people for money. To sit at a desk, call strangers, and actually get cold hard cash is a real skill. It is also a huge plus in politics. Some of my coworkers were really good at it, like, "You gave $25 last time we called. So yeah, can we put you down for $50 this time?"

I did love one part of the job—I loved talking about the environment. I loved the advocacy work. A guy named George, the phone canvassing director and my boss at CCE, also headed up a project every summer to protect piping plovers. Small sand-colored shorebirds that were near extinction, they needed a safe place away from the water's edge to nest. George hired me to monitor them as they laid their eggs.

It was an amazing experience and remains one of my fondest memories of life on Long Island. Every day, I would put on my sneakers, my tan shorts, my mirrored sunglasses, and my Australian slouch digger hat with a big Tweety Bird decal. Then I would head to Jones Beach—one of the most popular beaches on the East Coast with over six million visitors a year. It's an amazing barrier island with white sand that directly faces the Atlantic Ocean.

The problem is that the piping plovers nest right near the water's edge. All those millions of visitors spell trouble. My job was to check each morning on these magical, endangered birds. I never touched the birds or the eggs, but I would carefully monitor them. Each day, I would peer at their nests and see if the eggs had hatched. Sometimes I would see the little beige chicks chirping. I guess I was pretty memorable, because soon I was being greeted by the retirees who drove their RVs to the beach parking lot. "Here she comes, the boid gal!" they would cry out in that unforgettably nasal, consonant-dropping Long Island accent. "How them plovers doin'?"

During the same period, I met the older white woman who ran CCE. Sarah Meyland was the first woman I had ever encountered who was openly gay and spoke of her present and previous relationships. I had suppressed my sexuality since that horrible night in high school. Cheerful and athletic in high school, I had nonetheless walled off my true identity even from myself. Observing Sarah was the first time I had an inkling that maybe I, too, could find love sometime and enjoy a long-term partnership with a woman.

Through CCE, I also met an activist and educator at Hofstra University at the time, named Charol Shakeshaft. She was engaged in working with underserved girls. The summer after I graduated from college, Charol convinced me to work at her educational organization, Interactive Inc. Located in Huntington, New York, it was an easy fifteen-minute commute from my parents' new house in Wheatley Heights on Long Island. I was a counselor for a summer project called the Girls' Action G.R.E.E.N. (Girls Ready for Environmental Education Now) Project, funded by the National Science Foundation through Hofstra University.

Long Island is surrounded by water—the pounding surf of the Atlantic Ocean on the south side and the tranquil bluefish-filled waters of the Long Island Sound to the north. There are lush salt marshes, cattails, sailboats, seagulls crying out overhead. The beaches range from quiet inlets to the popular Jones Beach and the world-famous celebrity magnet of the Hamptons. Because of its enormous physical beauty and its proximity to New York City, the Hamptons at the tip of Long Island has served as a summer playground for the 1 percent for decades.

While a long way from the Hamptons, I had spent most of my formative years on Long Island, and some of my sharpest childhood memories took place on the beach—a quick drive from my parents' houses in Hempstead and Wheatley Heights. Every single time I feel overwhelmed or depressed, I go for a twenty-minute walk outdoors. Guaranteed, I have more energy and less stress afterward. Watching the sun set over the water while seated on a beach boulder has given me some of the most beautiful and meditative moments of my life.

But most of the young girls I met as a counselor at the Girls' Action G.R.E.E.N. Project had no such memories. Coming from underserved communities on Long Island—Hempstead, Uniondale, Roosevelt—they had never once seen the ocean or felt the sand between their toes. They had never breathed in the heavy salt air or heard the rhythmic crashing of waves against the shore. I was saddened at how little exposure these girls, on the cusp of being young women, had ever had to nature. Sometimes it seemed to me as if their senses had not been given a chance to be awakened. So often they would tell me that their parents forbade them from leaving their houses or apartments. They were to go directly from school to their homes. To their families, places of beauty, parks, and isolated outdoor areas meant gunfire or physical and sexual violence. Staying inside meant safety, but it limited their lives. I realize that without cross-country, my life might have been equally circumscribed.

I had had the same upbringing, and my parents had imparted the same message. And looking back, I can't blame them. Hempstead was a rough place with open drug dealing going on within sight of our home. I know my parents worried constantly about our safety. It is hard to encourage a sense of freedom and opportunity in children if everything is clouded with fear and worry. I can't emphasize enough how crippling this kind of anxiety can be to young people; to always be in a defensive crouch. And how it drains any sense of agency, any sense that they can shape their lives.

Our job at the Girls' Action G.R.E.E.N. Project was to open up the girls' experience of the outdoors. The catalyst for this program was a report showing that young girls start to lose interest in math and science by the age of twelve. This cuts them off from potential careers and opportunities. We were immersing these seventh and eighth graders in the outdoors in the hopes of getting them excited about the environment, nature, and STEM (Science, Technology, Engineering, and Math).

At the end of the summer, Charol asked me to stay on to work with the girls year-round after school and gave me a director's title. My immediate supervisor for the Girls' Action G.R.E.E.N. Project was a woman named Veronica; she was also a senior staffer at CCE. The now-year-long project became a partnership with CCE, Interactive Inc., and Hofstra University. During the summer, we piled the girls into a van and took them on field trips across Long Island. We saw the hydrangeas blossom at Planting Fields Arboretum and the magnificent sixty-five-room Coe Hall, a relic of Long Island's Gilded Age and the famed mansions on its "Gold Coast." Its lush grounds were designed by the Olmsted brothers, who inherited the country's first landscape architecture firm from their father, Frederick Law Olmsted, known for designing Central Park in Manhattan and Prospect Park in Brooklyn. We took in the vast array of magnificent flowers at Old Westbury Gardens. Perhaps most memorably, we visited Sagamore Hill, President Theodore Roosevelt's home before and after his years in the White House. With its sweeping veranda overlooking the grounds, the estate surprised the girls with its salt marshes, seaweed-strewn beaches, and multitude of birds. We wanted to reveal to the girls the variety and grandeur of this island where they lived. We hoped this would help them start to understand how important our environment is and why we need to protect our water, land, and animals. And, during the school year, I would visit the dozen-plus girls at their respective schools and do after-school workshops focused on nature and the environment. It was rewarding to see the girls mature and become committed to the project over the year.

This job took me back to one of my more memorable part-time jobs at the Theodore Roosevelt Sanctuary and Audubon Center. For over a year, I gave presentations to visitors. I also traveled to classrooms on Long Island with my new friends in a white van. And who were these pals? Let's see. There was a seven-foot snake, various owls, a red-tailed hawk, and turtles. I still have a scar where a turkey vulture's beak, its main ripping tool, pierced the skin on my forearm while the bird perched on a leather sleeve on my arm during a demonstration for fourth graders!

That unpleasant experience did not quench my passion for nature. I have reveled in being outside ever since I could remember. This hands-on experience of accompanying girls into nature during my time with G.R.E.E.N. reignited my interest in all things ecological. It also awakened me to the concept of "environmental justice." Underserved communities suffer from polluted air, water, and ground because of chemical contamination. So often, it is the least powerful who are exposed most to environmental hazards like lead and mercury.

This was the case in Flint, Michigan, where the drinking water was found to be contaminated with lead.

The effect of lead on children is terrible. It can lead to permanent brain damage, particularly if consumed by young kids, toddlers, newborns, and pregnant women. It can lead to decreased IQs and adversely affect academic performance and memory, causing a lifetime's worth of problems.

The people of West Virginia are also poisoned by fracking and coal runoff. With pollution, you really see the toxic impact of well-off people's NIMBY (Not in My Backyard) protections.

Now that I was carving out my own way instead of hewing to my parents' dream of medical school for me, I found real clarity. Combining my love of nature with my passion for helping the underserved seemed like a path forward in terms of a career. I was strongly influenced by the founders and leaders of Interactive Inc. Charol was married to an attractive man in his late fifties, Dale Mann, who was also her business partner. Dale was almost always the smartest person in the room. A professor emeritus at Columbia University Teachers College and SIPA, he was a pioneer in e-learning, i.e., using emerging technologies to create new and more engaging forms of instruction.

Charol, in her late forties, was equally passionate about and recognized for her work. A professor in the education department at Hofstra University, she wrote extensively about gender equality and sexual violence in schools. She was intent on lifting up women of color. Charol had adopted a young black girl named Evie, and she treated me almost as a second daughter. At times, it seemed that I butted heads with Charol as much as I did with my mother. Charol would often say, "Karine, you are ornery," when I failed to follow her advice. I was so insulted! Then I decided she was right (many years later)!

Charol was remarkably encouraging. There were a handful of smart, ambitious young women around my age in the office. Dale and Charol talked to us all the time about the value of a graduate degree. Education, they said, was something that no one could take away from us. It would give us a jump start to change the world for the better in whatever field we loved best. And they certainly led by example. Some of my coworkers did indeed go on to get their PhDs. After breaking the news to my parents about my MCATs and the fact that medical school was off the table for me, I promised them that I would get a master's degree one day.

Now I saw an opening.

Sometimes you meet people who have a profound effect on

you. Dale and Charol were that for me. I was mesmerized by the stories Dale told about his days at SIPA. He had attended the program during part of the Cold War—the historic period beginning after World War II in the late 1940s and ending with the fall of the Berlin Wall in 1991. In those decades, there was tremendous tension between the Communist superpower (the USSR) and its satellite nations and the capitalist superpower (the US) and its allies. Because there was so much hostility, which people feared could escalate into a nuclear hot war over the smallest provocation, citizens from capitalist and Communist countries rarely met. During the 1970s when Dale was a graduate student, SIPA was one of the few places where people from nations on both sides were able to exchange ideas and get to know each other. Dale told me SIPA allowed him to "reach across the globe" at a difficult time.

Founded in 1946 at the end of World War II, SIPA is a graduate school at Columbia University. Located in New York City, the school's students come from over a hundred countries. Its original mission was to educate diplomats. It expanded its mandate to include people passionate about effecting social change and other avenues of public service.

Eager to emulate Dale and become more engaged in advancing environmental justice on behalf of the underserved, I applied to start at SIPA in the fall of 2001. I never thought I would be accepted, but I took the chance. Dale wrote a letter of recommendation that I'm sure tipped the scales for my acceptance. I am so grateful that Dale and Charol took the time to share their experiences with me, to mentor me. Each day, I try to do the same with my own students.

I also credit my parents. I know they wanted me to become a doctor. They wanted me to follow their playbook, and they were disappointed when I didn't. But because they always told me that I was the best, they instilled a sense of bravery and purpose that I didn't even know I had. They raised me to have mountains of grit, and that enabled me to figure out a new path. If they had the courage to pick up and move from Haiti to Martinique and then to France and the United States, I could absolutely muster the pluck to try something new—even applying to a prestigious Ivy League university. My parents didn't want me to give up on medical school. Then, with the snap of their fingers—and a thick acceptance packet in the mail with Columbia's name and return address in the upper left-hand corner—they became my biggest cheerleaders. I realized that what my parents really wanted for their children was to be educated professionals and that, as is true of everyone, their lexicon was limited to what they had seen. In Haiti, there were only three paths to financial security: medicine, law, and engineering. Soon, my mother loved driving her car with a large blue-and-white Columbia University decal on the back window even if she didn't quite understand what I was doing at SIPA.

The two years I spent on Columbia's campus getting my master's degree in public administration were magical for me. I would imagine the bricks under my feet turning to yellow as I walked through campus from 116th Street and Broadway to 116th Street and Amsterdam Avenue. It was like a scene from one of my favorite childhood movies, not the 1939 *Wizard of Oz* but rather the 1978 remake *The Wiz* with an all-black cast starring Diana Ross and Michael Jackson. Walking to the SIPA building was like setting off on a life-changing journey. I truly came into myself intellectually, emotionally, sexually.

But there was a price to pay.

That first semester, I lived with my parents on Long Island, because I could not afford to live in the city. The commute took just under an hour by car with no traffic, two hours with traffic and an hour and a half on public transportation. The travel back and forth got to be too much, especially with late classes and group projects. For the second semester, I obtained gradu-ate housing.

In January 2002, I moved into a three-bedroom apartment on the northwest corner of 121st Street and Amsterdam Ave-nue, four blocks from SIPA. This was the first time I had ever lived away from my parents. My father and my brother Chris drove me in and helped me carry my few belongings upstairs. I was breaking a cardinal sin of Haitian family life, and my par-ents were not thrilled to have me living away from them. Tra-ditionally, Haitian women live under their parents' roof until they marry. And if they never find a husband, they remain there. The single life is not part of the culture, and only women dis-loyal to their families live on their own.

They could justify my move in some sense, though, because the way they saw it, I was still in a protective bubble—graduate housing run by Columbia University. And they boasted to *every-one* that I was attending a world-renowned Ivy League institution.

My building was called Kings College, but there was noth-ing princely about it. The not-yet-completely gentrified area teemed with scruffy graduate students. The nearby stores were mostly mom-and-pop bodegas. Even though my rent was less than $800 dollars a month for my sardine can of a room, I had to take out a $10,000 loan to afford my new life in Manhattan. I had the smallest room in that apartment—even smaller than my room at my parents' first apartment in Queens. My bed-room window faced the alley we shared with the buildings on 122nd Street. It was veiled in darkness twenty-four hours a day because a large brick wall blocked any possible light.

I had two apartment-mates, both women, and it was the first time I lived with white people. Amy was graduating from the film program at the School of Arts at the end of the semester in May 2002. When she moved out, I took her room and lived there for my second (and last) year at SIPA. It had tons of natu-ral light pouring in and was twice the size of the room I'd been renting. I now had to pay about $850 a month, but the extra space and light made the increase worth it. The only downside that I was completely unaware of, or had not considered, before making the change was the room's position. The larger room was located on the street side of 121st Street, which was right behind the garbage pickup of Columbia University Teachers College. For weeks, possibly months, I could not sleep well in the room. I could set my alarm by the New York City Sanitation Department with their vehemently boisterous and obnoxious garbage trucks that roared through 121st Street to pick up the industrial-size steel garbage dumpsters at 5:00 a.m. I was dumbfounded by how much garbage Teachers College produced. This was life in the Big Apple!

When I transferred rooms, a brand-new roommate moved into the apartment. She was a young woman from India. Just like us, she was at Columbia University to attend graduate school. One of the advantages and allures of living in New York City is the opportunity to come into close contact with different cultures and people. It is that very richness that former New York City mayor David N. Dinkins captured in his 1990 inaugural address when he said: "I see New York as a gorgeous mosaic of race and religious faith, of national origin and sexual orientation."

I loved the city's endless variety of people. Although I had often thought of myself as being an outsider because of my Haitian background, our new roommate made me realize just what an American I truly was. Indra had never lived outside India and seemed intent on setting up her own version of her childhood home. Incredibly fragrant aromas wafted out of the kitchen where she was always stirring pots of curry and lentil dahl while wearing the most beautiful silk saris in deep pink and green.

We were all loving the "gorgeous mosaic" of our living situation until one afternoon when Indra asked to speak with me and our third roommate.

Apparently, Indra had gotten married back in India over the 2002 winter break. When and where she got married was not the problem. The problem was her statement, "My husband, Akhil, will be joining me in New York City." These were already close quarters for three women all sharing a small apartment and, most important, one minuscule bathroom. What would it be like adding an unfamiliar man?

To say the least, we were not pleased. Indra promised that Akhil's "visit" would be for only a few weeks, but he ended up staying for my entire final semester at Columbia. Our friendship with her soured quickly. It all felt like an awful con game. It was never clear what Akhil was doing with his time in New York while Indra was in class or studying at the library. He tried to stay out of sight. Just as I opened the front door with the key, I would hear scurrying footsteps and the door to Indra's room would creak shut. But his toothbrush and shaving kit on the bathroom sink, as well as that off-putting sense of someone being in the apartment even if unseen, were a constant reminder that he was there. All of the comfort I had developed about being in my own space—able to walk around in my underwear if I pleased—vanished. I no longer felt at home in my home.

My second year at Columbia, I was one of the lucky ones who received a full scholarship that covered my tuition. This relieved a lot of the financial pressure that I felt that first year at Columbia—though I still had to take out a loan each semester to pay for my housing and food.

I want my story to give hope to readers who are late bloomers. I think I experienced at Columbia what most people experience at age eighteen when they go away to college for their freshman year or join the military. For them, living away from their parents and high school friends allows them the opportunity to envision themselves in new ways, small and big. The nerd becomes a bit of the party animal. The shy person emerges as the squad leader. The closeted guy acts on his desire for another man. The evangelical questions the existence of God for the first time. Or at least takes a few sips of beer.

My college years at New York Institute of Technology lacked these opportunities. I lived at home. I studied like a madwoman to become a medical doctor. I never dated. And I certainly never acted on my attraction to other women. Any feelings I might have had were buried on long, punishing cross-country runs through the back roads of Wheatley Heights. I helped my parents figure out their bills and remained every inch a traditional young Haitian woman whose family wanted to protect her. Security, not adventure, was vital to my parents.

Even physically, I remained my parents' little girl. I've always been slender and petite, unlike my siblings, who both tower over me. Like my dad, I look younger than my actual age. Because of this, I think people often underestimate me.

Back then, I was still having my mother process my hair. For black women, hair is a big deal and a fraught topic. There is a reason the political activist Angela Davis's magnificent towering afro remains a powerful cultural touchstone of the civil rights movement and the 1960s. But as comedian Chris Rock's 2009 documentary titled *Good Hair* reveals, black women's hair remains a topic that stirs up deep, often conflicting emotions.

The inspiration for the documentary originated when Chris Rock's adorable little daughter asked her father why she didn't have "good hair." The movie probes the history of black hair in America—from weaves to wigs to the relaxer known as "creamy crack" used in perms. And what all of this means.

In my case, I had a double whammy situation. I was a black, closeted lesbian whose loving mother owned a hair salon. My mother adored doing hair, most of all, the hair of her two beautiful daughters. (My sister loves having her hair done to this day, making her the good daughter and me the bad, ungrateful one.) It was something she did for us, and something we did together.

A black women's hair salon is more than a place where you get your hair cut or dyed. It's a gathering spot that every Saturday provides a meeting place for gossip and support. This is not a Hair Cuttery where you are in and out in forty minutes. On a busy weekend, I could spend six hours at my mom's salon, ER Unisex, in Far Rockaway. (ER was short for Elaine, my mother's first name, and Roslyn, her business partner's.) Years later she dissolved their partnership and opened Elaine's Unisex. No matter the name or location, my mom's hair salon was part of our family and our culture. Heck, Madam C. J. Walker—whose parents were enslaved—was one of the very first self-made African American tycoons and philanthropists. Her massive turn-of-the-twentieth-century fortune was founded on the hair products she manufactured for black women.

One thing I could count on was that there were certain constants every time I went. The first thing that always hit me was the stinging ammonia smell of perms and other chemicals that made my nose hairs tickle. ER Unisex had five black-cushioned salon chairs lined up on the right side of the shop facing a wall of mirrors and a black-and-white tiled floor. My mother always used the third chair, in the middle, and rented out the others.

Shanise, one of two of the regular hairstylists, rented the chair closest to the front door. As soon as you walked in you were likely to hear 1990s and early 2000s R & B booming from her workstation. Shanise was so in love with the singer Joe that she would play his CD *My Name Is Joe* on a nonstop loop.

A tall forty-something West Indian from Jamaica, Shanise talked with a faint accent. She wore her hair long down her back, and dressed with style. Big earrings, lots of spandex, manicured nails, bright colors. If you mentioned that you had an ailment, Shanise would offer a remedy. She even had a cure for acne. "Hey, Karine," she said once. "Try mixing honey and lemon in a bowl, spread it on your face, leave it on for a few minutes, then wash it off!"

I did just what she said, and it worked.

Evelyn's chair came next. Shanise's sister-in-law—they had married two brothers—she was a fair-skinned African American woman in her late thirties with two young daughters. She was shorter than Shanise and had a sense of chic, urban flair: leather jackets and fitted pants. They were both nice, friendly women with their hearts in the right place. But they loved to gossip about everyone—customers who came through the door and celebrities on the covers of the magazines my mom kept in neat piles for her clientele to flip through.

My weekday drop-bys were a lot calmer than Fridays and Saturdays—"the chaos days," as I thought of them, because between the customers and the bootleggers, the bell on the front door of the shop sang all day long.

The first bootlegger of the afternoon might be an African American man in his late forties. "Good afternoon, ladies!" he'd say as he swung open the door. "Today we have a sale—two shea butters for five dollars." He'd point to the big black bag on his shoulder. Besides beauty supplies, he'd hawk CDs and DVDs, a boom box on his other shoulder blasting out a hit album. He would hold up the plastic case to show that his CDs were legit. In the other hand, he held a DVD of the hottest movie then in theaters (recorded inside the theater by someone with a shaky hand). Part of this Saturday ritual would be a hairstylist or customer asking what he had on offer and what was good. Sometimes the bootlegger got lucky: someone bought his goodies. And inevitably a regular would complain about the CD or DVD they bought the week before, which the bootlegger then had to replace for free.

If there was no interest, he swung back out the door to try his luck down the block. But before you knew it, the bell tinkled and the next bootlegger had entered the shop, yelling, "Three for five dollars!"

This time, it might be the short, heavyset thirty-something

Latina. She'd wear the same uniform every weekend: a long white shirt over a sparkly black spandex bottom, a fanny pack around her waist, a baseball cap with a ponytail sticking out in the back. She barely spoke English. Her heavy bag was packed with socks and underwear. My mother, who bought my siblings their back-to-school underpants and T-shirts from her, was a regular customer.

Twenty minutes later, the next bootlegger of the day jingled the front doorbell. This one? Maybe a young black man in his twenties. He also had an accent, but from what part of Africa, it was hard to tell. His hair in long dreadlocks, this bootlegger wore a dashiki with blue jeans, and a large beaded necklace with a huge wooden pendant of the African continent hanging from his neck. His specialty was flirting with the ladies getting their hair done—a sales technique he used to try to sell them oils and incense. But when this effort to lay on the charm fell flat, back out the door he headed, bruised ego in tow.

Despite the familiar environment, I hated getting my hair done. Every four to six weeks, I would have the roots of my hair straightened with the strong-smelling, harsh chemical relaxant, aka "creamy crack," made from sodium hydroxide. This thick, heavy liquid removed the natural curl by breaking down the protein in the hair. Sometimes if my mom was super busy and left the chemical on too long, my scalp would be burned.

After removing the chemical, my mom would apply a toner. Then I would have to sit under a dryer for hours. I resented the time it took to get my hair done. After I graduated from college, I gradually became more self-aware. I began to recognize that there was an element of racial self-loathing in spending so much time trying to make my hair appear more Caucasian, less "nappy."

And yet, there was such a sense of community, of sisterhood, of connection to other black women that my mother's hair salon gave me. On one hand, I felt enveloped and accepted. And on the other hand, I felt trapped and angry. My sister, Edwine, does not share my conflicted emotions. She has continued to perm her hair and often wears a long, fabulous wig or weave. Her nails are always done, and she never leaves the house without makeup and thick fake eyelashes. She is all glam all the time.

It's the push-pull of tradition. In that salon, we were performing a weekend ritual that has linked black women for decades whether in the United States or the Caribbean. The barbershop serves the same function for black men. Our place. Our ways. But sometimes that sense of community can feel stifling to an individual.

The idea of rejecting it also made me feel incredibly guilty. Justifiably, my mother was proud of her skill as a hairdresser and of the gumption that motivated her to get her license and run a salon, no mean feat for an immigrant woman who left school at a young age. Plus, that salon kept me and my siblings housed, fed, and schooled! In my mother's house, nice Haitian women showed off their soft, processed straight locks. To be honest, I am lucky she didn't insist on keeping my hair in the thick, beribboned braids of my childhood, as she did back when she was able to exert complete control over what I wore and how I looked!

So despite moving to the city, I still made the trek to the salon. I wouldn't have the courage to let my hair be natural until I joined the John Edwards presidential campaign in 2007.

While I maintained the status quo with my hair for the time being, at Columbia, at age twenty-six, I felt free to experiment in other ways. For the first time, I went to women's bars—Henrietta Hudson Bar & Girl and Crazy Nanny's to play pool and dance. It was thrilling to walk onto a darkened dance floor and admire and be admired openly by other women. I still love the music from that time: Destiny's Child, where Beyoncé got her start; Jay-Z, who I would later see perform at a 2009 Obama inaugural ball; Missy Elliott. I couldn't get enough of the lovely Alicia Keys's signature song, "Fallin'." My friend Joselyn and I would go out at least three times a week. Even though I have never been a drinker or a druggie, in those days before New York's smoking ban went into effect, I would come home reeking of cigarette smoke and sweat. I'd have to peel off my clothes right at the front door.

Then I met Daphne, who was a year ahead of me in the same MPA program at SIPA. She was out, proud, and whip smart. She had penetrating blue eyes and tons of attitude. Daphne became my first girlfriend. I had to explain to Daphne that if she met my siblings or parents, it was imperative that we pretend we were just close friends. Sometimes we would walk along the streets of the Upper West Side holding hands and kissing, lost in the raptures of first love. Then I would freeze, terrified that the yellow cab I spotted behind us just might be my father's. Later, I would twist and turn in bed, keeping Daphne up, worried that my father had seen me and been devastated.

Eventually I wrote down his medallion number so I could check any passing cars and stop worrying. It was a temporary solution.

Daphne and I broke up after almost a year, but it was not as devastating as every breakup song I'd ever heard on the radio led me to believe it would be. I knew even when we started dating that I was not the right woman for her. But our relationship was important to me all the same. It allowed me to be myself and to take one step closer to being an out gay woman.

This journey at Columbia was life altering and thrilling. But breaking away from a loving, close-knit, immigrant family with a mother and father who had sacrificed everything for their children felt wrenching.

Finally, a massive panic attack on the New York City subway made me realize just how stressed I had become despite being happier than I had ever dreamed possible.

Ironic, I know.

In the fall of my second year at SIPA, I had gotten on the

Number One train at 14th Street. It was midmorning, and the subway wasn't particularly crowded. The car filled as we hit the local stations. I will never know what triggered my panic attack at Penn Station at 34th Street. My heart began to race—it was beating so fast and so hard that my eardrums felt as though they were being pounded like percussion drums. I worried people could see my heart about to burst through my jacket. With each passing stop, the subway car doors opening and closing, taking a breath became more difficult for me. Darkness came down like a black curtain over my eyes, and I realized that if I didn't get off the train, I would fall onto the filthy floor and people would step over me like I was a passed-out drunk or drug addict. Someone might call the transit cops, and I would end up either in Rikers prison or the Bellevue psych ward.

Using the metal pole in front of me, I pulled myself up, letting the people behind me push me forward out of the car and onto the platform. I slumped onto a wooden bench at 96th Street. I don't know how long I sat there, sweat pouring off my forehead. To give you an idea of how freaked-out I was, I left my backpack sitting on the ground of the subway station.

I never, ever allowed my backpack to touch the floor, nor did I even sit on a bench in the subway. The reason? Because I had personally witnessed the rats that scrabble through the New York underground like they own it.

Which, of course, they do. But at the time, I didn't care.

After two hours or so, I finally summoned the courage to leave the subway and start walking up to Columbia. It was a long walk, but anything seemed better than getting back on a subway car. It was weeks before I summoned the courage to ride the subway again. That evening, as I crossed the streets going north on Broadway, the sunset streaking the sky pink and purple, I made a decision to seek professional help from a therapist.

The next day, after my Environmental Law class, I walked into the student union in Lerner Hall and up the stairs to student counseling. Growing up in a Haitian household, you are taught at a young age that family business—i.e., secrets—stayed in the confines of your home. It was forbidden to talk about your family to anyone outside your immediate relatives. Aunts and uncles maybe, but not even second cousins were close enough.

It was also taboo to go to therapy. It was considered weak, because you should not complain—or focus too much attention on yourself. The answer to every obstacle or ailment was to stay quiet and work harder. But all of the existential pressures of family, school, life, my sexuality, my suicide attempt, the terrible sexual abuse I had suffered as a child at the hands of a relative had finally taken a toll on me physically. It was time to take care of my emotional health. The anxiety attack I'd experienced was so scary and debilitating, it was enough to make me overcome the guilt I would normally feel about breaking a family rule. And once I realized what a relief it was to talk with a trained, nonjudgmental outsider, I felt a burden I didn't even realize I was carrying had been lifted. I know I have mentioned this before, but it's so important I believe it is worth repeating: please seek help if you are struggling, even if it goes against your family's teachings.

I really want to stress this. So often we try to bury trauma in America. Our national narrative celebrates the story of brave, stoic people who leave their homes and their pasts behind—as well as the grief, poverty, and trouble that might have motivated the journey to these new shores. But this creation myth can carry a lot of heavy, often invisible baggage. My family is a perfect example. So many secrets, so much unexpressed pain. I only began to feel true to myself after I entered therapy and was able to distinguish between Karine the daughter and Karine the adult individual.

Most important, if I hadn't seen a therapist, one subway ride could easily have derailed my plans that spring for an epic journey.

CHAPTER THREE

Haiti, Here I Come

"I will never go back to Haiti."

That's what my mother would tell me whenever I asked her if she wanted to visit the country of her birth again. My mother's experience was emotionally scarring. She has had a hard, hard life. She and her twin sister were raised by their father and his then wife until the age of five. (Their biological mother was never in the picture.) Then, during a cataclysmic famine, her father gave each of the twins to different families who adopted them. This was not uncommon. Many people could not feed their children. At that point, my mother lost all contact with her twin sister. Later, when my mother tried to find her twin, she was told she had died. This was an unspeakable blow. My mother met her biological mother only when she was sixteen years old.

My mother's adoptive parents did not provide a happy childhood for her. They treated her not as a daughter but as a servant to babysit their own biological children. In 1970, when she was nineteen, my mother moved to Port-au-Prince and tried to continue her education at night school, where my father, then twenty-eight, was her teacher. My parents got married in 1971. A year later, my brother Donald was born in Haiti. Had he lived, he would have been older than me by a little more than two years. When Donald was seven months old, my mother left him in Haiti with her biological mother, so she could reunite with my father in Martinique, where he had moved during her pregnancy. My father had left when my mom was six months pregnant with Donald in hopes of getting work. Many Haitians would move to islands like Martinique and Guadeloupe, which were both colonized by the French. The culture and food were similar to Haiti's so my parents felt comfortable there.

My mother did what she thought was best: she could make more money without having to split her focus between a job and an infant. When she and my dad were financially stable, she would return to Haiti to get baby Donald.

My mother said Donald was an easy, quiet but very observant baby who rarely cried. It was his curiosity she most remembers, the way his dark eyes would drink in everything she did, following her around the room. Leaving him behind is her biggest regret, her overwhelming heartbreak in life, the torment that she remembers first thing in the morning and last thing at night. The little boy died before he was even old enough to walk, and my mother has never forgiven herself for leaving her precious firstborn son with her mother.

My mother has tortured herself over Donald's death for decades. From the day she heard in Martinique that her baby died in Haiti, my mother has dreamed of him, particularly around his birthday, June 19. She sees his sweet chocolate face and hears him crying out for her. My mother left me with my father in Paris in 1977, when I was three, to return to Haiti for the first time since Donald's death. She didn't have the money to both pay for and attend Donald's funeral in 1973. At last, she had saved enough to buy a little tombstone for his grave to commemorate his short time on earth. Even as a child growing up in Queens, I knew there was a certain day just before school let out for the summer when my mother would not leave her bed, lying there weeping.

When my mother left Haiti that second time, she vowed not to return, unable to forgive herself. But neither did she forget. None of us could. My parents had only one photo of Donald— a shopworn eight-by-ten black-and-white print that sat on the bookshelf in the family room beside our prized encyclopedia set—but it had a powerful presence in our house. When you walked into the room, you almost couldn't help but look for the photo. He was frozen in time at six months, sitting up in a sailor suit, very little hair, and a big smile. I used to stare at it, amazed at how much we looked alike, with our wide-set eyes and deep dimples.

When I was growing up, my mother prayed constantly—and most of her prayers were about Donald. She begged God to help her find peace, but it would not come.

I often thought, then and now, how my life would have been different if I had had a protective big brother. Would he have stopped my relative from sexually abusing me? Would I have had someone to share the burden of helping my parents adjust to a new country? Would we have been "partners in crime" as kids, helping to protect each other as I saw my two younger siblings do? I thought of Donald as I read Michelle Obama's terrific autobiography, *Becoming*, because the former First Lady writes so affectionately about her own big brother, Craig Robinson. In their Chicago neighborhood, in school, and at Princeton University, she was always known as Craig's little sister. He smoothed the path for her, and she loved him for it. I often wondered, how would my life have been different if I hadn't been the bossy eldest child but the darling, protected little sis?

Carrying decades of grief, one of the last things my mom ever wanted to hear me say was "I'm going to Haiti!" In her mind, Haiti had already taken one child, and she could not bear it if it took another. So in the spring of 2003, when the opportunity presented itself for me to go to Haiti for the first time, I couldn't bring myself to tell her. Instead, I waited until the eve of my departure to break the news.

"I want to die in my country and be buried in my country."

Ten out of ten times that would be my father's answer when asked "Do you miss Haiti?" He has always been a proud Haitian man. This idea of the country was the polar opposite of my mother's. My dad would daydream out loud with my siblings and me, sharing his hope to go back to the country of his youth. He would remember the beauty, the calmness, and ease of living in the countryside. For him, New York was too fast, too hard, too overwhelming. He saw it as a rattling jungle day and night, seven days a week. When I told him about my final graduate school project, which included traveling to Haiti for a week, he was thrilled. He hadn't been to Haiti in more than two decades. Hearing his eldest daughter talking about visiting Haiti for the first time sent him on a nostalgic journey. He hung on to every detail, as if he were traveling there himself.

The weekend before I left, I visited with my parents on Long Island. I had told my father the news weeks earlier, and he had already agreed to take me to John F. Kennedy International Airport to catch my flight on Sunday. Now the plan was to break the news to my mother.

Trying to get my mom's attention is always an arduous task. She is one of the busiest people I know. She has an unmatchable hustle. In those days, her Saturdays usually consisted of working a full-time job as a home health care aide as well as running her beauty salon and styling hair. On Sundays, she would spend ten hours at her Pentecostal church. The only way for me to get on her calendar to have this conversation was to literally step into her world. Attending church with her on Sunday was out of the question. By that time, I would be on a plane. And to be honest, spending ten hours praying and repenting would have been a no go for me even if I wasn't traveling. Growing up Catholic and going to Catholic schools as I did, spending more than an hour in church seemed excessive.

I called my mom earlier in the week to let her know that I was coming home for the weekend and ask if she minded doing my hair on Saturday. She agreed, but there was a quid pro quo. Getting my hair done meant me waking up early on Saturday to drive her from Wheatley Heights, Long Island, to Far Rockaway, Queens, for her home health care aide job. That would take an hour. I'd then have to be back by 1:00 p.m. to pick her up and make the five-minute drive to her beauty salon. The tricky part for me: When exactly during that day would I tell her about Haiti? I was in a pickle at this point. It was bad enough that I was going to Haiti, which I knew she would hate. But on top of that, I had waited until the last possible moment to tell her. I had let myself believe that by waiting (and waiting!) to give her the news, I was making it easier for her to agree to it. She would have no choice but to go along with it. If I had given her a few weeks' notice, I knew she would try to stop me. The truth, though: I was just being a chicken and avoiding conflict for as long as possible.

I should have done it first thing. Just ripped the Band-Aid off and gotten it over with. But as soon as we buckled up on Saturday morning, memories of our complicated mom/daughter dynamic welled up inside me, and it was as if my well-planned words about "the trip" got stuck in my throat. I just could not face her anger, fear, and grief. My mom is a passionate woman with deep emotions. She can yell, but when she's *really* angry, she bottles it up and ignores you. That's the worst.

After I dropped her off at her job, I sat in the parking lot for ten minutes infuriated with myself. Now what? Not telling her that morning meant waiting twelve hours for us to be alone again. My plane would take off in less than twenty-four hours. I was cutting it dangerously close—and I was already operating in dangerous territory to begin with.

I was jumpy all day. But I couldn't bring myself to tell her on the way to the salon, either. The whole time my mother stood behind my chair at the salon, I wanted to just blurt it out, but I knew this was the wrong time. When my perm was done, I moved the car to a coveted spot in front of the shop to load our belongings into the trunk. Sitting behind the wheel on that chilly spring afternoon, I watched as the store owners on either side of my mom's salon closed up shop, banging down their steel window gates. I could see the hairstylists packing up to head home through the big plate-glass window. The neon letters of the shop name beamed: *ER* in red and *Unisex* in white.

My mom has a habit of carrying around multiple bags wherever she goes—a change of clothes, food, shoes, and a stack of mail so important to her she never leaves it at home. With a nanosecond's notice, she is ready for anything. She even has a jar in her car for peeing in just in case of an emergency during her almost two-hour ride to and from work. (My mom is too afraid to drive on the highways which means sticking to the local streets that take twice the time.) This bag-carrying habit makes people sometimes look twice at her. My mother is a beautiful woman who has always looked far younger than her age. She takes enormous pride in her nails, her clothes, her jewelry, her grooming, her trim figure. She rocks bright red lipstick and has the complexion of a teenager! But she totes enough bags to qualify as a bag lady. She carries all this luggage because she needs a variety of outfits and shoes to match her multiple jobs and identities. What my mother wears—high heels and leggings—when she is the proud owner of her own beauty shop is very different than the plastic clogs and floral scrubs she sports as a home health care aide.

At last she closed up shop and got into the car, bags and all. We set off and it was now or never. But was she ready for my news?

Touching my freshly permed hair, I looked at my mom beside me in the passenger seat and drew in a deep breath. It was as if the other cars on the Southern State Parkway melted away. "Mummy," I said, pausing to muster all of my courage. "I have to tell you something. It's actually great news. Columbia University has been working with the Haitians Living Abroad Ministry on a project on how universities in Haiti and Columbia University can work together. And tomorrow I will be going to Haiti with five other students from Columbia University."

The closest experience I could possibly compare this to is when someone proposes marriage to a loved one and all you hear and see from them is silence, fear, and total confusion.

"What Haiti are you talking about?" she demanded. "You are going to Haiti tomorrow to do what? I don't understand. Why would anyone let you go to Haiti? I did not say you could go to Haiti. How are you going to get to Haiti? How long are you going for? Where are you going to in Haiti? Why is Columbia University allowing you to go to Haiti? With who are you going? Does your papi know that you are going to Haiti? Did you tell him? What did he say? Where are you staying? Why are you going there? Why would you want to go there?"

Finally she stopped, and after two minutes of silence, I looked over at her to see if it was safe to start answering her questions. Her face looked cold, stoic, emotionless. She didn't look back at me. Her gaze was focused on the road ahead, the hood of the car leading us home. The one familiar movement that I did notice was her hands. When my mom is upset or nervous, she rubs them together, usually while fiddling with a tissue. I leaned over with my right hand and touched her rubbing hands. She didn't flinch. She didn't even move away. It was as if I wasn't even in the car with her. She was in a place of her own.

If there's one thing I have learned living with my mother, it's knowing when to speak and when to stay quiet. For the last thirty minutes of the ride, it felt like the grim reaper was sitting on the armrest between us. When we got home, she got out of the car, slammed the door, and went straight to her bedroom—slamming that door, too. To this day, my mom and I have never spoken about the car conversation or my trip to Haiti.

I've never needed an alarm clock. I woke myself up at 6:00 a.m. on Sunday, March 9, 2003. I was in my old room at my parents' house, which had originally been the master bedroom. Although there are five bedrooms on the second floor—plenty of room for everyone—my mother had decided years ago to turn the small apartment attached to the house on the first floor into a new master suite for herself. As Edwine, Chris, and I reached high school and college, my mother and father stopped being a couple. They were just two people raising kids together. They lived under the same roof but led separate lives. The reasons for my parents' emotional chasm were never discussed. Another family secret. We just took it for granted that my dad slept in the guest bedroom across the hall from my room. My brother Chris's room was next to his.

For me, the best part about sleeping at my parents' house was waking up to songbirds adding their voices to my morning routine. I have always loved getting up early. I view it as an opportunity to set the tone of the day before anyone else can. It is my way of having a leg up on the world. Nothing compares with the stillness of early morning. It is quiet (except for the birds singing), which helps me ease into the day. Early mornings feel less polluted, not just with air, but with voices, bodies, angst, and stress.

My parents' Wheatley Heights house sits on a one-acre lot

with a fenced-in pool. There was a skinny two-story-high tree right outside my window, and from my bed I could see the birds sitting on the branches. This was the serene opposite of the gray cityscape and screeching garbage trucks outside my apartment window in Morningside Heights.

After a few minutes of my morning serenade by the song-bird chorus, I rolled out of bed, took a hot shower, and spent an hour packing the brand-new black suitcase I had purchased for the trip. While the weather in New York was going to be in the forties all week, Haiti would be in the nineties and humid for my six-day stay. Goodbye, winter coat, sweatshirt, and wa-terproof boots! Hello, shorts, sandals, sunglasses, and sunscreen! The most important item I was taking with me was the $10,000 worth of camera equipment loaned to me by Columbia Univer-sity's Graduate School of Journalism.

The Haiti trip was a twofer. I was taking a graduate work-shop at Columbia which set up the trip as well as a course at the Journalism School, where I was working on a documen-tary on the Haitian diaspora. The advantage of being a gradu-ate student at SIPA is that you're allowed to take classes at other schools within the university. Knowing that, I zeroed in on the Journalism School. I had always had an interest in journalism, especially in documentary storytelling.

The story I originally wanted to tell was about my father. Driving a New York City taxi has been the longest job he has held since immigrating to America decades ago. For years my dad has woken up at 4:00 a.m., six days a week, to drive his yel-low cab. It could easily be a twenty-hour day for him. By that time in 2003, he owned one taxi medallion, which was a cov-eted prize—worth five hundred thousand dollars back then—in the New York cab industry.

Throughout the years, I got to meet taxi-driving friends of my dad's, most of whom were other Haitian men. I learned that before coming to the United States, many of them had been doctors, lawyers, business owners. Others had been engineers or teachers, like my father. I wanted to tell the story of how these professional men transitioned from a country where they had status and relative wealth to the United States, where they were working long days for very little reward. Usually, they were not only supporting their families in America but were also supporting other family members back home in Haiti.

As a kid, whenever I got an idea in my head, a project or goal I wanted to accomplish, I did everything possible to make it happen. I had that same strong sense of determination in my twenties—and it's still with me today. The summer of 2002, I started mapping out how I was going to fulfill my longtime quest of making the documentary. Since college, when I had more freedom to go to the movies, I had loved documentaries. Among my favorites were *Mandela*, *Four Little Girls*, and *Buena Vista Social Club*.

I scoured a Journalism School bulletin for the 2002–2003 academic year until I found a documentary seminar course being offered that coming spring. The course was taught by the legendary documentarian June Cross. Professor Cross had won an Emmy in 1997 for *Secret Daughter*, her autobiographical film about how her white biological mother gave her to be raised by a black family. Her mother would pretend that Cross was her adopted daughter during the summers Cross spent in Los Angeles with her mother and her husband, Larry Storch, who starred in a 1960s TV show about the Wild West, *F Troop*.

It wasn't going to be easy to get into Professor Cross's class, but I was determined to do the best I could. Since I was set to graduate that May, it seemed like a make-or-break chance.

In mid-January 2003, I walked across the 116th Street campus from SIPA to the J-School and rushed up the stairs. Although I arrived early for the 5:00 p.m. class, the room was packed. I was blown away. I guess I wasn't the only one on campus who dreamed of making a documentary or who thought their story was Emmy material!

There was tension in the air from the start. About fifty students had shown up, and there were only fifteen slots. To be chosen as one of the lucky fifteen, we each had to write a synopsis of the story we wanted to create on film. Not being a journalism student, I was at a disadvantage. I had never written a synopsis before. I searched "writing a synopsis" online and sat down in my apartment to bang out multiple versions of my Haitian taxi drivers idea. The first day of class I added my final edited version to the papers piling up on top of Professor Cross's desk. We would learn our fates before the next class the following week. Leaving the classroom, I thought I had a fifty-fifty chance. While I wasn't a Journalism School student, I believed that I had a compelling personal story. A unique story that only I could tell.

I got the great news a few days later by email. I got into the class! I was over the moon. I ran to my apartment, went straight into my room, closed the door, and screamed and jumped around with joy (for once, not self-conscious that Indra's husband, Akhil, could hear everything). I had hoped it would come true, but I still couldn't believe it. When the second day of class arrived, the chosen fifteen met with Professor Cross in a smaller room than the week prior. That was the editing room, the workspace where we would learn about documentary filmmaking. But there was still another hurdle: while fifteen of us were chosen to participate in the course, only *five* of the fifteen story pitches submitted to Professor Cross would be selected to be turned into documentaries.

As hopeful as I was that second evening in class, when I learned then that my story was one of the chosen five, I was stunned. Me! The science nerd who had studied premed as an undergrad and was now working on a master's degree in public administration. I was going to make my own documentary!

Each story had a team of three. Professor Cross matched me with two guys, Bernard and Alesandro. Bernard, from Denmark, was getting his PhD from the anthropology department. Ale, as we called him, was a journalism student from Greece.

Professor Cross let me know that by picking my Haitian taxi driver story, she was taking two big chances. First, she thought it would be an uphill battle to film it in twelve weeks. I hadn't locked in a single interview with a Haitian cabbie. My story was only an idea, nowhere close to becoming a reality. The second risk came in putting our group together. Ale was the only journalism student—the only one who knew how to handle a camera or had any storytelling experience.

It turned out that Professor Cross's professional concerns were right on point. My father was all in on this project, trying to recruit taxi drivers. Despite his help, we had hit a massive brick wall three weeks in. Haitian taxi drivers, including the only one we had interviewed, didn't want their stories to be told. They were worried that family members back home might see the documentary and learn they were now cabdrivers, not New York City big shots raking in money in their former professions. For many Haitian American men, being a cabdriver was an embarrassment. They wanted to keep it a secret.

We scrambled for days trying to figure how to stop our film from flatlining. Then a solution surfaced. Haiti was going to celebrate its bicentennial in 2004, the two hundredth anniversary of Haiti's independence, making it the first black republic. The idea was to tell the story of Haiti's history through a personal narrative. It took a lot of searching, but we found a compelling figure in Father Guy Sansariq, then a sixty-nine-year-old Haitian priest who became a bishop in 2006. At the time, he served at a Roman Catholic church, St. Jerome's in the heart of Little Haiti in Brooklyn, at the intersection of Newkirk and Nostrand Avenues in the Flatbush neighborhood. Father Sansariq had a tragic and riveting story. The regime of "Papa

Doc" Duvalier, the murderous Haitian autocrat, had executed this gentle priest's entire family decades earlier in Haiti. Now Father Sansariq was considered to be a guiding light and confidant to his Haitian American parishioners as they tried to make a new life in a foreign and often hostile world. By telling his story, we would tell the larger story about the Haitian diaspora.

It wasn't easy to convince Father Sansariq to sign on to the project. He was a humble man who didn't want to be in the limelight, which made sense considering his calling. But I think he liked our group and sensed our sincerity. The truth is, we kept badgering this kind man, and perhaps we just wore him down. We truly wanted to tell his story in a thoughtful way. The last person we needed to convince was Professor Cross, who, despite her doubts, signed off on us changing course and telling Father Sansariq's story.

I have often wondered why she didn't just choose another of the proposed documentaries and put us to work on that one instead. All of us were novices. We had only twelve weeks; we were now way behind. I'm grateful that she didn't give up on us. Professor Cross wanted us to be successful. But as she made crystal clear, there would be no hand-holding. "You know what you need to do," she said calmly. "Now go do it!"

A friend of mine always tells me about a boss she first hated, then grew to admire. An anxious, driven people pleaser, Lizzie worked for an older woman at a book publisher in Manhattan. This woman would give Lizzie assignments, then expect her to complete them without giving her much direction. Panic-stricken, Lizzie would ask for more detail. "You'll figure it out" was the woman's refrain.

At first, Lizzie was in a constant lather of worry and anxiety, furious at her boss. Then, as the months passed, Lizzie realized how rare it was to work for someone who forced her out of her comfort zone, who demanded that Lizzie learn to create solutions on her own instead of micromanaging every step of a project. After hearing this story, I unashamedly seized on this mantra: "I'll figure it out." Since then I have used it on political campaigns all over the United States. In the end, Lizzie's boss gave her a gift. So often I see young people, particularly young women, who are paralyzed with this sense that there is a right way to do things and a wrong way to do things. In reality, there are many ways to do things and often what works for one person doesn't work for another. In politics, you want to achieve your goal in the most direct, impactful, and least expensive manner. There is no ironclad rule book that provides solutions to problems in politics, school, book publishing, or life, alas. You just have to "figure it out" on your own.

There is also no guaranteed control in life as I learned to my horror. Hands down, the moment when I thought I'd fail to make the documentary was one of the very worst experiences of my entire life. It's the kind of memory that still makes me break out in a cold sweat when, always unbidden and never desired, it swims up out of my subconscious.

After we gained Father Sansariq's trust and cooperation, Bernard, Ale, and I went to visit him at his rectory. In a reverential manner, he stood before us. In his leathery hands he held a shoebox of old photos, many black-and-white. "Just remember," he said, "these are the only photos of my family that I have. The only copies are here." These family photos were of his relatives back in Haiti who had been killed or "disappeared" by the murderous Duvalier regime of Papa Doc and Baby Doc. Here was this elderly priest sharing with us the only vestiges of his lost family and his lost life in Haiti.

Did we head to a copy shop and make copies of everything he gave us that very afternoon—then drive them back to his rectory in Little Haiti? Did we refuse to accept the precious shoebox until he had the photos copied himself? Did I at least strap those photos in a zippered pouch that I wore bandolero-style across my chest? Oh, how I desperately wish we had!

Instead, we effusively thanked the good padre for his photos and stashed the shoebox in a nondescript shopping bag in my car's back seat while we looked for a place to eat lunch. Yes, we did lock the car.

You know what happened.

Somebody—we never found out who—smashed the window and grabbed the shopping bag with the shoebox inside. This is a common crime in New York City. I screamed when we came back to the car after lunch. We ran from garbage can to garbage can, from disgusting dumpster to reeking bags of garbage on the street. Block after block we searched. Surely the miscreant had opened the shoebox, realized that it was just old photos, and tossed it.

No such luck. We never found the shoebox, and telling Father Sansariq that we had lost his photos was just terrible. Amazingly, he took it in stride, smiled bravely, and said it didn't matter because he held his relatives' faces in his heart. The loss still pains me today.

Then, unexpectedly, the trip to Haiti for our second-year SIPA seminar course was approved. After this terrible start, it felt as if all was coming into place. Not only was I going to Haiti, the country of my parents' births for the first time, I was also going to get an opportunity to film it for my documentary on Father Sansariq and the Haitian diaspora.

We could use the footage I would shoot in Haiti and weave it into the story of how the priest served as a shepherd for his flock as they moved from the Caribbean to the United States. We could show how Father Sansariq helped new Haitian immigrants obtain green cards, find places to stay, get jobs, and enroll their children into schools.

Finally, it was the morning that I was to depart for Father Sansariq and my parents' homeland. I stood in the hallway of my parents' home on Long Island. My heart was thumping with anticipation.

With my backpack on my shoulders, my dark blue camera bag packed, and my new black suitcase ready to go, I headed downstairs to the garage to put my bags in my father's yellow cab. On the way, I stopped by my mom's room at the bottom of the staircase. As I knocked on her bedroom door I could not help but stare at the white sticker she had applied to the doorframe above her room. In flaming red uppercase letters it cried out "THE BLOOD OF JESUS." (Pentecostals believe that the blood of Christ washes away all sin.) When there was no answer, I opened the door and immediately realized that she had already gone to church. She left that morning without saying goodbye to me.

I felt sad, really sad. But I was not surprised. My mother was enraged that I had made a decision to visit Haiti, the country she associated with her suffering over her painful childhood, and most of all, the terrible death of her firstborn son.

Sunday was my father's day off. He was standing over the kitchen counter drinking a cup of coffee and eating a chunk of traditional Haitian *pain*, a chewy wheat bread shaped like a baguette, while scanning the day's *New York Daily News*. He was waiting patiently for me so we could start our journey to JFK Airport to catch my flight to Port-au-Prince, Haiti's capital.

The sun shone through the skylight in the plant-filled kitchen. I stood still for a few seconds, closed my eyes, and quietly said goodbye to the songbirds, thanking the universe for the adventure I was about to experience. A few feet away, I faintly heard my dad ask in his heavy accent, "Ka, are you ready?"

Taking this trip was special for reasons other than that I was visiting Haiti for the first time. In less than a year, both Haiti and Columbia University would be commemorating major milestones. In 2004, Haiti would celebrate two hundred years of independence, and Columbia University would celebrate its founding two hundred and fifty years ago. Of course, Columbia University, which was founded in 1754 by the royal charter of England's King George II, has had a much calmer history than Haiti!

These two anniversaries led to the SIPA Haiti Capstone Project seminar. Headed up by Dean Lisa Anderson, SIPA was exploring how to collaborate with Haitian universities and colleges. A year prior to our Haiti trip, Dean Anderson had met with a top aide to Haitian president Jean-Bertrand Aristide, Leslie Voltaire. The minister of Haitians Living Abroad, Voltaire had given a speech at Columbia in April 2002. He spoke about how he thought the Haitian Revolution of 1804 was being "ignored by Western historians, even though it went further in the redemption of humanity than did the French or American Revolutions." This series of conflicts between Haitian slaves, colonists, and troops—both French and British—has been called the most successful slave rebellion in history. And Minister Voltaire was correct, of course, in that the Haitian Revolution was rooted in the same ideals of personal liberty as the American and French Revolutions. It led to Haiti's independence from France and made Haiti the first country to be founded by former slaves.

That speech led to the first of many conversations between Dean Anderson and Minister Voltaire about how SIPA could work with Haiti to elevate and acknowledge the upcoming paired anniversaries. The Haiti Capstone Project was the result of those conversations. The project's mission was to collaborate with the Ministry of Haitians Living Abroad to organize an international research center in Haiti on development issues in the country. This would be a research center where professors and students like me could come to Haiti to work on projects. Dean Anderson would serve as our faculty advisor.

During my first year at Columbia, I had made a cherished friend who was also an important contact. Pascal was a master's of International Affairs student. I was the newly minted co-president of the SIPA Student Association (SIPASA), the liaison between the SIPA student body, the Office of Student Affairs, and the Columbia University administration. During that time, SIPASA sponsored Thursday night happy hours held at different bars, restaurants, and places of interest around Manhattan. The irony was that even though I was a copresident representing the student body, I would rather put needles in my eyes than attend a social event. But it was part of the job.

I had to adjust to Pascal's slow, measured conversation. Growing up in fast-paced New York City, I was used to people who spoke quickly. Pascal was different. Listening to him was like watching molasses drip down a tree. Every word was deliberate. I learned to put time aside if I planned to engage in a back-and-forth discussion with him—and I wanted to talk with him as often as we could. He was born in Gabon, in Africa, but both of his parents were born in Haiti. That fact was important to them and their son. Pascal and I became friends right away. He encouraged me in my quest to reconnect with Haiti.

It wasn't until I met Pascal that I realized how ambivalent I was about my Haitian heritage. Yes, I loved my parents and extended family, but I had never considered visiting Haiti. We ate a lot of Haitian food like *Pwason Boukannen* (grilled fish), *Diri Kole* (rice and beans), and *Bannann* (plantains) but I never considered learning the language of Haiti, Creole. If I were honest, I would admit growing up I was, well, ashamed of being Haitian. Part of me had absorbed both a sense of stigma that the AIDS epidemic had created around Haiti and my mother's bitterness toward her birthplace. I had spent so much of my life trying to fit into American life. Now I had met a man who had grown up in an African nation who was deeply connected to his Haitian roots. And was very proud of them!

It also struck me that I was meeting a lot of international students at SIPA. Learning about their backgrounds pushed me to learn more about where I was from.

Pascal convinced me to join him in taking the Haiti Capstone Project seminar with Dean Anderson, for which I remain eternally grateful to him. It was a group of ten students from different SIPA programs and backgrounds. The trip to Haiti was part of the seminar—and a way to get the Capstone Project underway.

Only six of us were going on the trip. We were a diverse group. There were Andy, a Congolese man; Sheila, an Australian woman; James, an African American man; Carly, a white American woman; Pascal; and me. None of us, except for Pascal, had visited Haiti before.

Pascal saw the Haiti trip as a way for him to contribute to his country. His parents had moved from Gabon back to Haiti—his father in 1996 and his mother in 1999. They had a home in Port-au-Prince. Pascal's father had his own architectural practice. He and Pascal were very close to Minister Voltaire. This made their family powerful and influential. Without Pascal and his dad, our trip to Haiti in 2003 would never have happened.

But days before our flight was scheduled to take off, we still had not heard from Minister Voltaire's office in Port-au-Prince regarding the agenda for our trip. It made all of us, including Dean Anderson, apprehensive. She was already concerned—rightly so—about sending students into a country that witnessed repeated eruptions of violence. There was no point in visiting unless we had arranged ahead of time to meet with government officials and leading academics. We were not tourists; we were researchers.

Pascal came to our rescue. He left for Haiti four days before the rest of our team. Twenty-four hours after landing, he visited Minister Voltaire's office and watched him work the phones, locking in meetings for our six-day trip.

We were on our way!

Driving with my dad was like being in the Broadway version of a *Fast & the Furious* movie—more comedy, fewer cars flipping over. I used to worry that my dad would lose his mind if he continued to be a New York City cabdriver for too long. In the car, he seemed so agitated—his right hand twitching on the steering wheel. With the radio always tuned to an all-news station like 1010 WIN, he would make jokes about the random people crossing the crosswalk in front of him or about another driver who just cut him off. The biggest bane of my father's life: leisurely "Sunday" drivers who kept below the speed limit at all times and stopped at the first glimmer of yellow instead of gunning through the light on red. When I rode with my father, I felt like the character Bruno from the TV show and movie *Fame*. Bruno also had an overbearing but loving dad who drove a yellow taxi in New York City, except my dad was far less emotional than Bruno's.

My dad pulled up to the curb of the departure drop-off at American Airlines. Looking at him was like looking at the male version of me but almost forty years older. We're both short and have smooth dark chocolate skin. Like me, he has spent the majority of his life looking two decades younger than his real age. At sixty-one, age was finally catching up to him—he had a few gray hairs starting to settle in on his crown. Now he looked about fifty. My father would go back and forth from a beard to a goatee, always keeping his hair less than an inch short. Growing up, I was probably closer to my father than to anyone else in our family. Besides our looks, our temperaments and mannerisms are similar. We also share the same dry sense of humor and confident strut. While I love my mother tremendously, she can be difficult. But my interactions with my father were straightforward and close.

Before I jumped out of his cab, my dad, as always, gave me some money. Never a big hugger, my father leaned in to embrace me. This awkward but meaningful gesture was followed by "Okay, be careful and call me."

"I will, Papi!" I told him.

★ ★ ★

The flight manifest to Haiti's Toussaint Louverture International Airport in Tabarre, right outside Port-au-Prince, from New York's JFK International Airport was fairly full. It included all of us from our group except Pascal. I sat by the window and while the plane sped down the runway, making my seat vibrate, I closed my eyes. As soon as the wheels were up, I leaned my seat back and tried to imagine what our experience must have been like when my parents and I traveled from France more than two decades before to immigrate to America, arriving at the same airport. That was the last time my mother was on an airplane. I was too young to remember that day. But on this flight to Haiti, it felt as if I were making a full, perfect circle. This journey was meant to be.

It seemed like no time before I looked out of the window to see the island of Hispaniola. Home to two countries—Haiti and the Dominican Republic—it is the second-largest island, after Cuba, in the Caribbean and the most populous one. Haiti is even poorer and more politically unstable than the Dominican Republic.

We had started our descent into Port-au-Prince on the western side of the island. After the intense confrontation with my mom and Pascal's last-minute maneuverings, it all felt surreal. The closer we got, the stronger the butterflies in my stomach fluttered. The thought of being in Haiti excited me, and the thought of contributing to the Haiti Capstone Project thrilled me. I could hear and feel the wheels on the plane stretch down for island contact. When the wheels firmly kissed land, the Haitians on the plane started clapping and shouting *"Gras a Dye!"* They were thanking God for a safe arrival in Creole.

As soon as our plane slowed to a stop and the door opened, I hoisted the heavy, unwieldy camera bag onto my shoulder and made my way down a set of shaky white stairs. The air was hot, humid, and uncomfortable. I was still wearing my New York uniform of jeans, long-sleeve shirt, and sneakers. With everyone from the plane now on the tarmac, we joined the line outside a tiny room of the airport. Not only was the room claustrophobically small, there were only two Haitian immigration officers to handle an entire planeload of passengers—hence the line. The beauty of it all—being sarcastic here—is that when you finally got into the room, there was no air conditioning! In an absurd way, it was cooler out in the hot blazing sun than it was to be inside.

After the five of us got through immigration, we were swiftly ushered to the VIP room as guests of Minister Voltaire. He was not at the airport to greet us but had made sure we would be taken care of, and our luggage was sitting in the VIP room waiting for us. The next stop was customs, where the officer barely raised his eyes at us. *"Bon aller,"* he said in French—"Good to go." You were only spoken to in Haitian Creole if the officers knew you were Haitian or you spoke Creole to them. French was for foreigners.

What was happening in the Haitian world outside the terminal was beyond chaos. It was pandemonium. With my backpack on, camera bag over one shoulder, and pulling my black suitcase by the handle, I stood in front of the airport sweating from the heat and exertion. My colleagues were standing around me like we were in a bubble. We couldn't believe the madness that was unfolding around us as we were led by Minister Voltaire's driver to two waiting Jeeps—his and Pascal's father's—just a dozen steps away. A group of twenty to thirty young men, from about twelve years old to their early twenties, surrounded us as we walked toward our vehicles. They reached out to touch our bags, and to pull at them, begging us in Creole and then in broken English for money or aggressively offering to help us with our bags for money. We had been warned earlier inside the VIP room to not give up our bags to anyone we didn't know. If we did, we were told, we would never see our belongings again. We were being physically harassed by this group of kids two dozen deep. As the crowd started to close in on us, Minister Voltaire's driver grabbed my camera bag and carried it to the car. Seconds later we quickly jumped into the Jeeps.

For the first time since stepping outside the airport, I looked at my classmates' faces. Everyone looked shocked and scared by what had just transpired. The biggest surprise was the fear I saw on our driver's face. It was obvious he wanted to shield us from this experience. He was trying hard to get us out of the airport and to the hotel as quickly as possible.

The forty-five-minute drive to Hôtel Prince was a rollercoaster ride. The roads were in bad shape. I sat in the back seat hanging on to my seat cushion and the seatback in front of me. Our heads bobbed up and down like bobbleheads with every bump the tires hit. No one said a word. The driver was working diligently, using every muscle in his body to keep the car steady as we bounced along. Suddenly, I noticed that he had a handgun sitting next to him on the seat. This was Minister Voltaire's driver, so I thought maybe it was common practice since he drove a government official. But later, when I mentioned it to Pascal, he told me that many Haitians in Port-au-Prince keep a gun in their cars, usually under the driver's seat. It is not normally left out in the open—unless the driver fears he may have to fire in case of an imminent attack.

I stared out of the window next to me. All I remember of the drive was that it was hot and dusty and loud—horns honking all around us. With every bump, my mind felt like it was going into a deeper part of my subconscious. I could not stop thinking about what had occurred outside the airport, the aggressive kids who accosted us instead of welcoming us to their country. They were younger than I was, and yet there was no hope in their eyes. It gave clarity to the importance of our project and what we wanted to accomplish.

It was 6:30 p.m. when our two vehicles pulled up in front

of the Hôtel Prince. It sat on top of a hill in the quiet, central Port-au-Prince neighborhood of Pecot. After we checked in, we walked out to the open-air terrace. From the hilltop we had a panoramic view of the city. Being there felt a bit discon-certing. Obviously, it was a relief to be safe in our small castle on the hill, with its amazing sunset, but right below us was the life-and-death struggle to survive of the Haitian people. I was struck by the unexpected contrast between palm trees and views of the turquoise water—which imply relaxation—and the lives of people who were unspeakably poor. It was the survival of the fittest. You can sense the desperation even from this safe hilltop.

Next, I wanted to explore our hotel. The lobby, decorated with worn antique furniture, had high ceilings, parquet wooden floors, a mahogany staircase. The front veranda had old tiles. It all added to the hotel's character.

As I walked, I could hear my sneakers squeaking on the wooden floor. I was so entranced with this new musical instru-ment that I missed the warm "Hello!" from the young Haitian man who greeted me from behind the front desk. In his early twenties, with a slim build, cropped hair, and dark skin, he had an enormous smile. His perfectly crisp uniform reminded me of my well-pressed school uniform when I was in Catholic school back in the States. I mentally compared him to the frightening young men and boys we had just encountered at the airport. I wondered about his story, how he landed behind the desk at the hotel and what his aspirations were. His "Hello" was not just friendly but confident. You could barely hear his Haitian accent. He had already figured out that we were Americans. I soon learned that his name was Willem. I remember thinking that "Willem" was not a Haitian name I had heard before, so I asked him questions about his family background and where his first name came from. His flirtatious wink as he answered me caught me off guard.

Four of us stayed at the Hôtel Prince—Sheila, James, Carly,

and me. Pascal and Andy were at Pascal's parents' home a few minutes away.

Exhausted, we chose to have dinner at the hotel restaurant and then turn in for the evening. We were all in the seminar but didn't know each other well. And, now we were on this life-changing trip together. I had *Diri Kole ak Pwa Wouj* (red beans and rice) with steamed vegetables and *Bannann Douce* (sweet plantains). It was the perfect meal for a vegetarian like me.

But it was not the food that got me hooked on Haiti. It was Cola Lacaye, a Haitian soda in a glass bottle that comes in three different flavors: fruit cola, fruit champagne, and banana. It was so sweet; it was like drinking liquid candy—and just as addictive. As an adult, I am a pretty health-conscious eater, so soda is a no-no. But being in Haiti gave me the perfect excuse to relax my self-imposed rules. From that first dinner, I ordered a Cola Lacaye every time we sat down to eat during our trip. Years later, I found out that Cola Lacaye was distributed in Brooklyn, New York, and tracked it down. I loved the ritual of twisting off the cap on the glass bottle with its *psssh* sound, inhaling the sweet smell of the fruits, and looking at the bright, fizzy liquid as I poured it into my glass. I just had to keep reminding myself: in Haiti, NO ICE! The water was undrinkable. I once ended up brushing my teeth with Cola Lacaye, to dubious effect!

The next morning, I woke up just before 6:00 a.m. as usual. Normally, I would get up for a run, but today I was just excited being in Haiti.

Outside, the air already felt heavy—heavier than I'd ever experienced—as if preparing for the humidity that was drawing everyone in with its opening act.

Then I noticed mango trees! I decided to go in search of fresh mango juice at the hotel restaurant. With mango trees above my head, I sat down and enjoyed the refreshing fruit. Sitting there with my island drink so lush and yellow, I started to get antsy. I thought to myself, *I am finally here in the country of my parents' births, my ancestors lived and died here, I need to get out and go explore.* I stood up straight with pride and put on my shades.

I walked to the street outside the hotel to get a better sense of my surroundings. Standing there with my sunglasses on, I tried not to let the humidity overwhelm my permed hair and me in general. I spotted about a dozen preteen Haitian girls in heavily starched plaid school uniforms walking toward me. Their hair was braided and adorned with colorful ribbons to match their pinafore dresses. I had forgotten that while we were on a trip staying at a hotel, it was still a regular Monday morning for the people who lived on the island. I seemed to have caught the girls' attention, too, as I could see them looking at me and talking. As I got closer, I could hear that they were speaking in Haitian Creole. When I was about twenty feet away, they started to point at me and call out, *"Blan, blan, blan, moun blan!"* I froze, confused. Why were they calling me *blan*? The direct translation of *blan* to English is "white," and *moun blan* is "white people." In my entire young life no one had ever mistaken my dark-skinned complexion for white.

From their excited reaction, you would have thought I was a famous entertainer or actor or the Supreme Pontiff himself. I turned around, perplexed, walking back to the hotel. I later learned during our trip that *moun blan* or *blan* is a phrase used to describe foreigners. I heard the phrase a few times that week. It was a hard reality for me to reconcile with. Back home in America, I was seen by most people as "exotic," a foreigner with my dark skin, broad nose, full lips, and big eyes. I never felt like I fit in. If it wasn't my Haitian culture, then it was my looks. It didn't matter how hard I tried; I was an "outsider," the "other." My whole life, I have felt a sense of "You are not one of us." How could it be that I finally made it to Haiti and I was still seen as a foreigner, an "other"? I felt rejected by Haiti. Suddenly the trip became more complex than I had anticipated.

★ ★ ★

New York City traffic had nothing on Haiti. Throughout our stay, everywhere we went there was a traffic jam. *Tap tap* (quick quick) are flamboyantly decorative, painted pickup trucks and buses functioning as shared taxis in Haiti. They look like loud pieces of art on wheels. The *tap tap* vehicles move in lawless unison with people walking in the streets. The hustle and bustle of the city was intense and overwhelming. A few times Minister Voltaire's driver had to use the siren on his car dashboard to get us through the chaos. Haiti's infrastructure seemed nonexistent. The roads were barely roads, cars drove up on sidewalks, and people walked in the streets. There was no clear distinction between the two. As we drove through the maze of the city, the combination of heat, humidity, and dust felt suffocating. An hour later, we were all standing with Leslie Voltaire in his Ministry of Haitians Living Abroad office for our first meeting of the day.

Leslie Voltaire was a *grimo*, which is a Haitian word to describe a light-skinned black male. His hairline receded ever so slightly. What visually stood out the most was his goatee—hair that covered only his chin, no mustache, no hair on his cheeks. Voltaire was soft-spoken, kind, and even-tempered. When he stepped in a room, I felt calmness all around him. He was only a few years younger than my father. While they looked very different from each other, their demeanor was identical. Maybe that is why we got along.

Voltaire had an impressive résumé which, along with his Haitian heritage, he carried with pride. He was an architect and an urban planner who had received his degree from Cornell University. Voltaire was not only brilliant but also thoughtful. He had spent more than a decade as a college professor in Haiti, which made him a perfect partner for our project.

That day, we stayed inside the confines of Port-au-Prince. We pulled up to Université Notre Dame d'Haïti (University Notre Dame of Haiti). With its manicured grounds and palm trees, the small campus offered a contrast to the concrete of Port-au-Prince. It reminded me of a small American elementary school in southern Florida.

We were welcomed by Sabine Malbranche, a professor of urban planning and architecture at Notre Dame. She escorted our group to a class of a dozen or more students. I was surprised to see that they, too, were all wearing uniforms. American college students would never stand for uniforms, other than the self-imposed jeans, sweats, or pajama bottoms. But these uniforms served to showed the world that the students' families could afford to pay for school. You could see the pride in their faces and confidence in their body language. The students were clearly smart and eager.

Visiting with students was key to moving our project forward. That week, we also visited Université Quisqueya (Quisqueya University). The word *Quisqueya* (or *Kiskeya*) is one of the former names of Hispaniola Island, believed to mean "mother of all lands" in the Taíno language spoken by the original Arawak people of the Caribbean.

That afternoon, we were given a tour by Professor Mirlande Manigat, an elegantly dressed university administrator and professor at Quisqueya. Sixty-three years old and educated at the Sorbonne University in Paris, France, she was a former First Lady of Haiti. Professor Manigat's husband was the thirty-fourth Haitian president, Leslie Manigat. He became president in a controversial, military-organized 1988 presidential election and was ousted four months later. (Mirlande Manigat later ran for president herself in 2010. She lost that election in a runoff against music entertainer Michel Martelly in March 2011. If she had won, Professor Manigat would have become the first female Haitian president.)

Our meetings were not just limited to university visits. We took a tour of the gorgeous white National Palace, the official residence of the Haitian president. (After it was severely damaged in the devastating January 12, 2010, earthquake it was subsequently demolished.) We admired statues and monuments of Haiti's revolutionaries and founding fathers in the city. My favorite statue was the stunning *Le Marron Inconnu de Saint-Dominique*, also known as *Nèg Mawon* (*Black Maroon*). It is a statue of "The Unknown Slave" with his left leg stretching long behind him, a broken shackle at the ankle. In his right hand he is holding a machete, and with his left hand he is fiercely blowing a conch shell trumpet at his lips, alerting the masses. The bronze statue is a breathtaking commemoration of the abolishment of slavery, the historic thirteen-year slave revolt against France that won Haiti its freedom in 1804. The iconic statue represents the Haitian people, embodying their strength, hope, and pride as well as the resilience that has sustained them through tragedy for centuries.

One visit that had a lasting effect on me was to Les Centres GHESKIO (GHESKIO Centers). GHESKIO is an acronym that stands for the Haitian Group for the Study of Kaposi's Sarcoma and Opportunistic Infections. The organization was founded in 1982 with a staff of two by Dr. Jean W. Pape, an internationally recognized infectious disease expert who is the executive director. GHESKIO launched in the early days of the HIV/AIDS epidemic. While in the beginning they struggled to keep up with the influx of patients, decades later they provide free testing and treatment of the tens of thousands of Haitians who were HIV positive. They also treat the tens of thousands of Port-au-Prince residents suffering from tuberculosis.

Pape grew up in Haiti. He received his medical degree from Weill Cornell Medical College on the Upper East Side of Manhattan in 1975. He returned to his country and built GHESKIO into an internationally renowned institution with a staff of over a hundred employees. Dr. Pape's work has saved countless lives from HIV/AIDS, childhood diarrhea, tuberculosis, and other life-threatening diseases. GHESKIO is the second-oldest institution in the world to battle against HIV/AIDS. (The Pasteur Institute in Paris is the first.)

Dr. Pape and a handful of his colleagues met with us. Being at GHESKIO that day was surreal for me. Before my career as a Columbia University graduate student, I, too, had wanted to save lives in Haiti as a medical doctor. I couldn't help but think of Dr. Chantal.

Something deeply disturbed me in Haiti. There were stray dogs everywhere. They scavenged on top of garbage piles. They looked at us with starving, pitiful eyes. They hid behind any object they could find, fearful of humans. When they moved, they looked like walking skeletons covered with patchy matted fur, many limping due to a broken leg—lost souls walking the city. I must have seen a dozen bony dead corpses lying inanimate by the side of the road as well.

I grew up with family dogs. One of the wonderful experiences of having a dog is the excitement they show when you come home after a long day. Our dogs were every inch as much a part of our family as my siblings and I. There is something so moving and vulnerable in the all-in adoration dogs show their owners. To me, a house isn't a home without a canine companion right there at the door greeting me.

In contrast to my pets at home, the stray dogs in the streets of Haiti showed no emotion. They did not bark. Their tails looked bruised and stiff, no wagging to show happiness or even any life. The people around them seemed to ignore their existence. The exception was when the vendors would yell at the strays to stay away from their goods. I realized that what I was seeing should not be all that surprising. How could people who are living in these dire conditions be able to feed or care for a dog? They have to worry about feeding themselves and their families. They are left with no options. The dog is thrown out or left to fend for itself.

When I finally asked one of the drivers about the stray dogs, he told me that they were called *chien peyi* or "country dogs" in Haiti. Due to their poor health and drinking contaminated water, many are infested with parasites, which are a major health threat to people. Unfortunately, the Haitian government did not have the financial resources or manpower to solve the *chien peyi* problem.

As our agenda moved us through the city and the week, I started to think more about my Journalism School documentary film. One of my objectives for this trip was to shoot B-roll of Haiti. The overwhelming experience of the island thus far had my brain churning, trying to work through how I would capture the country's many layers. Many who visit Haiti portray the island at its worst, focusing primarily on the poverty and the political corruption. Haiti is so much more than that. I wanted to show Haiti in an honest and raw way but also be respectful of its history. Winning its struggle for independence, Haiti set the tone for black and brown freedom across the world. That is a proud legacy that we own in our hearts, our souls, our minds, and our bodies.

Voltaire had kindly arranged a driver for me when I set out to film. He also hired a local videographer to take me downtown to capture footage. On one afternoon, I took off with the driver and videographer to go shoot. They were very nervous about this assignment. In their minds, I was this naive, young American girl who wanted to film in some of the most dangerous slums of the city. I assume that Voltaire made it clear to them that if anything awful happened to me, they would be held accountable.

Our first stop was Cité Soleil (Sun City). The driver and videographer told me we had to get there before the sun set. Getting caught anywhere near Cité Soleil after dark is a death sentence. At the time of my visit in 2003, Cité Soleil had been taken over by numerous armed gangs who roamed the streets, each controlling their own district of the city. Every day was filled with murders, rapes, kidnappings, robberies, and shootings at the whim of gang members who terrorized the neighborhood.

Cinder-block homes with tin metal roofs were interspersed with tin shacks and huts made of random scavenged material. The area was crippled by unemployment, a lack of public services, and unsanitary conditions. The majority of the homes in Cité Soleil didn't have access to a latrine. The inoperative canal system served as the sewage system. I had never witnessed—nor begun to imagine—this level of poverty.

The videographer suggested he would go ahead of us to check out the neighborhood. He said he knew someone who might be able to help us. We needed to get permission from a gang member to even attempt to film the neighborhood. I was sitting in the vehicle when it hit me: unlike the noisy neighborhoods we drove through in the city of Port-au-Prince, it was eerily quiet where we were. You did not have to see the violence to know that it was there, like a thunderstorm ready to strike at any minute. The driver and I watched the videographer talking to a young teenage boy who was standing semihidden at the corner. After a few minutes—which felt like hours—the videographer ran back to our vehicle. He jumped in quickly and motioned the driver to drive us away—fast. As we accelerated to full speed, the videographer nervously explained to us that the young boy was warning him that we had pulled up on a "silence before the storm" moment—his gang was about to take down a rival gang.

Besides the country's deep poverty, I also wanted to film a wealthy neighborhood in Port-au-Prince. On our way to the next location, I pulled out my camera to shoot Haitian women carrying white buckets or brown baskets on top of their heads. The path was narrow because alongside them was the contaminated canal filled with garbage and who knows what else. On the other side of the canal were mostly Haitian women vendors standing under small umbrellas of different colors: yellow, blue, green, and rainbow. These women were selling food and merchandise. The area was tightly packed with people trying not to knock each other off the narrow walkway into the disgusting canal.

We finally arrived at the last location on my shoot list. A wealthy neighborhood outside Port-au-Prince, it was filled with well-protected, manicured compounds and gated homes with more than one fancy car in the driveway. There seemed to be no real middle class in Haiti; you were either poor or wealthy. The divide was stark. There were degrees of being poor, the slum cities being the poorest of them all. But if you were wealthy, you were wealthy.

On another day, Pascal's father took the seminar group to visit a friend of the family who lived in the mountains outside the city. On top of a hill, this beautiful house was surrounded by well-tended lawns, flower beds, and trees. The security gate opened to let our two-car caravan onto the expansive grounds. Driving up to the home, we passed a gorgeous man-made waterfall. It was hard to see that thick, cascading, strictly ornamental plume of blue water and white foam and not think of the slum dwellers queuing up for hours in search of clean water in the city below.

One night, our group decided to go hear the band RAM. We wanted to experience Haiti's flavorful musical culture. Playing horns and traditional drums, RAM weaves together voodoo culture, Haitian roots music, politics, and rock and roll.

The band performed at Hotel Oloffson in the middle of downtown Port-au-Prince every Thursday night. The hotel is wrapped up in character and history. It is the inspiration for the Hotel Trianon in Graham Greene's 1966 novel about Haiti, *The Comedians*, which explored the regime of Papa Doc and his murderous secret police, the Tonton Macoute. It is an original gingerbread mansion delicately placed within a blooming tropical garden. It is clearly the place to be on a Thursday night.

The people—locals and NGO employees—were mostly in their midthirties to forties. We got a table close to the band, some of us ordered dinner and drinks—and we danced!

The only person missing from the group was James, who was sick that night with a stomach issue. The irony is that throughout our stay on the island, he refused to eat any Haitian food; he wanted only American food like burgers and BLT sandwiches. He was the only one who ended up getting sick.

On our final day, I watched the Haitian sunrise one last time. The air felt young. I closed my eyes, inhaled deeply, and replayed all that we had seen during the past six days. The trip had overwhelmed me.

I was startled not to feel a deep connection with Haiti.

Often, I walk through life wondering, who am I, really? I ask myself, are there people in the past who would help explain me to myself? While I have my mother, father, and siblings, I don't have a large circle of cousins and relatives. We have "cousins," but they are the offspring of family friends who we treat as our relatives. We had family when I was growing up, but they were chosen, not biological. Both my mother and father came from unhappy circumstances and had cut themselves off from their families of origin. Because Haiti doesn't have a well-maintained government system for birth certificates, marriage records, or title documents, there is no way I can trace my heritage and ancestry backward through time. This is a deep sorrow to me.

This has always left me with questions. I had hoped to find the answers in Haiti. I loved the country, but I cannot say that I felt an instant, uncomplicated bond.

I thought now might be the time to try to make more of a connection when it seemed as if I was the only human being awake on the island. As I sat on the terrace, I kept my eyes closed and prayed—for my ancestors, for my people, for my country, for my parents.

Then it was time to go. Voltaire's car pulled up in front of the hotel. He escorted us back to the airport. We literally went from the Jeeps to the VIP room, onto the airplane. There was no hassle, no danger, no fear.

I am sad to report that the research center was never set up. Political turmoil in Haiti the following year led to a coup d'état. Voltaire's political ally, Jean-Bertrand Aristide, was removed. The last time I saw Voltaire was when we did the presentation of our Haiti project at SIPA. After our presentation, we had lunch with him and Dean Anderson at the faculty house and took a group picture together. It was then that Voltaire told me I should go into politics.

"*Moi?*" I asked him. I was startled but flattered.

"*Mais, oui,*" he said with a smile.

It was a thought that was already percolating in my subconscious.

CHAPTER FOUR

How I Got into Politics

I was terrified. A crowd of three thousand people looked up at me as I stood behind the pulpit at the Cathedral of St. John the Divine, the magnificent Gothic church at Amsterdam and 113th Street. I was a featured speaker at the SIPA graduation. I had never spoken in public before. I was nervous, but thrilled. This was a special day for me—but also for the joyful parents, family members, students, and faculty. Sitting in the audience as well: my parents; my sister, Edwine; and my brother Chris—so proud of me for getting a master's degree in public administration from an Ivy League university, a first in my family.

I tried to ignore the sweat pooling under the pale blue polyester graduation robe I had rented and instead focus on the soaring splendor of the cathedral. Even though I couldn't pick them out from my perch, I knew that the stained-glass windows featured not just the usual ecclesiastical figures but American heroes and activists like Martin Luther King, Jr., Albert Einstein, Susan B. Anthony, and Mahatma Gandhi. That thought gave me a confidence boost.

My real secret weapon was my friend Mohammed Hadi, the writer and journalist who went on to work for the *Wall Street Journal* and *Business Insider* after graduation and is now at the *New York Times*. He had helped me think through what I wanted to say and prepare my speech. And I admit: I got a huge rush out of having all those people listen to me. I was no longer the silent little girl whom the nuns fretted over. I had found my voice. I thought of myself as part of a continuum, adding my thoughts to a long line of female change agents.

The first political speech I watched was former representative Barbara Jordan during the 1992 Democratic National Convention. I was seventeen, and I sat alone in front of the TV in the living room of our house on Long Island. Except for their infatuation with "Dukaka" in 1988, my family wasn't interested in politics. I later realized that while we were focused on Dukakis, we had missed a pivotal historical political moment—the possibility of the first black president. For the second time, Jesse Jackson was a Democratic candidate for president. But 1988 was different from his first run. He expanded on his 1984 success, and it almost paid off. In March, a few months prior to the Democratic National Convention, Jackson's upset win in the Michigan primary put him on the precipice of winning the Democratic nomination. At one point, R. W. Apple, a seasoned political reporter at the *New York Times* even dubbed 1988 as "the Year of Jackson." Poll numbers showed that he was set to take Wisconsin. Some pundits later attributed his unexpected loss there to the "Bradley effect," named for Los Angeles mayor Tom Bradley, an African American who lost the 1982 California gubernatorial race to the white candidate George Deukmejian. The theory (which not all political scientists embrace) is that some voters who actually plan to vote for the white candidate pretend otherwise when asked by pollsters for fear of being thought to be racist. Their answer then skews polling numbers.

Whatever the reason for Jackson's defeat in Wisconsin, it established Dukakis as the Democratic frontrunner.

Four years later, Jordan, a dark-skinned black woman wearing glasses, seated in a wheelchair, stirred the convention with her deep voice, her oratory, and her forceful presence. She was the first black woman in politics I had ever witnessed. In a world of pretty, pearl-wearing charmers, Jordan was substantive and authentic. Looking back, I understand why I must have been drawn to her: she was a powerful black female pathfinder. In her speech, she mentioned that in 1976, when she made history as the first African American woman to deliver a keynote speech at the Democratic National Convention, Democrats won the presidency. She encouraged Democrats to repeat that moment again in 1992 for Bill Clinton.

I turned eighteen less than a month after the convention, but I was not able to vote that November, because I was not yet a US citizen. That would finally happen on June 3, 1997, at the US District Court for the Eastern District in Brooklyn, New York. In a roomful of people in New York City, varying shades of brown and black and white from different countries, speaking different languages, my father and I stood side by side as we took the oath together to become United States naturalized citizens.

Our shared naturalization ceremony was an amazing experience. There were no fireworks or people shouting "Woo-hoo!" or anything like that. After all, we're talking about a city where there were probably dozens of ceremonies a month. But we did get a certificate proclaiming that we were now US citizens and with the date of our oath and a passport-size photo. It freezes that moment of what one looked like in time. I felt like I had finally joined a special club I had always wanted to belong to. My excitement and pride were marred only by the fact that my mother, who did not get to attend school past the fourth grade, was not able to pass the test. This made the moment bittersweet, because the three of us had come together on the plane from Paris, France, so many years ago.

The test, I'm here to say, is not easy. There's a total of a hundred questions from which a US citizenship and immigration officer asks each applicant ten questions. You have to answer six correctly to pass. You might be asked about US geography, American history, and the different powers that belong to the states versus the federal government. You have to know which branch of government does what, and what rights are guaranteed by the US Constitution. A lot of Americans who have been citizens since birth can't answer these. I've seen surveys over the past few years that show an embarrassing lack of knowledge among Americans of US civics and history. One example: 34 percent of people believe the Bill of Rights (the first ten amendments to the Constitution) includes the right to own your own home. Another example: 10 percent of people believe that the Bill of Rights guarantees the right to own a pet.

It's so sad, but somehow it doesn't surprise me. My eleventh-grade history teacher at Kellenberg taught us civics, but this is not true for all high school students. Some students and their parents in Rhode Island are even suing the state for graduating kids who are not prepared to "function productively as civic participants." This includes important activities like knowing the basic philosophies behind the different political parties, understanding what income taxes are, and being knowledgeable enough to serve on a jury.

My speech at the Cathedral of St. John the Divine felt like a victory lap. It was an opportunity for me to contribute. I was proud to be a full-fledged member of the American body politic. I felt I really had something to say, and the audience drank it in. I talked about keeping our idealism alive as we entered the workforce. Most of the students at SIPA are change-the-world types—people

who study conflict resolution, people who want to help humanity, people who want to assist underserved communities around
the world. I urged them to hold fast to that part of themselves; to
not give up on their dreams as the reality of making a living set
in. My experience growing up had already taught me that reality
can set in pretty hard when it hits.

All that year, I had been trying to figure out what to do next.
I had thought that maybe I would continue my schooling and
get my PhD. Among the areas I considered concentrating in:
sociology, anthropology, environmental law, and environmental
justice. But there were other factors I had to consider.

I want to address some really hard truths here, including the
hardest one:

Money.

The fact is, I am not sure I would—or more important—
could get a master's from Columbia University today. College
and graduate school have gotten so impossibly expensive. This
makes me really sad, because attending SIPA at Columbia and
earning a graduate degree transformed my life. I felt I grew intellectually and socially. I met and became friends with people
from countries like Gabon and Pakistan. I learned that there
is an amazing world of opportunities out there. But earning a
master's degree today would involve taking on a massive burden of debt, and I'm not sure I could do that, particularly since
I have a daughter to think about educating and sending to college, and I know others face a similarly tough decision.

I am a first-generation college graduate. And in families like
mine, when you have gotten ahead, made something of yourself, you are expected to help your parents and your siblings. My
success becomes their success. I was lucky that I didn't start graduate school with a lot of debt from college. I had gotten scholarships to attend New York Institute of Technology and had lived
at home, saving a lot of money. But I still owed $5,000 when I
graduated. I would have gotten a stipend as a PhD candidate,

but I felt that I needed to start earning money. I had expenses my parents couldn't help me with. Even today, despite earning a full tuition scholarship for my second year, I am paying student loans from Columbia to the tune of more than $25,000.

Money aside, I wasn't at all sure about what I wanted to do in life. It's a big, hard decision for everyone. It's one of the reasons being in one's twenties can be so agonizing. The program at SIPA was demanding. My fellow students were ambitious and seemingly laser-focused on their career paths. But in those days, I might wake up in the morning thinking of one thing only to change my mind by lunchtime. And by the time I put my head on my pillow at night, I would be entertaining another career path. I found this professional uncertainty scary and anxiety provoking.

I fell into politics almost by accident. I had run for copresident of my class at SIPA on a bit of whim. My fellow student leader had a strong, don't-mess-with-me personality. You couldn't have put two more different people together, but we made a good team. She was outgoing. I was fairly quiet. But we both spoke up on behalf of our classmates. At the time, there was a big change to the SIPA curriculum in the works, and we worked to make sure the voices of the student body were heard. We brought people together.

Yes, I know. You hear the words *student government*, and you perhaps conjure up Reese Witherspoon playing the odious Tracy Flick in the 1999 movie *Election*. You remember—the high school student obsessed with being elected president. Conniving and hypocritical, she embodied all the reasons people avoid student government. But honestly, if you want to get into politics, try running for a low-level position just for the experience. Lots of college positions are left empty so you could run unopposed. The more experience you get, the wiser and more informed your decisions will be! I know a college student who moved heaven and earth to get a summer internship with her congressman from Long Island. The experience made her realize that she was not cut out for the political life at all. She found the staffers cynical, unhappy, and resentful that their careers and fates were inextricably tied to the secretive, often abusive congressman. This is an undeniable element of political life: the politician is the Sun King—or Queen—of his or her office, and the staffers mere satellites in this court of intrigue and endless currying of favor.

The closer we got to graduation in May—as I thought about *my* experience—politics seemed increasingly appealing. As I worked on various drafts of my speech, I realized that I loved being able to help mold policy. As copresident of SIPASA, I had found that I could push for changes that would benefit me and my fellow students. I also was very lucky. I had mentors at Columbia University who encouraged me to get involved in politics, such as Leslie Voltaire, the minister of Haitians Living Abroad.

Voltaire saw in me a leader, a young Haitian American living in the US who he hoped would play an important role in helping Haiti. Like a father telling his child, "You can be anything you want to be, just dream big!" Voltaire wanted me to succeed in politics. He thought I should run for office and eventually become a US senator from New York State. You never know!

David Dinkins, the former New York City mayor—and the first African American mayor of New York City—has also encouraged me. A longtime professor at SIPA, he joined the faculty in 1994, a year after he lost his reelection bid to Republican Rudy Giuliani.

Always immaculately tailored with matching bow ties and pocket handkerchiefs, the dapper, white-haired Dinkins, then in his midseventies, was an unforgettable presence at SIPA. He strode through the hallways while grad students from around the globe discreetly gawped. He encouraged me to consider politics as a career. With his trim white mustache, he also could be very grandfatherly! I remember him pinching my cheek one day in the elevator and telling me that I could be his granddaughter. Touched, my eyes filled with unexpected tears. I had grown up without ever meeting a single grandparent. Having this kind, accomplished statesman show encouragement and affection moved me. It made me realize what a supportive, important presence a loving older person could play in someone's life. I know my parents loved me, but they could never enter into my world of politics and constant job changes which they found confusing. By contrast, long after I graduated from Columbia, Dinkins was always so eager to hear about my work with various politicians—from Anthony Weiner to Tish James to John Edwards to President Obama. He listened, asked questions, and, when requested, offered sage, insightful advice. Later, it was a thrill to visit Dinkins and his wife, Joyce, whom he married in 1953, at their Upper East Side apartment so Suzanne and I could show off our two-month-old daughter, Soleil.

While Dinkins had a courtly paternal way about him, Ester Fuchs, another important mentor, was a force of nature. With her striking bangs, pronounced eyebrows, and large brown eyes, she seems always to be in motion. She was the only professor who encouraged us to explore our feelings about September 11 on the day after.

The daughter of a Queens cantor, Fuchs is the very opposite of an elitist academic removed from the real world. For decades she has been a catalyst for good, an internationally recognized expert on urban politics and policy. She is a deeply engaged civic activist who worked with Mayor Michael Bloomberg from 2001 through 2005. From the moment I walked into my first Columbia seminar back in 2001 to today when she suggested that I teach a course at SIPA, Fuchs has been encouraging me. I consider her to be a friend and a role model. I admire the way she engages passionately with the larger world, always working to make things better for her fellow citizens as well as taking time to mentor individual students.

I am certainly not the first person to stress the importance of mentors. But I cannot overstate how important these people are when they see something in you that you might not yet see in yourself; who encourage you and offer you a hand up to help you get where you want to go. Often, they hear about jobs even before they're posted, and pass the information on, putting in a good word for you. They can also caution you on pitfalls and people you would do well to avoid. They are cheerleaders and crossing guards.

One thing I learned: Don't just be grateful, show your gratitude. Don't be shy about dropping a quick note saying thanks, writing a breezy email with an update on what you are doing, or calling to wish a mentor a happy Thanksgiving or happy New Year. It can be very difficult for former powerful movers and shakers to recede into the shadows of retirement as they grow older. Being remembered by someone whom they once mentored validates their decision to help you. And you might find yourself in this position one day, too.

Every day I say thanks that Charol Shakeshaft and Dale Mann from Interactive Inc. and Ester Fuchs, David Dinkins, and Leslie Voltaire from my time at Columbia saw something in me that I hadn't yet perceived myself.

Their good advice and encouragement were especially important to me. My parents were thrilled with my Ivy League degree. My mother bragged about me not just to all of her patients but to her clients at the hair salon, and my father couldn't let a passenger out of the cab without telling them he had a daughter at Columbia. But they had both been confused and worried when I told them that spring that I might pursue a career in politics. My parents had left Haiti because of the abject poverty, because of the political environment, because of the dictatorship government. Politics to them was a complex career choice at best. They saw politics as being very dangerous, soul-crushing, and unseemly.

To them, politics meant literal death squads like the secret police, the Tonton Macoute (Bogeymen), that the Duvalier family, father and son, used to terrorize the population of Haiti and to stifle any resistance to the corruption and cruelty of their regime. It wasn't until I joined the Barack Obama campaign and he won the presidency that they came to fully embrace my career choice. And that was five years after I graduated from SIPA.

So mentors are key. But for all the help they can give, they are not a substitute for personal grit. In the previous century, people even used the expression "pounding the pavement" as a synonym for job hunting. (It refers to when people literally went door-to-door to apply for work.) Today, of course, many if not most job seekers simply upload their résumés online. But my search predated that technology. Do you know how I got my first job after SIPA? I combed through the Help Wanted sections in the *Daily News* and other local newspapers, circling job descriptions that looked even remotely interesting to me. Then I narrowed those down to positions and places where I could actually envision myself working. One place I mailed my résumé was to the office of New York City Council member James Gennaro. He was in his first term, having been elected to represent the Fresh Meadows neighborhood in Queens just a year earlier, in 2002. He appealed to me because he was the head of the Environmental Protection Committee. He was advertising for a director of legislative and budget affairs.

I didn't feel remotely qualified. But my résumé appealed to him because I had just graduated from Columbia and had demonstrated an interest in environmental advocacy. This explains why people often stretch intellectually and financially to go to as prestigious a school as possible. It's not so much the degree that makes a difference. It's the connections you develop and the positive impression it makes.

But let me be clear: Even with my Ivy League degree, Gennaro's office took a huge chance on me. Politics, more than most fields, is about who you know. And I was a blank slate as far as they were concerned. That would soon change. This is the last time I got a job that didn't come through word of mouth.

I was also not an obvious choice for another reason. Gennaro's district was largely Orthodox Jewish, and in politics it's typical to hire someone who is similar to the community they'll be working in. Case in point: the young budget director who interviewed me to be his replacement was an Orthodox Jew. Yet, somehow, I got the job!

I was based in the district office at Union Turnpike 185-10 two days a week. Even though it was in Queens, where I had spent half of my childhood, it was a world away from the hustle-bustle of Queens Village. Fresh Meadows dates back to Revolutionary War days, and it had retained almost a village-like feel. Until recently, there had still been a privately owned working farm—the last of its kind in New York City.

The first thing I had to do was to get up to speed quickly on the Orthodox Jewish culture. I instinctively understood that I was an extension of the councilman. Maybe because of a childhood where I had to immerse myself in different cultures—French, American, urban, suburban, traditional Haitian—I'm able to adapt easily to new situations. Still, I was terrified of saying or doing something that would reflect badly on Gennaro—that could cost him voters in the next election. For political staffers, like doctors, Rule Number One is "First, do no harm."

It was imperative that I learn the "rules of the road" so that I could be respectful. The women wore skirts and dresses below their knees, and, if they were married, they wore wigs. Their real hair could be viewed only by their husbands. The men wore a prayer shawl, or tallit, with special knotted fringes at the ends

known as tzitzit. I had to constantly remind myself that the men
were not allowed to shake a woman's hand—and vice versa—
unless they were married or a close blood relative.

I made a conscious effort to dress in modest professional outfits. Because I had so little money, I used to haunt the sale racks
at a discount store near City Hall. I had a uniform: a pantsuit
in an array of dull colors—black, navy blue, brown. I would
wear either loafers or low-heeled pumps—never higher than
two inches. I had a long-sleeve white button-down shirt and
a pink one. For spring and summer, I would wear a V-neck in
light colors. But if I was with constituents, the jacket never came
off, no matter how hot it got. Sleeveless was verboten. At this
point in my life, my mother was still perming my hair straight
so I would wear it long or up in a bun.

As budget and legislative director, I had to learn about the
different Jewish organizations we were helping to fund. That's
when I started building my all-important Rolodex. I spent the
other three days a week in Gennaro's City Hall office, which
was not actually in City Hall but across the street, at 250 Broadway in Lower Manhattan. I felt a little jolt of *Wow! This is cool!*
every time I glanced up at City Hall, a gorgeous, imposing, early
nineteenth-century building. Designed in the shape of a U, it
houses the mayor's office in the left wing (if you're facing the
building) and the Speaker's office in the right wing. Originally
made of marble (replaced by Alabama limestone in the 1950s),
with graceful arched windows and a center, domed tower, it is
the oldest continuously operating city hall in the country. A hub
of near-constant activity, with protests and press conferences on
the front steps.

My job was to establish a beachhead there; to secure funding
for the initiatives Gennaro wanted to do. It was Government
101—a crash course on how government works at the local
level. Gennaro was head of the city council's Environmental
Protection Committee. He believed that the most urgent envi-

ronmental concern was contamination from the World Trade Center towers after 9/11. In the days immediately following the attacks, Christine Todd Whitman, the administrator of the Environmental Protection Agency (EPA), had reassured New Yorkers that their air "is safe to breathe and their water is safe to drink." But it later turned out that the smoke plume and dust blanketing Lower Manhattan was loaded with carcinogens, including mercury, lead, benzene, dioxins, and asbestos. Residents of Lower Manhattan—who assumed that it was safe to return to their homes—were all exposed. Standing on the steps of City Hall, Gennaro told reporters that the EPA made "great strains" to clean its Lower Manhattan offices at 290 Broadway but did not use the same care in ensuring residences in the area were safe.

Workers clearing the Ground Zero site were also exposed to the tainted soil. An article that ran in the *New York Daily News* in October 2001 headlined "A TOXIC NIGHTMARE AT DISASTER SITE Air, Water, Soil Contaminated" had spelled out the dangers. It quoted one expert saying: "I don't know how the government defines a Superfund site...but I'd certainly treat Ground Zero like one."

While the fallout from 9/11 was Job Number One for Gennaro and the committee, his to-do list also included water safety throughout Manhattan and toxic waste in Queens. Interestingly, one of the issues he focused on—whether or not dry-cleaning chemicals leaking into the area's groundwater had led to an increased cancer rate in the neighborhood of Jamaica—is making headlines again today. In Johnson County, Indiana, a plume of trichloroethylene, or TCE, from a long-closed dry-cleaning plant has spread toxic vapors into local homes. Residents link the carcinogen to a cancer epidemic among Johnson County children, even as the Trump administration has weakened restrictions on the sweet-smelling fluid used by the majority of the nation's dry-cleaning facilities.

There were several things I loved about my job. It was fun

and inspiring that most of New York City Council staffers were young like me. This made for instant and long-lasting friendships. I got to know Kathleen Gaspard, the scheduler for then councilman (now New York City mayor) Bill de Blasio. (Kathleen went on to work for the US Department of Labor and the Institute for Policy Studies.) Kathleen's brother Patrick Gaspard later hired me to work at the White House. I also became close to Terrance Stroud, a Brooklyn native who worked for then councilwoman Maria Baez, a Democrat who represented the Fourteenth District in the Bronx. Her City Hall office was right next door to Gennaro's. Terrance returned to New York after getting his law degree in Indiana, and he has dedicated his career to New York City and State politics.

I also liked working for a New York City councilman because, let's be honest, when you're talking about New York City, everything is on a large scale. Particularly its bare-knuckle political battles. And yet, you can witness firsthand the impact local politics have on individual constituents.

Gennaro, tall and clean-cut with dark hair silvered at the temples, was a good guy—a Democrat who was always on the right side of the fight. He was the rare politician with a background in science. He had graduated from Stony Brook University with a bachelor's degree in geology. Before he ran for office, he was an environmental policy analyst for the New York City Council. As I watched him interact with constituents, I sometimes thought that his personality was better suited to behind-the-scenes policy work than to the smiling, handshaking, baby-kissing life of an elected official. Gennaro was a quiet man who did not fit the mold of a charismatic politician. But during the year that I worked for him, I appreciated his passion for protecting the environment. After I left, he was able to pass a law reducing New York City's greenhouse gas emissions 30 percent by 2030 and he has gone on to work with Andrew Cuomo, the governor of New York, to help prepare the state for the extreme weather that is the result of climate breakdown. He's found a role that suits his passions.

But I have long since moved on. Young and ambitious, I was confident after a year with Gennaro that I had crushed the job as legislative and budget director. Certain that I had learned all there was to learn, I felt ready to move up to a chief of staff position. That wasn't going to happen under Gennaro. Even that early in my political career, I felt I had developed a knack for understanding which politicians had a future and which didn't. The first time I met Bill de Blasio, now the New York City mayor, I could tell that he was super ambitious; that he was going places. This isn't defining some politicians as losers and others as winners. It's more recognizing that some politicians burn with an all-encompassing desire for a bigger stage, for more media attention. They lust to be at the top of the ticket. Often this is unbridled ego. Other politicians are content to serve their constituents to the best of their abilities. Often the latter are much more admirable than the former.

All these factors meant that I was easily swayed when another New York City Council member, James Sanders, approached me. He told me that he had been impressed by how I represented Gennaro at City Hall. "If you're thinking about your trajectory," he said, "let's talk."

A proud former US marine, Sanders was the head of the council's Economic Development Committee. He was African American, and he represented the Far Rockaway, Queens, district, where my mom had her hair salon and worked as a home health care aide. I had spent a lot of time there as a kid—so much so that it was like a second home. I liked the idea of working for a black official who represented an area that I knew so well.

Leaving a job can often be a hard decision, and I've noticed that there's a tendency—not just in politics—for people to overstay. After all, you're jettisoning the known for the unknown. It takes a real leap of faith. Even though it can be scary, it's good to be aggressive; to seize opportunities. When you stay too long, you risk being pigeonholed, and it's hard to grow beyond the particular expertise you've developed.

One lesson I learned, though, was that I should have done a better job doing my research on what Sanders was like to work for. I walked into a very different kind of setup than James Gennaro's orderly, hierarchical, every-meeting-with-an-agenda office. There was no org chart in Sanders's far more freewheeling and unstructured office. Rather than following the to-do list I had written out the night before, I had to jump into whatever Sanders wanted accomplished. Word to the wise: you adjust to the politician; the politician does not adjust to you!

But I didn't mind the chaos, because the new job came with a big promotion. Sanders not only made me his deputy chief of staff but promised me that when his chief of staff left to get married, I was a shoo-in for her post.

From the moment I arrived at work, I felt at home. These were my people, and I wanted to advocate for them and their needs. The Rockaways, as it is affectionately called, is a diverse community that includes public housing, small businesses, and a large elderly constituency. It is primarily black and Latinx, dotted with Jewish enclaves. Sanders's Far Rockaway office was on Mott Avenue, the neighborhood's main artery, a street lined with mom-and-pop shops. On one block, you can get your hair and nails done; pick up fried chicken, Chinese food, or grab a slice of pizza; fill up your gas tank; get documents notarized; and find yourself a lawyer. One of these shops was *my* mom's. By that time, she had dissolved her partnership and moved from ER Unisex to Elaine's Unisex, just down the street, at 1847 Mott Avenue. A few short miles east of Mott Avenue, you can step off the concrete and onto the beach to hear the waves of the Atlantic Ocean crashing toward land.

The 101st Precinct of the New York Police Department was housed on Mott in an elegant, classical brick building with arches and pediments over the windows, its doors concealing the fast-moving conveyor belt of young black and brown boys in handcuffs within. They were even younger than my little brother, Chris. Seeing them made me feel dejected. Many of these boys would come in covered with dirt, their clothes torn, signs that they had made a run for it before getting apprehended by the police.

It fell to me to drive Councilman Sanders everywhere. (I had a car and he did not.) I would pick him up for work in the morning and chauffeur him all day, right through his evening events. I had inherited my dad's old taxi, which we had repainted a deep shade of green. Councilman Sanders got so comfortable sitting in the shotgun seat, it sometimes felt as if he forgot I was in the car. I have a friend who had similar chauffeuring duties for his boss. Once, as he was regaling me with stories, he told me that sometimes, to his disgust, the boss would clip his nails as they drove along. "I would think, *Why are you doing that?*" my friend said. "*It's so gross!* Once," he added, "I remember thinking, *I need a new job! We have clearly crossed a line here!*"

Occasionally, instead of waiting for Sanders in the car while he nipped inside to attend a meeting, I would swing by my mother's salon to see her. It was a hub of gossip, drama, and laughter, and I loved that I could check in and catch up.

My mom had a small private room in the back corner of the shop that she had furnished with a twin-size bed and cable TV. Sometimes she would sleep there, since it was so close to her job as a health care aide, but mostly, she'd use it between jobs to eat the Haitian food she had prepared at home—rice and beans, chicken, steamed vegetables—or nap, or just to catch her breath and get off her feet for a few minutes.

The room had always functioned the same way for me. I was still getting my hair treated back then. Usually my mother's last customer of the day, I would go there to unplug until it was my turn. I felt like I was in a quiet hut, out of sight and mind. Then

I would step back into the hustle-bustle, ready to sit through the hours-long perm process.

Now that I was full-time politico, time like this just to chill was rare.

One of the tricky parts of working in politics is that because it's a job that demands you to be all in, it can be hard to know where to draw boundaries. That's how I became a bridesmaid in Sanders's wedding to his fiancée. She was also—case in point—his chief of staff, and I was meant to replace her. But more about that later.

Besides my first stint as a bridesmaid, Sanders also gave me my first opportunity to run a campaign. When he asked me to head up his reelection effort in 2005, I said, "But, Councilman, I have zero experience with that."

"I don't care," he said. "I'll teach you, and you'll learn."

He gave me a book to read about the basics of campaigning, *Get Out the Vote! How to Increase Voter Turnout*, by Alan S. Gerber and Donald Green, but I didn't read more than a couple of chapters. I never had the time. (This is one of those situations where you should do what I say and not what I did. If a higher-up ever gives you anything to read, read it. Stay up all night if you have to, and then come in with a few questions. It will show how eager you are. The opposite is also true. I have a friend who was given a book to read by her boss when she was a summer intern. Two weeks later, when the boss asked her about it and she admitted that she hadn't cracked the book yet, it was effectively the end of her career there. She was never given the responsibility she craved, and she wasn't asked to stay on in a permanent capacity.)

Politics was pulling on my heartstrings, energizing me, for a reason that had nothing to do with Councilman Sanders that summer. Like many other millions of people who watched the keynote address at the Democratic National Convention on July 27, 2004, I had been introduced to Barack Obama. He was then a relatively unknown Illinois state senator who was running for US Senate. He walked onstage, waving, with a big, friendly, infectious smile. The crowd rose to their feet and waved large blue placards with the name "Obama" printed in white; the lettering done in all caps. Though still unseasoned, Obama, who by the end of the night would establish himself as an orator and set in motion his meteoric rise, was confident and relaxed. I loved his humility when he said, "Tonight is a particular honor for me because, let's face it, my presence on this stage is pretty unlikely." And I identified with him, because in some ways he was an outsider to America. His father had grown up in a tiny Kenyan village. "He grew up herding goats, went to school in a tin-roof shack," Obama said. "My grandfather was a cook, a domestic servant to the British." This resonated with me, because my mother had worked as a domestic. But his family, like mine, had bigger dreams for their children.

This was the first time since 1988, when I had watched Michael Dukakis, that a man with a strange name not only had my attention but inspired me to do more and be better, showed me that I could be anything I wanted. They both had the immigrant story and the hope of achieving the American dream, carrying with them the hopes of their parents. I was so moved by Obama's speech, I so wanted him to become a US senator that I felt I was working for the wrong politician. I seriously considered quitting my job with Sanders and moving to Chicago to volunteer for Obama. Not doing so, not following my passion and taking a chance to move to Chicago is one of my greatest regrets. But working in an unpaid job after graduating from Columbia University just a year earlier would have been not just financially irresponsible, but financially impossible.

It is also an uncomfortable truth in politics that when you are a paid staffer, you are taken more seriously than a volunteer is. All the same, I would have loved to have gotten in on the ground floor with Obama. Even as a volunteer.

Sanders was right about running a campaign. I did learn, and he won. It was a big election, because Sanders had angered the Queens Democratic Party. They thought he worked too closely with Michael Bloomberg, who had switched his party affiliation from Democratic to Republican in 2001 when he ran for mayor. The Queens machinery wanted Sanders out, and they put up a candidate named David Hook to run against him in the primary.

Quick civics lesson: In a political campaign, there is the primary election and the general election. The primary election is when a candidate runs against other candidates *from the same party*. This is why it is important to register as a Democrat or Republican because it allows you to vote in primary elections. For example, in Maryland, only registered Democrats can vote in a Democratic primary because it is a "closed" primary state. Only fifteen states have "open" primaries, where any registered voter—Democratic, Republican, or Independent—can vote.

Sanders rented a tiny run-down house a couple of blocks from his house in the Rockaways that we used as his campaign HQ. I was exposed to a new world. I worked closely with the labor union 1199, ACORN (the Association of Community Organizations for Reform Now, which advocated for low- and moderate-income families until it lost its funding amid controversy and was forced to close its doors in 2010), and a political consulting firm. We created signage. That term means things like signs and placards with the candidate's name boldly featured on them. These we placed around the district, particularly at street intersections. Nothing is better for a candidate than when people ask for yard signs to place on their lawns or apartment windows. This spells voter engagement, that intangible sense that people are connecting with the candidate and developing an emotional bond. So easy to spot, so difficult to cultivate, believe me. Most important, we started planning our GOTV: the single most important acronym in politics. Get Out the Vote.

In a typical primary, you will get only a tiny percentage of the voters to the polls.

I had responsibility for day-to-day decision making, choosing, among other things, which events were important for Sanders to attend. It was important to balance fundraising and connecting with potential voters. These are the same lessons I teach my students today in my Campaign Management class at SIPA, my alma mater, where I am a lecturer.

Another first: I rented my first non–Columbia University apartment. It was just off Cortelyou Road in Ditmas Park, Brooklyn. My parents were not pleased that I was living by myself or that I was so far away from their house in Wheatley Heights. But I was delighted. I was paying $850 a month for a one-bedroom, thousand-square-foot apartment, a steal even back in the mid-2000s. Plus, I thought the neighborhood, named for the Dutch family that farmed the area in the 1600s, was gorgeous. With its spacious Victorian houses, wide wraparound porches and large front yards, it has been compared to Greenwich, Connecticut. At the same time, there was a seedier side. It wasn't far from the Haitian community where Father Sansariq's church was, and where my car got broken into when his precious photos were stolen. One Friday evening in the middle of the night, someone smashed a window on my dark green car and stole the car radio.

Just as I had often fallen asleep in the garage when I drove to the Wheatley Heights house at night from the New York Institute of Technology, I was so overworked and exhausted from my job with Sanders that many times I left my key in the door of my apartment. It was a sign of how overwhelmed I was. My neighbor, a white woman with a couple of kids, looked out for me. Whenever she found the key in the door, she would take it out and let me know.

As liberated as I felt to be on my own, I was also intensely lonely. I didn't know anyone in Brooklyn. I had chosen it more or less by default, because Queens was too close to my family and I couldn't afford a place in Manhattan. I wasn't out at work, but I was out everywhere else—including on Match.com. But it didn't take long for that whole superficial dating routine to get old.

That's when I met Inez. She was Jamaican and almost a decade older than me with a big corporate job and a personality to match. With her emotional highs and lows, she reminded me of my mother. The first thing I fell for was Inez's hair. She alternated between a gorgeous, Angela Davis–style afro and a long weave à la Beyoncé. I was trying to find my way not just as a gay woman but as an adult and trying to tap into my Haitian roots. Inez helped me with all of that. When she broke up with me on the phone after a few months, I was seriously bummed. To cope, I would often head to my parents' house on Friday afternoons for some weekend TLC. Glad for the chance to take care of her "baby," my mother would jump into mom mode, spoiling me by cooking all of my favorite childhood dishes. She didn't ask any questions, and I volunteered nothing about why I was there. I would spend forty-eight hours watching movies on TV and walking on the beach before returning to my single-lady apartment on Sunday nights, fortified to go back to work.

When Sanders hired me and made me deputy chief of staff, he had promised that I would replace his chief of staff after the wedding. I didn't realize at the time that I would also be called upon to *be* in the wedding. Someone in the bridal party had had a heart attack and had to drop out. Everything about the wedding was on a preternaturally gigantic scale. Sanders used this personal milestone, which took place on Saturday, July 9, 2005, two months before primary day, as a campaign event. Their nuptials, held at the First Presbyterian Church, the largest church in Far Rockaway, were open to the public. Ditto the reception, held in tents on the church grounds. Hundreds of people attended. The bride's train stretched all the way down the aisle behind her.

One of about two dozen attendants, I felt like an understudy who was bumped up at the last minute—reluctantly so. I had to have my long black bridesmaid's dress made for me. I also had to buy my black stiletto heels at a particular shoe store on Flatbush Avenue in Brooklyn. Everyone had to wear their hair swept up in a bun. My mother, who fixed my hair, and my father came to the wedding. They were thrilled to see their little girl all dressed up having a visible role in a huge political and social event. I know they dreamed that someday I would be the star in bridal white. They loved seeing me dressed in all this feminine finery.

I was chagrined. I felt ridiculous. I hadn't gotten that dressed up since my date with Brendan to the Kellenberg senior prom!

On September 13, 2005, the day of the New York City Democratic primary, we turned Sanders's office into a war room so we could immediately respond to any situation in the district. At 6:00 a.m. when the polls first opened, my stomach was in knots and I couldn't even take a sip of tea. But as the returns rolled in during the day, my nerves were replaced by excitement. That night, we all crowded in to celebrate Sanders's victory. In a district like Far Rockaway, if you won the Democratic primary, you were virtually guaranteed victory in November. I do not even recall whether Sanders faced a Republican challenger. This situation is common across the United States. For example, in a blue state like California, the Democratic primary is very important. But in a red state like, say, South Carolina, it is the Republican primary that is very important. Someone like Senator Lindsey Graham worries more that he will lose in a Republican primary in 2020 to someone more conservative than he worries that he will lose in a general election to a Democrat.

As you can tell, I got hooked on campaigns. I found that they gave me an adrenaline rush. Most last six months or a year—two years, max, if it's a presidential candidate—and I discovered that I loved the horse race. At the outset, there's no way to predict the winner or loser. For instance, although Obama's 2004 speech had lifted my heart like no other, I did not imagine that four years later he would be able to build a winning movement based on young people's enthusiasm. Ditto for a certain kooky-looking, white-haired independent from Vermont—Bernie Sanders— who crushed it with millennials in 2016.

I always say that politics is like gambling. It can become an addiction. That's why so many political operatives jump from one campaign to another.

But after James Sanders won reelection, he pulled me aside. Looking abashed, he told me that I wasn't going to get the top job. "It's for personal, not professional reasons," he said. "You did good work for me." He and his jealous new wife had decided it would be more appropriate to bring in a man to replace her. One chief of staff heading down the aisle with Sanders was quite enough.

At least Sanders thought I had done a good job, and I could keep my current position. But at that moment, I was so hurt that fact didn't make me feel any better. I left the office and drove to my mom's beauty shop, walked straight to the back, and went into her private room. I lay down on the bed, pulled up the thin little blanket, and wept.

An afternoon of nursing wounds was all I required. Then my self-respect kicked in, and I started revising my résumé. I flipped through my Rolodex like a maniac. A few weeks later, when I told Sanders I was leaving for a new job in Washington, I cried again. Even though I had wasted no time in figuring out my next step, I had still suffered deep-down disappointment, and my bruised ego hadn't healed.

Here, I have to add a footnote. At the time, it was devastating to me that I didn't get the chief of staff gig. But as often occurs, in retrospect, it was the best thing that happened to me. If

I had gotten the COS job, I am not sure I would have taken the leap to go into national politics. I may not have left New York City to work at Walmart Watch, the subject of the next chapter.

That job led me to the next job, in Chapel Hill, North Carolina, working on John Edwards's 2008 presidential campaign. So not getting the chief of staff was the kick in the butt I needed to take a chance—to have courage to be brave and to step out of my comfort zone. What at first felt like a failure opened up whole new horizons for me.

CHAPTER FIVE

Sometimes Politics Means Leaving Home

Washington, DC, was a culture shock for me, a New Yorker. New York City has a population of almost nine million and soaring skyscrapers. I now found myself living in a city of 570,681 residents—570,682 when I counted myself!—where by law, no building can be more than twenty feet taller than the width of the street it faces. When the Washington Monument was completed at 555 feet 5⅛ inches in 1884, it was the tallest building in the world. (Even the Empire State Building in midtown Manhattan is more than twice as tall at 1,250 feet.) I couldn't get over how quiet the streets were at night and how few good restaurants serving vegetarian food there were. Back then in 2006, you were hard-pressed to find a restaurant serving *anything* after about 9:00 p.m. Quite simply, there's a different, slower vibe to DC. Perhaps I agreed with President John F.

Kennedy's crack about Washington—that it's "a city of South-ern efficiency and Northern charm."

Now, of course, I realize there are the vast suburbs in Mary-land and Virginia, but back then, I never ventured outside the District. It's also true that the Obama administration raised the level of cool in the city.

I moved to Washington, DC, not for a campaign or for a can-didate. I moved to Washington, DC, to advance the needs and rights of some of the least compensated, most exploited workers in the country: the people who man the cash registers, stock the shelves, and greet the customers—Walmart employees.

The way I got this new job was old-fashioned networking. It was a reminder of the need to leave every job on good terms. Yes, I know—some people are now no longer giving two weeks' notice when they exit a job. Don't do that. Burning bridges or trash-talking former bosses is never, ever a good tactic. And I have worked for some weird people. Everyone who stays in pol-itics long enough has.

People often equate "networking" with being one of those hateful people at a cocktail party who scan the room looking for victims to harass by asking for favors and thrusting their busi-ness cards at people. I am a shy person, so that is the last way I would approach anyone. But if you stay in touch with people by email and text and take an active interest in them and their ca-reers, you create a bond with people you already like. Someone very wise said, "Never have the first conversation with someone start with your asking for a favor." Even remembering to wish people happy birthday thanks to the magic of Facebook is a start.

In New York I had met and become friends with Scott Levin-son. He was an outside political consultant hired by the James Sanders campaign. He liked me and really wanted to help me. We stayed in touch, and he connected me to Andrew Gross-man. Talk about a small world! Andrew Grossman's best friend was a guy called Patrick Gaspard. Patrick's little sister was my friend from the New York City Council, Bill de Blasio's scheduler, Kathleen.

Andy Grossman was the head of Walmart Watch, an exciting nonprofit venture sponsored by the labor union SEIU (Service Employees International Union). The second-largest labor union in the United States, the SEIU focuses on organizing service workers—health care workers like my mother as well as janitors and public employees. I was hired to be the state and federal outreach coordinator for Walmart Watch. Our mission was to make Walmart a better corporate citizen.

Here's the hard truth. Sometimes everyday people don't grasp just how much money and power is concentrated in the hands of a few families and corporations. Literally. The combined family worth of the Walton family is over $175.2 billion. Just get your "please don't let me bounce my rent check or I'll have to cut back on my kid's insulin this month" mind around that kind of staggering wealth.

Founded by Sam Walton in Bentonville, Arkansas, in 1962, the multinational corporation operates over eleven thousand Walmarts and Sam's Clubs in twenty-seven countries, operating under fifty-eight different names.

In the United States, they employ well over two million Americans—the single biggest private employer in the country. But their wages are so low the employees often qualify for food stamps, Medicaid, and other subsidies. In other words, while the Walton family has a triple-digit billion-dollar bank account, we the American taxpayers subsidize their gargantuan fortune. (The company has recently raised its hourly wage to $11 an hour.)

My blood boils at this kind of economic inequality. It astonishes and horrifies me that according to the Institute for Policy Studies, "Wall Street banks doled out $23.9 billion in bonuses to their 177,000 New York–based employees [in 2016], which amounts to 1.6 times the combined earnings of all 1,075,000 Americans who work full-time at the current federal minimum wage of $7.25 per hour." The 2016 Wall Street bonus pool was large enough to have lifted all 3.2 million US fast-food workers, or all home care aides, or all restaurant servers and bartenders up to $15 per hour. Meanwhile, the Koch brothers—who fund groups denying climate change—have an estimated fortune of almost $52 billion each.

Obscene, that's the word for it.

The dream that everyone in America has a fair shot in life is being destroyed by a handful of billionaires who manipulate the political system to enrich themselves and impoverish the rest of us.

It also imperils our nation. We are not the first society to face a vast chasm between the haves and the have-nots. When the have-nots rise up and protest, upheaval ensues. Think of the Russian Revolution in 1917, which toppled Czar Nicholas II (hereditary ruler of Russia). Or the French Revolution in 1789, ending the reign—and lives—of Louis XVI and his wife, Marie Antoinette. Just listen to the wisdom of the ancient Greek biographer Plutarch:

"An imbalance between rich and poor is the oldest and most fatal ailment of all republics."

Walmart's rock-bottom prices come with a hefty price tag. Walmart has decimated Main Streets all across America. Where once there were family-owned stores and flourishing town centers, now there are empty storefronts and despair. As one writer put it, two things have destroyed rural America: meth and Walmart.

By the way, not all big-box stores are terrible. Costco pays a living wage and provides health insurance to employees.

My job at Walmart Watch was to encourage elected officials across the United States to demand that Walmart give more back to the communities where it was making its money. I would call mayors, state senators, governors, and their staffs emphasizing that Walmart could provide a lot more to its underpaid, over-worked employees. I spent a lot of time pushing for health care legislation and a community benefits agreement. The idea was that if Walmart was going to build a big-box store, the com-munity and employees should be able to demand concessions in return.

This job was a big change for me. I was accustomed to work-ing within a single political district within one New York City borough. Zipping around the district in my father's old taxi with a council member doing his back-seat driving, I knew every street, every intersection—hell, every street sign and pothole.

Not to mention the people. I knew the voters and the mov-ers and shakers. The rabbis and the undertakers. The bar owners and the hot-dog-cart employees. Everybody.

Now I had entered a new world. Suddenly I was flying all over the United States. I hadn't grown up getting on planes. The first and only flight I had taken as a child was from France to the United States at age five. And I had flown to Haiti and back when I was at SIPA. In our family, we drove everywhere and never took a vacation.

Now, with my little wheelie suitcase in hand—the same one that had accompanied me to Haiti—I was parachuting into states I knew only from maps: Georgia, Texas, Tennessee, Montana. I mean, all over the country! I discovered what exactly "frequent flyer miles" were. I'm lucky. I am one of those people who have only to hear the sound of the engine getting ready for takeoff and I'm falling into a deep coma that lifts upon touchdown. I really felt for a friend of mine, a committed union organizer who hated to fly. Hated. To. Fly. She was the kind of person you see at an airport bar at 9:00 a.m. pounding down vodkas. I saw her recently and she told me that Ambien had made a big improvement in her life when she flew.

Walmart Watch really stretched me. In my city council gigs,

I had been interacting with fellow New Yorkers. White, black, Asian, Latino, Orthodox Jewish, Roman Catholic, secular— I understood them and where they were coming from. But in rural America I was meeting devout white evangelicals who were as foreign to me as I was to them. They were super friendly— almost excessively nice for my East Coast sensibilities—but it was startling to hear Bible proverbs and Jesus cited constantly. I knew deeply religious people—at my mother's Pentecostal church, or the Catholic school I attended—but I was surprised to see how these evangelicals invoked their Christian faith in every situation, from the weather forecast to good outcomes in terms of organizing. It was helpful to me to start framing our arguments about Walmart in terms of "WWJD." What would Jesus do? I knew that he wouldn't think it was morally right that one family feasted while millions starved.

I remember meeting a community activist in Georgia. I loved the way Kaylee could talk the birds out of the trees. She was as friendly as a country cousin with a remarkable gift for remembering names and how many grandchildren someone had. There was no medical ailment or family issue she didn't recall and ask about. She would sit with her knitting at an organizing event and people would flock to her.

She was a reminder of the lesson that in any political situation you should think about how to appear approachable. "Frowny face" just doesn't cut it. When you grow up in New York, walking around with a big smile isn't done. Our default mode is set at "brusque verging on hostile." But that didn't work when I was traveling for Walmart Watch.

I also realized that small talk has a big purpose. Like most young people, I wanted to be interesting and original when I spoke to people. Plus, I was shy. So I avoided discussing really boring, predictable, clichéd topics like the weather. The result: awkward silences with me feeling tongue-tied. As I met with local politicians around the country, I realized that making small talk about the weather or the traffic really does break the ice and make social interactions easier. What really works well is if you ask the person next to you a question about themselves: "Tell me how you met your husband" or "What's your favorite way to spend a Saturday?" The point of good manners isn't which fork to use, it's to make other people comfortable. And more open to hearing your perspective.

That's the point of campaigning after all. It is to persuade people to your way of thinking. Note my use of the word *persuade*. Not *harangue* or *argue*. Fighting hammer and tongs with your Trump-supporting uncle might feel therapeutic but it rarely changes anyone's mind. What does help is gently noting to your uncle that the Republicans are all in on cutting Social Security and Medicare so they can continue to give $1.5 trillion tax cuts to billionaires and corporations. With the federal deficit skyrocketing, other areas of federal spending will have to be cut and the Republicans are very clear that putting "entitlement programs," as they call them, on the chopping block is their game plan. It sounds cynical, but most people are motivated by self-interest for themselves, not for others. I.e., your uncle may not care that migrant children are dying on the border, but he does care that Medicare may not pay for his dialysis.

Being successful in politics is often dealing with the world as it is, not as it should be.

I also used a lesson I remembered from high school: The Roman Catholic saint who founded the Jesuit order, St. Ignatius of Loyola, famously urged people to assume good intent. This means trying to give people the benefit of the doubt. When I met someone who spoke to me in a molasses-thick, slow Kentucky accent, I would make an effort to hear them with an open mind and heart without prejudging them or worrying about how weird they might find me!

I sometimes wondered: Was I being manipulative in framing the question of Walmart Watch in religious terms? I don't think so. In politics as in life, it is important to meet people where they are. For example, in Texas, where individual rights are by tradition highly prized, it would have offended my listeners to hear me bang on about how unions create collective power and help raise up groups of people. To them, that would run counter to the frontier pioneer spirit they were so proud of. By contrast, if I were speaking to a group in Michigan with its long and glorious union tradition of mass strikes in the automobile industry, they would have found invoking the spirit of coming together in a union to fight corporate oppression a powerful and inspiring message.

Working for Walmart Watch also made me realize just how enormous the United States really is. When you grow up in and around New York City, you imagine all of America is as densely populated. You think every neighborhood teems with different ethnic restaurants and delis open twenty-four hours a day. More than once, I would arrive at a hotel and discover to my horror that the only dinner available to me was coming out of the snack vending machine next to the ice dispenser. Often I was driving for hours on empty highways, staggered at the long stretches where I saw no one. I used to worry about falling asleep behind the wheel. I was glad, however, that Walmart Watch always sent us out in pairs or threes. With good reason, you can feel very vulnerable as a young woman in America.

I also had one of the funniest experiences of my life thanks to Walmart Watch. I had flown to Bozeman, Montana. First, it takes an entire day just to get there—there are no direct flights from Washington, DC, and you have to fly on a smaller passenger plane to land in the state. Second, it's a beautiful place, with gorgeous towering mountains and picturesque views.

We were staying at the Holiday Inn Express, and the morning after we arrived in Bozeman, a woman from the housekeeping staff passed by me in the hall. Then she stopped and turned around. "You must be an actress," she called out.

"I wish," I said, smiling. "But, no, I'm not."

"Really?" she said, flashing a look of disbelief. "I have never seen anyone who looks like you before in my life. The only time I've ever seen black people is on TV."

Wild, huh?

CHAPTER SIX

Flawed Candidates—They Are Everywhere

Yes, I worked for Anthony Weiner.

Yes, *that* Anthony Weiner.

Carlos Danger himself.

Guess what? Weiner was, hands down, one of the most gifted politicians I have ever encountered. He could read a room instantly. Work the crowd at any parade like a born showman. He was passionate, whip smart, and *never* at a loss for words. His speeches were effective, and he was a genius with graphic presentations. Anthony Weiner could have been an amazing NYC mayor, US senator from New York, or the governor of the state. The political fairy godmothers bestowed upon him all the gifts. All of the gifts except, well, dare we suggest self-control?

To refresh your memory if you've forgotten: Born in New York City in 1964, Anthony Weiner was hired by then representative Chuck Schumer's office right out of college in 1985.

After six years with Schumer, Weiner ran for the New York City Council in 1991, winning one of the fifty-one seats. At twenty-seven, he became the youngest city council member in history.

When Chuck Schumer decided to run for Senate, Weiner aimed for Schumer's congressional spot—New York's Ninth Congressional District—and won it handily in 1998. He was an effective advocate for his constituents, for his city, and for his state for seven terms. He was particularly good on health care. Weiner was clearly an up-and-coming star in Democratic politics. It didn't hurt that in July 2010, he married the woman whom Secretary of State Hillary Clinton called her second daughter, Huma Abedin. President Bill Clinton officiated at their wedding.

But trouble loomed. Weiner resigned from Congress in June 2011, after a photo of a man's bulging crotch was discovered on Weiner's Twitter account. In May 2013, Weiner decided to run for mayor of New York City. It wasn't long before his comeback became another comeuppance. In July 2013, Weiner admitted that his sexting did not stop when he left Congress. On October 28, 2016, James Comey informed Congress that the FBI had reopened the Hillary Clinton email investigation, right before the presidential election because of an investigation into Weiner's contacts with a fifteen-year-old girl in North Carolina. (Abedin and Weiner had apparently shared a computer.) On May 19, 2017, Weiner pleaded guilty to a charge of transferring obscene material to a minor. In November 2017, Weiner, fifty-four, began serving a twenty-one-month sentence at Federal Medical Center Devens in Ayer, Massachusetts. He was released in February 2019. He had to register as a sex offender.

Wow. The documentary *Weiner* captures both his charisma and the collapse of his career because of sexting. It also conveys the manic excitement of working on a high-pressure campaign. There are the scads of fresh-faced, eager volunteers and people seated at phone banks cold-calling voters. Phone banking is not easy since many times your phone calls are unanswered. Worse, there are the times you get a real live voter who promptly either hangs up or curses you out. Among the volunteers phone banking for Weiner: his sweet-faced mother, Frances. It's a good documentary, and I urge folks interested in politics to watch it. But a warning: few campaigns generate the red-hot media scrutiny of the press like Weiner's. Plus, New York media is a world unto itself. Small island, millions of people, hundreds of publications, and dozens of TV stations. This is unique in America.

I worked for Anthony Weiner for three to four months in 2008. I had been a paid staffer on Senator John Edwards's presidential campaign—another flawed candidate I will discuss in detail later. But when Edwards came in third in the all-important 2008 South Carolina Democratic primary, behind Barack Obama and Hillary Clinton, I couldn't get out of town fast enough. The tea leaves were clear. John Edwards had been born in Seneca, South Carolina, making him a native son, and had grown up in neighboring North Carolina and served as its US senator. When a "favorite son" gets trounced in his home state and its southern neighbors, it signals that the campaign is DOA. I bolted back to New York, where I had put a long-distance relationship in the freezer for six months.

Back home in New York, I needed work, and Weiner needed a press secretary. This gig seemed like it had plenty of promise and opportunity. As I mentioned, he was a successful congressman who had his eye on running for mayor of New York City but hadn't yet announced.

Media was incredibly important to Weiner. He could command the camera, proffering the pithy quote with nary a pause. Seriously. Quite simply, he was an extraordinary communicator. He wasn't a great orator like Barack Obama, but he could galvanize a room. He liked local press, he liked local TV, and they liked him. One of my jobs was to get up around 3:00 a.m. and, over the next two hours, read all the websites—both national and local—and send him articles and summaries about any coverage of interest to him or, more important, coverage *of* him. But as popular as he was with voters, Weiner was a famously difficult boss. Staff turnover was constant. His behavior—screaming at employees, throwing phones—was written up in a July 2008 *New York Times* article, published right after I left. No question, he could be incredibly abusive, but he kept his temper around me during the time I worked for him. I also didn't get to know his then fiancée, the tall, beautiful, elegantly dressed, and silent Huma Abedin.

It was during this job that I learned a political truism I have never forgotten: the most demanding elected officials to work for are the ones who started as staffers. During his time with Schumer, Weiner had held almost every job in the office so he knew exactly what each position required and how it should be executed. He didn't take no for an answer—ever.

I will never forget my initial interview for the job as press secretary with Weiner at his New York City congressional office. Striding in late, Weiner was talking on what looked like at least two phones. (I would quickly discover that the congressman was a true tech fiend, on top of all modes of digital communication. Woe to the staffer who couldn't keep up.)

In person, Weiner appeared even thinner than he looked in photos. Tall and wiry with a knee that never stopped jiggling, Weiner sprawled in a chair, put his phones on the desk facing downward, and gave me a huge grin. Then in classic wise guy New York style, he made a crack about my abandoning the now-imploded John Edwards campaign.

"Ya gonna do that to me?"

I laughed out loud. After months below the Mason-Dixon Line working in North and South Carolina, where the manners were polite, the accents gentle, and the conversation often oblique, I was back with the people I had grown up with. Brash.

Maybe obnoxious. Often downright rude. But New Yorkers—
black, white, Jewish, Catholic—like to cut to the chase. Get to
the point. We are horseradish people, not mayonnaise people.
Weiner offered me the job on the spot, and I accepted. I liked
him then and I liked him after I left the job.

Three years later, when I got the breaking news alert on
my phone about his resignation from Congress because of his
sexting habits, I was both sad and surprised. Anthony Weiner
was a good public servant, fully focused on helping his constituents. It just reminded me of what my mother always said:
"You can never really know what goes on behind closed doors
in someone's house, *mwen renmen anpil* (my dear)."

I wasn't burned by my association with Weiner. To be honest, it was just a blip on my résumé. Even a fun nugget to bring
up at cocktail parties. Unscathed, I left Weiner's office to go
work for the Obama campaign in Chicago, which opened up
so many extraordinary avenues. But there were folks who devoted years to Weiner, who himself was a true workaholic. They
gave up weekends, dinners with family and friends, possible romantic relationships, their entire personal lives, really, to meet
their boss's sometimes over-the-top demands and put up with
his often-withering criticism to advance his career.

And then that boss becomes an international embarrassment
and star of a full-blown scandal. That is a devastating blow.
We're not talking about his wife, Huma Abedin, the mother of
their son. We're not talking about Hillary Clinton, whose 2016
presidential campaign was severely damaged by Weiner. We're
talking about your typical low-level political junkie who now
needs to find a new job and pay the rent but whose political career and years of hard work and effort are now summed up in
a punchline to a bad sexting joke.

It's demeaning and demoralizing to sit for a post-Weiner job
interview and have all the questions focused not on how you

think your skills can contribute to this office or campaign but instead on when you realized your boss was a sexting maniac.

I wish I could alert you, dear reader, to certain telltale signs that the political candidate you are working for night and day will self-destruct and take you down with them. If I told you to avoid narcissists, then you would have to stay out of politics altogether. Most, if not all, politicians have massive egos, a burning desire for center stage, and a sense of mission. These men and women want to make history and change the world. Easygoing they aren't. To be a politician, you need an ironclad ego and a rock-hard belief in yourself and your cause to call up friends and strangers to ask for donations. To wear out shoes going door-to-door canvassing. To sit for endless interviews. To attend tedious cocktail parties and conventions looking for donors with fat wallets. To repeat again and again—literally hundreds of times—your stump speech. And to sound as though you mean every single word of the speech and are uttering it for the very first time. Perhaps most difficult, politics requires you to expose yourself, and yet more painful, your family, to press scrutiny. That is a big sacrifice. And it is growing larger with every election cycle.

So there's the rub. What makes a politician successful is also what can turn them—sometimes—into entitled narcissists who believe they can get away with things mere mortals cannot. You, the volunteer or staffer, should believe in the politician's mission, their goal of changing society, more than in the politician him or herself.

I will, however, share some observations a very smart and prominent national political reporter once shared with me about narcissism and politicians. This woman observed that pretty much every single politician has a huge ego. "It's a job requirement," she said over cocktails in the lovely living room of the home of a well-connected Washington, DC, media couple.

"But the politicians who don't become crazy entitled psychos inevitably have an area in their life that is sacrosanct, i.e., an area more important to them than political advancement. For most politicians, it's their family, particularly their children." This is the parent who buys Disney on Ice tickets for the family, then discovers it coincides with the annual Democratic Party's brunch for the elected politicians and donors in the county. They skip the brunch, not the ice show. The true narcissist is the one who skips the ice show, attends the brunch, then makes staffers baby-sit his sobbing twins on their birthday. Weirdly, not only do the latter fail on a personal level, they almost inevitably fail in politics. It's as if the voters can sense that their ambition is all consuming—which generally makes them less likable. Opportunists are rarely appealing.

Politics is a hard business even when you work for someone like Barack Obama, whose administration and postpresidency are utterly free from scandal. And who truly seems like a devoted father and loving husband.

Which brings me to my time working for Senator John Edwards of North Carolina. I joined his presidential campaign in 2007. This was my first national campaign, and I learned an enormous amount.

In the wake of John Edwards's personal scandal, it's hard to remember that back in the 2000s, he was a charismatic national figure who brought the issue of poverty front and center. Like me, Edwards was the first person in his family to go to college. His father was a mill worker and his mom a mail carrier. Reared in a tiny North Carolina textile town called Robbins, Edwards became an enormously successful and wealthy trial lawyer. After the death of his sixteen-year-old son, Wade, in a car accident, Edwards decided to enter politics and successfully ran for the US Senate in North Carolina. Political pundits called him "[Bill] Clinton without the baggage."

Poverty was Edwards's central theme. The man's stump speech was all about the "Two Americas." In it, he stressed that in one

America, people led comfortable, easy lives with access to good schools, stable, well-paying employment, and top-notch health care. But in the other, they struggled against institutional barriers: poor paying jobs, unemployment, bad schools, unaffordable health care. In 2004, Democratic presidential nominee John Kerry selected Senator Edwards as his vice presidential running mate. (Today we largely remember the 2004 Democratic National Convention because its keynote address was delivered by a then state senator from Illinois named Barack Obama.)

Kerry's aristocratic, privileged upbringing—wealth, boarding school—paired well with Edwards's hardscrabble childhood. After the election, Edwards's accomplished lawyer wife, Elizabeth Edwards, became a national figure in her own right. In part, this was because of her struggle with breast cancer, which was diagnosed on November 3, 2004, the day that Kerry conceded to George W. Bush. Mrs. Edwards went on to write a national bestseller about the death of her son and her struggle with breast cancer, *Saving Graces*.

After that election, Edwards, who was no longer a US senator, founded the Center on Poverty, Work and Opportunity at the University of North Carolina at Chapel Hill. By the time people started talking about the 2008 presidential cycle, he was the front-runner. Dynamic, boyishly good-looking, an outstanding public speaker, oozing Southern charm—he had the whole package. He launched his campaign in New Orleans on December 28, 2006. He specifically chose a house that had been devastated by Hurricane Katrina back in August 2005. Could there be a better contrast with the Republicans who had all but abandoned the people and the city of New Orleans to their fate? I, for one, still remember President George W. Bush telling Michael Brown, director of the Federal Emergency Management Agency (FEMA), "Brownie, you're doing a heck of a job!" And that iconic photo of Bush looking down at New Orleans from the window of Air Force One. Safe. Distant. Unmoved. Passive. At least 1,836 people lost their lives in the churning muddy water after the levees broke.

Mind-blowing.

I joined the campaign in February 2007. I had watched the New Orleans kickoff a couple of months earlier and felt inspired. I believed in John Edwards and his commitment to alleviating poverty. Heck, I still believe in Edwards's agenda! When he announced, he said he was committed to fighting climate change, providing universal health care, and withdrawing troops from Iraq. It also seemed the wise and sensible decision to take the Edwards campaign up on their offer for a paid position and health insurance. There was also the practical fact that he announced his candidacy about six weeks earlier than Barack Obama, and I wanted to work on a presidential campaign.

Let me explain what happened. Remember that I originally moved to Washington, DC, because I wanted to expand from local politics to national politics. My goal was to work on a presidential campaign. When I was in New York working for Councilman Sanders, wise people told me that in order to make that happen, I would need to add solid national experience to my résumé and do some serious networking. Enter Walmart Watch. Besides the satisfaction of working to curb a big-box store's worst excesses and the excitement of traveling the country, my job helped me accomplish my next goal. Sometime in the fall of 2006, my phone started ringing. My Walmart Watch boss, Andrew Grossman, had connected me with Steve Hildebrand and Paul Tewes. Both men, from the Midwest, had serious street cred in the Democratic Party. Both men had worked on major Democratic campaigns. Tewes had run Wisconsin senator Russ Feingold's winning reelection campaign in 1998 and had been Al Gore's Iowa State Caucus director in 2000. Hildebrand had been the campaign manager for South Dakota senator Tim Johnson's successful reelection effort. They were a big deal.

And they offered me a job. Two jobs, really. They were starting to staff the Obama campaign, and they asked me if I wanted to become the deputy political director in Iowa, which, as the nation's first caucus state, plays more and more of a role in determining who wins their party's presidential nomination. When I said I wasn't that excited about Iowa, they put another plum on the table. How about coming to Obama's national headquarters in Chicago with my role there TBD?

I'm embarrassed to say now that despite my stint at Walmart Watch, I was still naive. Sitting with them in Washington, I didn't really understand who they were. Even as a person of color—or possibly, especially as one, I didn't think the country was ready to elect a black man. And I did not want to crunch around in freezing, snowy Iowa or freezing, snowy Chicago. It wasn't just about the bad weather. It was about wanting to be in my comfort zone, in my safe space. And the whole Obama operation seemed pretty tentative to me.

All I know is that soon thereafter, another top national political consultant, Nick Baldick, who had worked with the SEIU, among many other organizations and candidates (he was national campaign manager for the 2004 John Edwards presidential campaign), passed my résumé on to the Edwards campaign. It seemed like a no-brainer for me. I walked the five minutes from our Walmart Watch office in Dupont Circle to the Mayflower Hotel. I was going to meet with David Medina, the national political director for the 2008 John Edwards campaign, and David Bonoir. A longtime US representative from Michigan and top figure in the Democratic congressional leadership, Bonoir had been tapped by Edwards as his 2008 campaign manager. They offered me a job on the spot as the Southeast political director. I snapped it up.

So I headed down to the postcard-perfect, tree-lined college town of Chapel Hill, North Carolina—part of the state's famed Research Triangle—where Edwards had opened his headquarters.

I learned so much on the campaign. On a personal level,

David Medina was openly and unapologetically gay, which meant a lot to me at a time when I was struggling with how public I wanted to be about my own sexuality. David (whom we called Medina) was also an incredible political mentor. Uncharacteristically for politics—which is usually a loud, rough-and-tumble business, a lot like being a line chef in a restaurant kitchen—he spoke softly and remained cool no matter what the emergency. I mean, the man could not be rattled.

Medina, with whom I am still friends today, patiently taught me the fundamentals of national campaigning. How to write a political memo for the candidate, how to be a strategic thinker, how to read a room, how to secure endorsements. There was also little-*p* politics to learn—office politics. I had to learn how to navigate through the competing interest groups and layers. There were the people who had been with Edwards since before he was elected a senator, his senate staff, veterans from his 2004 presidential campaign and vice presidential run, and then newbies like me. I had experienced some of these things with Sanders, but on a much smaller scale.

In case you have not encountered these before, let me take a minute to explain. A memo for a candidate outlines the who, what, where, when, and how. You are giving the candidate a map of why they're there, who they're meeting, and what the purpose of the meeting is. Every meeting has a goal—either to get an endorsement, establish a relationship, continue a relationship, whatever—and a strategy. The overall goal is always to win that state but there are a thousand little moves you need to make in order to triumph. Maneuvers on a battlefield to serve your grand strategy.

Next, reading a room: If people show up to meet your candidate or to connect with you, that's a really good sign. They may not have made up their minds about who to support, but their presence means they're open. They want to be persuaded. And they are not shy. They let you know exactly what they want to hear from you. So you have to sell them on the plat-form. But how you talk to a roomful of pastors and ministers will differ from a roomful of college kids or a Mothers Against Drunk Drivers meeting. Knowing your audience is key. I was surprised and somewhat dismayed that I ran into a fair amount of resistance, because I was neither a Southerner nor a Tar Heel.

Medina put a lot of trust in me, for which I have always been grateful, because he essentially handed over his longtime rela-tionships to me. For the votes to add up, they have to start one-on-one, with individuals. Besides learning a ton, this was also a fun period in my life. Although I had been to Georgia and Ten-nessee with Walmart Watch, this was the first time I had ever lived in the South. I was apprehensive as a gay black woman, but I quickly learned that Chapel Hill was an oasis of liberal politics below the Mason-Dixon Line. Founded in 1795, the Univer-sity of North Carolina at Chapel Hill is an amazingly beautiful state-of-the-art campus with classically designed buildings, brick sidewalks that crisscross a grassy common, and a blue-domed rotunda known as the Old Well, the symbol of the school.

Edwards had established his campaign headquarters in an area called Southern Village, and staffer housing was in the complex. We all lived in that same development. We literally worked and slept within the same small radius in Chapel Hill. You could roll out of bed, get dressed, brush your teeth, and then, less than sixty seconds later, be walking into campaign headquarters.

Some politicos haul TVs, espresso makers, and other creature comforts from campaign to campaign—all in an effort to make themselves feel at home. Politics is hard on people who like stable schedules, fixed bedtimes, home-cooked meals, and days off.

I drove down from Washington, DC, with all my earthly possessions stashed in my dark green SUV. I had given up my apartment and had no idea what was going to happen next. I remember that drive like it was yesterday. Me at the wheel won-

dering what the heck I was getting myself into. I was both terrified and thrilled.

Quick bit of advice: Starting out on an adventure—whether
it's adopting a baby or joining a national presidential campaign—
exhilarates your spirit. You feel alive. But you will also be scared
and maybe really hard on yourself. Remember, always be patient
with yourself when you are trying something new. You're going
to make mistakes. Just accept that and keep on going!

I have always been a minimalist, so sleeping on an air mattress for a year did not bother me. I wasn't just traveling light.
I felt lighthearted. At the beginning of any political campaign,
there is so much hope and energy. You believe in the politician's
mission and you believe in them, the candidate. It reminds me
of a new start to a sports season back in high school. This year,
we'll make the championship! This year we can win it all. There
is nothing like a shared goal to bring people together. And in
adult life in America, there's nothing as thrilling as working
on a victorious political campaign, especially at the presidential
level. It's the political equivalent of winning the Super Bowl or
World Series.

In 2008, the folks on the Edwards staff skewed young. Al-
though Edwards had hired David Axelrod (who later helped
Obama get elected) for his 2004 campaign, in 2008 John and
Elizabeth Edwards wanted to run their own show.

I found that I liked living, working, and eating with a bunch
of other dedicated young people from all over the country. The
camaraderie can feel like the best part of college—or, for me,
grad school. Campaigns are notorious for partying and hooking
up for people who are looking for that. This wasn't my scene. I
had made a decision early on that mixing love and work is a bad
combination if you want to have a successful career in politics.
Perhaps because of my strict Haitian American upbringing, I remain a very private person who believes strongly in the separation
of the personal and the professional. Also, as I mentioned, I was

still coming to terms with how "out" I wanted to be. I wasn't ready to flaunt my romantic life. Perhaps it's no coincidence that most of my relationships were long-distance and with women in fields other than politics.

This decision might have led to dull nights alone on my air mattress binge-watching *The West Wing*, but I recommend it highly. There's no way around it: people gossip. And they gossip even more about women and their sex lives—straight or gay. Sorry, but it's true.

One really sweet moment happened with my parents during this period. They had driven down for a visit—my Haitian American parents, who had almost never stepped outside the New York metropolitan region. But here they were in North Carolina. When my papi opened up the trunk of the taxi, I could see all these coolers of home-cooked Haitian food (and also cooked tofu that my mom learned to make after I became a vegetarian in high school). There was so much, I had to store most of the food in my freezer. Instead of hiding my lunches under my bed like I did in elementary school, I was now hiding it in my freezer. At that time of my life I had taken on a habit that my mother started. I was regularly drinking Ensure, the vanilla-flavored ones that you could buy in a can. Yes, you heard it correctly: I was a thirty-two-year-old drinking Ensure—the liquid nutritional supplement favored by the elderly and the ill! My mom made sure to bring three dozen cans for my liquid delight.

But after I had spent more than six months in Chapel Hill doing outreach and making connections in the political and religious communities, I was asked to move to Columbia, South Carolina. So I stuffed my air mattress in its cotton bag and left nirvana.

I didn't like South Carolina. It put me on edge. Columbia was a totally different scene than Chapel Hill. Here I was, a young black New Yorker who was gay. In 2008, the Confederate flag still flew in front of the capitol, and I had to watch it flap in the breeze every day on my commute from my apartment to the John Edwards headquarters. It didn't help that HQ was a rented space in a depressing cookie-cutter office park and my apartment was a nightmare.

No, seriously. While most of the Edwards staff had chosen short-term apartments in an upscale area of Columbia where rents ran about $850 a month, I decided to rent an apartment for $400 a month in a less upscale and more inconvenient neighborhood. But I hadn't realized just how down-market my apartment was until about two o'clock one morning when I heard a lot of foot traffic and squeaking mattress sounds coming from above my ceiling. This wasn't one couple having sex. This was a door opening, door closing parade of different heavy feet thumping across the floor above me.

I'm not judgmental about sex workers, and I certainly admire the fire and sass of adult film star Stormy Daniels, who was paid $130,000 by candidate Donald Trump to cover up a July 2006 sexual encounter they had. (Trump's current wife, Melania, had just given birth to their son, Barron, in March 2006.) But living underneath a pay-for-play operation in a sketchy neighborhood was really scary. I mean *scary* as in I would creep around my apartment listening to the continual tread on the stairs for hours after midnight. I would lock and relock the deadbolt and shove a chair under the doorknob, thinking this might stop an intruder from breaking down the thin, painted wood door.

It's funny. People always think New York City is a big unnerving city with an out-of-control crime problem. Not so. New York City was then and remains among the very safest large metropolises of the United States, with a crime rate per inhabitant lower than the national average. Columbia, South Carolina, was much more dangerous.

Probably because I wasn't sleeping well, or really at all, I came to detest South Carolina. Everything about it was off-putting. The Confederate flag, the humidity, the covert stares I received every time I ventured into a white neighborhood, the simmering racial hostility that seemed to permeate the very oxygen I breathed. Even the occasional syrupy friendliness I would encounter freaked me out. I would keep thinking, *What's the agenda behind this apparent overture?* I know I am not being fair to an entire state, but hey, you know what they said about South Carolina in 1860 when it kicked off the American Civil War: "Too small for a republic and too large for an insane asylum." But I couldn't let these personal feelings get in the way of the job I was hired to do. When you are working for the candidate, you represent that person. You must be "on" all the time. Just to boil it down: "meh" won't fly.

This actually applies to all of life, I suppose!

The Edwards campaign had some momentum going. That included several celebrities who supported him. One was singer and longtime civil rights activist, the impossibly handsome Harry Belafonte. Actor Danny Glover was another. (Glover starred in *The Color Purple* with Whoopi Goldberg and is most famous for starring in the *Lethal Weapon* franchise.) I traveled with both men in South Carolina, and that was a blast. Their goal was to raise awareness for Edwards among African American voters.

The Edwards campaign had money. The candidate enjoyed the powerful backing of a specific and very well-heeled constituency: plaintiff attorneys around the country. Edwards was an admired lawyer who had earned a massive fortune from lawsuits he brought on behalf of his clients who had suffered injuries. One young girl had been disemboweled by a defective pool drain. Edwards won a $25 million award for the family in 1997. Another client was a child with cerebral palsy. During childbirth, the doctor had not performed a cesarean when the fetal monitor showed the baby was in distress. Corporations and insurance companies wanted to pass legislation which would limit awards. Not surprisingly, Edwards's fellow attorneys opposed these efforts, and so did he.

As a midlevel staffer, I wasn't in constant contact with the candidate. My main job was calling local politicians to find any endorsement I could nab. But, as I wrote in my journal on March 18, 2007, about a meet and greet at Bennett College, a historic black women's college in Greensboro, North Carolina, "I got to meet my boss, the next president, and his wife and kids! Everything just seemed so surreal. It just clicked. This was everything I'd been working for in my life—to be doing that job and standing there in that tiny holding room with JRE [John Reid Edwards] and chatting with his wife. Damn! How did I get there? Unbelievable!"

Two days later, there was a fundraiser with Boyd Tinsley, a member of the Dave Matthews Band in Charlotte, North Carolina. "The crowd was difficult to build," I wrote in my journal. "The senator was so happy with the job I did, he hugged me and said how lucky he was to have me on board."

The next day, we got devastating news at HQ. "Today was a scary day. At 2:30 p.m., we were told that JRE cancelled his last events in Iowa and headed back to North Carolina. EE [Elizabeth Edwards] had a follow-up doctor visit. What a horrible sadness in the conference room when the announcement was made that her cancer had come back." Ten days later, I recorded in my diary that EE's cancer was "treatable but not curable. The Edwardses' two little kids are six and eight. The Edwardses are an amazing family. The press conference was just wonderful. In thirty minutes people were crying and also revved up. I have never respected a couple as much as I respect this couple. They announced that they had decided that they were going to continue with the campaign."

Elizabeth Edwards inspired me. After an appearance on *The Oprah Winfrey Show*, I wrote, "EE was on *Oprah* today. It was a short but great segment. She said, 'Live your life until you die.' I don't know that's the exact quote but close enough."

I was also wowed by her husband. At an event at Benedict

College—another HBCU—in Columbia, South Carolina, I wrote in my journal about how a female student "totally disrespected him, and he handled her with such grace. He turned a possible horrible situation into a positive one."

I remember standing with John Edwards once in an elevator. Photos do not do justice to his boy-next-door good looks. The man had dreamy blue eyes, a dazzling smile, and the kind of thick luscious walnut-brown hair you see in TV shampoo commercials. He really rocked the jeans-no-tie-blue-blazer look.

What I recall best is how the candidate seemed utterly impervious to the mad flirting of an attractive blonde stranger who was chatting him up. I remember thinking that, yes, he really was devoted to his wife.

Did I or any of the other midlevel staffers have any idea that Edwards was conducting a torrid affair with the campaign videographer, a woman named Rielle Hunter? Or that the couple would conceive a daughter and then try to get one of Edwards's closest campaign aides to claim that he, Andrew Young, was the father? And that Young would agree to the pretense. Then Young, along with his own wife and three children, would travel around the country incognito with Rielle. All the while the tabloid publication the *National Enquirer* would be hot on the trail of Edwards, the Youngs, and Rielle. Photographs and front-page exclusives would follow. Elizabeth Edwards, meantime, would be blaming Andrew Young, according to Young's book, *The Politician*. The tell-all is a searing portrayal of what happens when ambition takes over your life and your moral compass.

But when I was working for Edwards, I didn't know any of this stuff. While stories about Edwards's love child were breaking in the *National Enquirer* in late 2007, the idea was too ludicrous to be believable. What's more, I had never read that tawdry piece of garbage in my life. Back then, there was a gulf between mainstream journalism and the tabloids. iPhones had just been introduced. In 2008, Twitter was only two years old and social media simply didn't have the death grip on people's attention it now employs.

One thing no one needed to tell me was that Edwards and his message were not connecting with voters. Between Barack Obama and Hillary Clinton, another white male candidate was as enticing as a bowl of cold grits. The polls showed it, the commentators were noting it, and my gut told me. In no uncertain terms.

There is a theory in Democratic political circles. Republican candidates can try for the presidential nomination more than once—take Richard Nixon in 1960 and 1968, and Ronald Reagan in 1976 and then again in 1980. Or John McCain in 2000 and then again in 2008. But Democratic voters like to fall in love with new candidates. So while John Edwards was dazzling and fresh in 2004, by 2008 the buzz was all about the new guy, Senator Barack Obama. John Edwards seemed like a tired retread bringing back bad memories from the failed 2004 John Kerry campaign. (Hillary Clinton is a unique figure since she was originally a First Lady.)

There's nothing more dispiriting than working on a dying campaign. The atmosphere resembles one of those sad birthday balloons with the air slowly seeping out as it deflates. You show up at the office. You're pumped. You attack the phones. You deliberately put pep in your voice. "Everything is going great!" we would blatantly lie to the movers and shakers we were calling. But the more we tried, the less it helped. In the 2008 Democratic primary in the first state where African Americans made up a large part of the electorate, the energy was all about Barack Obama. In South Carolina on January 26, 2008, Obama got 55.4 percent of the vote, Clinton got 26.5 percent, and Edwards got 17.6 percent. Timing is everything, and Edwards's time had come and gone.

My time in South Carolina had come and gone as well. I remember hauling my suitcase and deflated air mattress out the door of that horrible apartment the day after the primary, January 27, 2008. I felt bad about the woman who lived above me, but I could literally taste the relief of getting out of South Carolina. I threw my stuff in the trunk and hit the road. I remember catching one last sight of the Confederate flag and just shook my head. *You lost, people—get over it!* I thought as I accelerated north to home.

The endless scandals, corruption, and off-the-wall shenanigans of the Trump administration have blotted our collective memory of previous scandals, but John Edwards also pushed the limits of acceptable behavior. He would be investigated for whether he used more than one million dollars in campaign donations to hide his affair with Rielle Hunter. (The money was donated by an enormously wealthy woman named Bunny Mellon, who was a close friend of Jacqueline Kennedy. A world-famous gardener, Mellon designed the Rose Garden at the White House during the Kennedy administration and would later do the flowers for John F. Kennedy's funeral. Born in 1910, the elderly Mellon had met and admired John Edwards and wanted to help him.) By the time the mainstream media picked up the story of the Edwards-Hunter liaison in July 2008, I was already in Chicago, safely ensconced with squeaky-clean candidate Obama. I remember campaign staffers saying, "Oh, thank God he wasn't the nominee. We dodged a bullet with that one. Can you imagine if we went into the convention with a secret love child?" People were worried, because they didn't want the Edwards scandal to overshadow the big Obama moment. Everyone just wanted Edwards to go away.

Edwards's trial began on April 23, 2012. On May 31, he was found not guilty on one count of illegal use of campaign funding, and mistrials were declared on all the other charges.

Of all my career decisions, the one I most regret is choosing to join the John Edwards campaign in 2007 rather than Barack Obama's. Still, I feel sad about John Edwards. On one hand, I remain grateful that his team gave me a chance to work on a national presidential campaign. And I remain impressed that John Edwards, despite all his failings, really focused the nation's attention on poverty. He was right in 2004 that there are "Two Americas," and it is even more true today. Economic inequality has only grown worse since then. But the whole affair was so squalid. I try not to judge people and their personal decisions involving sex and love but Edwards was conducting an extramarital affair while his wife was dying. (She would die on December 7, 2010.) That is just plain wrong. He was also running for president and raising enormous amounts of money from donors. Staffers were working their hearts out for him. People really believed in John Edwards.

So I end this chapter on "flawed candidates" with this warning: believe in the mission, not the messenger. It is so easy to become jaded in politics and cynical about politicians. You begin to feel dirty just thinking about the endless "dialing for dollars," the trade-offs, the lobbyists, the favor exchanges, the media spin, the quid pro quo.

Fortunately, my luck—as well as the luck of the nation—had already turned. I was campaigning my loafers off for a candidate who, as I write these words, still inspires me and fills me with pride.

CHAPTER SEVEN

Barack Obama

Thank goodness my plane was on time. I flew from Chicago to Atlanta on the first flight out of O'Hare Airport. This was my first week (the first week of July 2008) as the Southeast regional political director on the Obama '08 campaign, and this would be the first time I would meet the Illinois senator running for president.

Barack Obama would accept the nomination on August 28, 2008. Forty-five years earlier to the day, on August 28, 1963, Martin Luther King, Jr., had walked hand in hand with fellow civil rights activists from the Washington Monument to the Lincoln Memorial in Washington, DC. They were among the more than 250,000 people—black and white—who converged on the nation's capital to participate in the peaceful March on Washington for Jobs and Freedom. The event, on an unseasonably temperate summer day for Washington's usually hot and swampy weather, drew momentum from earlier demonstrations in Birmingham, Alabama, where Commissioner of Public Safety Eugene "Bull" Connor had turned fire hoses and police attack dogs on the protestors. It culminated in the delivery of King's iconic "I Have a Dream" speech on the steps of the Lincoln Memorial. Although the speech is rich with imagery from the Bible and references to our country's founding documents, I've always thought that one of the most powerful lines is the one in which he speaks from the heart as a father: "I have a dream that my four little children will one day live in a nation where they will not be judged by the color of their skin but by the content of their character."

Which brings me to the reason I was in Atlanta. The Obama '08 campaign had arranged for the candidate to meet with one of those "children"—Martin Luther King III, who, at fifty, was the eldest son and eldest living offspring of the slain leader and his wife, Coretta Scott King. The meeting's agenda was to make sure that the remarkable confluence of history commanded all of the recognition it was due at the upcoming Democratic National Convention in Denver, Colorado. There, for the first time, a black man would accept his party's nomination as president, the highest position in the nation, and in some ways, the crowning achievement of King's vision for racial equality. Ironically, one of the hurdles Obama had faced on his path to the top of the ticket was proving that as a biracial man who grew up in Hawaii and Indonesia, he was "black enough"—that he could relate to the African American plight of being "an exile in his own land" that Martin Luther King, Jr., had spoken of with such eloquence.

So much of what remains in the collective memory of that long-ago August day occurred by happenstance. President John F. Kennedy had not originally supported the march, calling it "ill timed," and at first asked civil rights leaders to delay it. King had agreed to speak last after most of the reporters and TV cameras covering the protest had left to file or air their story, and most people, including King himself, agreed that his speech would be quickly forgotten. He had not originally planned to invoke the "I have a dream" refrain he had used in a couple of previous speeches in Birmingham and Detroit until singer Mahalia Jackson called out on that summer afternoon, "Tell them about the dream, Martin!" It's doubtful that his speech would have hit the impossibly high notes it did if she hadn't prompted him and he hadn't been willing to improvise.

Four decades later, my job to "staff" Obama during his meeting with Martin III called for exactly the opposite sensibility. To staff a candidate is political speak that translates to "leave as little to chance as possible—and for God's sake, don't let anything go wrong." One of my roles was logistical, helping to advance the meeting—which means arriving at the site before the candidate (then senator Barack Obama) to make sure everyone who needed to be in the meeting had arrived and there were no surprises. But more critically, I had to learn enough about the people involved and the subject at hand to be able to jump in with well-timed and helpful information if necessary—including if, for any reason, the conversation stalled.

Martin Luther King, Jr.'s birthday—January 15—had become a federal holiday when I was a teenager, commemorated every year on the third Monday of the month, and we had certainly read about him during Black History Month every February. So I thought the two-hour flight to Atlanta, the city where King was born and lies buried, would be more than enough time to brush up on a few facts and fit in a nap. I opened my reading packet and started with the year 1968, when King was assassinated outside the Lorraine Motel in Memphis, Tennessee. He was there to lead a garbage workers' strike the next day. He was thirty-nine, just a few years older than I was. He had accomplished so much, but his life had been cut off when he was far

too young. Who knows what trajectory the civil rights movement would have taken had he lived.

So much tragedy had been visited on his family. Six years after
King was murdered by a racist, petty criminal named James Earl
Ray and less than a hundred yards from his grave, his mother,
Alberta Williams "Mama" King had been shot and killed by a
deranged young black man as she played the organ at the Ebene-
zer Baptist Church. This was where her husband, Martin Luther
"Daddy" King, Sr., was pastor. Coretta Scott King had died in
2006, and the couple's eldest child, Yolanda, had died of a heart
condition in 2007, more blows to an already-fractured family.
The King siblings had had their share of disagreements over how
to handle their father's legacy, both within the firmament of history and financially. In 2008, Martin III and his sister Bernice
had sued their brother, Dexter, for taking "substantial funds" out
of their mother's estate and "wrongfully" appropriating money
from Martin Luther King, Jr.'s estate. Since then, the King children have taken each other to court on other occasions—as well
as anyone they believe has not compensated them appropriately
for use of their father's words, image, or possessions. In 2014,
Martin III and Dexter (now the president and CEO of the King
Estate, which oversees King's intellectual property) sued Bernice,
the CEO of the nonprofit King Center, over who had the right to
sell their father's Nobel Peace Prize and his traveling Bible. The
brothers won. More recently, the family was criticized for refus-
ing to donate the two coveted items to the National Museum
of African American History and Culture in Washington, DC.

It's easy to be judgmental, but I couldn't imagine how hard
it must have been for Martin III and the three other King children to grow up first in the public glare—and then in the long
shadow that their father's death had cast. Yolanda was born two
weeks before the start of the Montgomery Bus Boycott in December 1955, when Rosa Parks refused to move to the back of
the bus. And she was less than a year old when segregationists

firebombed the family's modest redbrick house in Atlanta in retaliation for the boycott's success. Martin III, just ten when his father was killed, had gone on to graduate from Morehouse College, an all-male, liberal arts, historically black college founded just two years after the Civil War that his father, grandfather, and great-grandfather had attended. He had held elected office and headed the Southern Christian Leadership Conference (SCLC), the nonviolent, church-based organization formed to end racial segregation of which his father had been the first president.

Although protests and historical turning points famously took place in other cities and towns around the South, including Birmingham, Montgomery, and Selma, Alabama, to name a few—Atlanta's concentration of historically black colleges and its thriving black business community helped it become what one writer calls "the natural headquarters for the Civil Rights Movement." Many of King's acolytes—John Lewis, Andrew Young, and Hosea Williams—had risen to political prominence there. Despite its own dark history of racial discrimination, the city, which twentieth-century African American activist W.E.B. DuBois once described as "South of the North, yet North of the South," had gained a reputation as a progressive stronghold thanks in no small part to a public relations campaign that dubbed it "The City Too Busy to Hate."

Sitting uncomfortably in the back seat of a cab long past its prime and snarled up in Atlanta's notorious traffic worried that the meeting would start without me, I imagined renaming it "The City Too Busy." But my sourness toward Atlanta dissolved once my cab pulled up in front of the library where the meeting was being held. Taking a deep, mindful breath, I realized the enormity of what I was about to witness.

Maybe it was a sign of my nerves, but I'm embarrassed by how silly the thoughts flitting through my mind were when I met the two men. Shaking Martin III's hand, all I could think was, *He's just a more heavyset version of his father.* And as soon as I met Obama, I thought, *His hair is really gray.* Then when we sat down in the library, I had another superficial thought: *Obama smells nice!*

Obama sat to my left, with MLK III on my right and his aide, Johnny Mac, across the table. Obama set the tone, as you might expect—totally calm and cool. I took notes to give to David Plouffe, the campaign manager; Steve Hildebrand, his deputy; Patrick Gaspard, Obama's political director; and Jen O'Malley Dillon. She was Obama's battleground states director, whom I got to know when we were both working for John Edwards, where she was the Iowa state director. (Jen, whose nickname for me was—and is—"Hot Ticket," had them hire me on the Obama campaign.) In reality I was too gobsmacked by the high-voltage stars in the room to remember a word they said. Afterward, I made a note to myself: "Do not let your excitement get in the way of the job!"

I also had a twinge of regret that day. Now that I had seen the candidate up close and gotten to know the people working on his campaign, I occasionally wished that I had gone with Obama from the beginning—especially as John Edwards's personal life continued to publicly unravel. As cool as it was to be a part of the general election effort, there is a lot of pride that comes with knowing you were there from Day One, before the first state-wide caucus or primary. It demonstrates a level of commitment that you believed from the beginning. It's not like anyone calls you out, but it gives you a certain insider cred.

But here's the flipside of that argument. You never know which road is for you. I was given two options. I picked one. Who knows what would have happened had I picked the other. I learned so much from David Medina that I was able to bring with me to the Obama campaign and, later, to the White House. And living first in North Carolina and then in South Carolina definitely made me braver. After watching that Confederate flag flap in Columbia, Chicago seemed like no big deal.

The convention was two months after the meeting with Martin III. When he and his sister Bernice spoke at the Democratic National Convention in Denver, he told the 75,000 people packed into Invesco Field at Mile High and the millions more watching on TV that his father would be "proud of Barack Obama, proud of the party that nominated him, and proud of the America that will elect him." But he also cautioned, "My father would be quick to remind us that realizing his dream is not Barack Obama's job alone. America needs more than a great president to realize my father's dream. What America needs is a great America."

During the months I worked on the campaign I often saw glimmers of this "great America." As the Southeast political director, the states I was in charge of were Florida, North Carolina, and Virginia, and I met good people working hard to improve health care, education, and environmental protections in each one.

But in one instance, I didn't even have to leave my temporary home in Chicago to experience what Abraham Lincoln called in his first inaugural address "the better angels of our nature." I was roomies with a woman named Ellyce. Still a practicing lawyer in her midseventies, she had worked with indigent clients for decades in Chicago. I lived in her moderately sized condo's second bedroom in her Lincoln Park neighborhood. For free.

A passionate admirer of Barack Obama, Ellyce had little money to donate. But she signed up to provide "supporter housing" for his campaign workers. "This is a way I can help him," she told me. So amazingly generous to open one's home to an absolute stranger. And Ellyce wasn't alone. This scenario played out all over the country—people sharing their homes with Obama supporters.

You might think a Jewish white woman closing in on eighty might not have a lot in common with a young Haitian American woman. But she and I became fast friends. I called her my

Jewish mom. She called me her Obama daughter. I was up at 6:00 a.m. and out the door to the campaign headquarters near Millennium Park and often didn't return until after midnight. But we chatted many Sunday nights. Ellyce's all-in enthusiasm for Obama and his quest for the presidency inspired me. She read every story, cheering him and us on. She wanted nothing but his victory.

Just as an aside: Today, whenever depression or rage or frustration smacks me down about the future of the United States, I think about Ellyce—her passion and her generosity. She's no billionaire Koch brother—thank God!—but she gave me a bed and a roof for free to support a candidate she knew would work for all of us.

There are millions of Ellyces in this country—good-hearted, justice-minded, intelligent people—who know Donald Trump and his wrecking crew have hijacked America. We don't have their millions but we have the passion and the commitment—which will always top mere money.

I attended rallies with Obama in my region. At one point, I went to Little Haiti in Miami to staff Patrick Gaspard. It was amazing to be there hearing Creole and smelling the food of my childhood while at the same time representing the person we hoped would be the next president. Patrick did local radio, and we worked together to produce a robocall that went out to the Haitian American community. It featured Obama saying, *"Sak pase"*—Creole for "what's happening."

Barack Obama is a hand shaker, not a backslapper. Some people thought he was aloof, but I found him jovial, friendly, and light-spirited. He never showed any type of stress. I also thought he was politically astute. And as the campaign advanced toward November, it seemed more and more like voters did, too. It was all about the "Obama Coalition." We needed a diverse cohort made up of African Americans, Latinx, unmarried women, millennials, and those with a college education in order to win.

The last couple of weeks before Election Day blur together in my memory. There was an air of anxious-cautious excitement at HQ—a sense of *Are we really here?* and *Oh, my God, we're about to elect the first black president.* There was an abundance of riches—people and money. Every day, someone new arrived to volunteer. People were taking a weekend, a week—even two weeks—off to pitch in. They would walk in and ask, "How can I be helpful here?" It was bananas! You just tried to find a space to put your laptop down and dive in.

On the night of Tuesday, November 4, 2008, when Barack Obama coasted past Republican nominee John McCain to win the presidency, garnering 365 electoral votes to John McCain's 173—I couldn't help but feel that Martin Luther King, Jr.'s dream had been reached at last; that, as King once said, "The arc of the moral universe is long, but it bends toward justice."

The new president-elect made his acceptance speech in Grant Park in Chicago, the same place where on another historic August 28—this one in 1968—tear gas–wielding police, National Guardsmen, and US Army soldiers had clashed violently with anti–Vietnam War protestors, a time when "the streets literally ran with blood," *Washington Post* columnist Mary Mc-Grory wrote in 1996.

I wasn't part of the history-making moment at Grant Park in 2008. I stayed back in Northern Virginia, where the night before as many as 100,000 people—the campaign's second-largest crowd ever—had shown up to see Obama at his final, pre–Election Day rally. He must have felt a jumble of emotions on a day that started with the death from cancer of Madelyn Payne Dunham, his beloved maternal grandmother, who helped raise him, and ended with his speech at 11:00 p.m. in the pouring rain. Only then did he fly home to Chicago so he would be in place to cast his own ballot the next morning.

I attended the rally in Manassas, the site of two bloody Civil War battles. Obama was uncharacteristically more than two hours late for his final rally. I still remembered seeing the young faces of black boys and girls waiting to not just see the next president of the United States, but also the first black president. Their parents who were in attendance were so proud to be there to see Obama, too. It was getting so late that a few of the children had fallen asleep in their parents' arms. A few other Obama staffers (Michael Strautmanis, Greg Lorjuste, Karen Richardson, and Stacey Brayboy) and I danced onstage to entertain the crowd while we all waited. The main entertainment that evening was supposed to be the legendary Stevie Wonder. By that time, Obama had hundreds of celebrities flying around the country in battleground states and key border states doing events on the campaign's behalf. It felt like a movement. For a reason I cannot remember, Stevie Wonder had to cancel so the audience got the five of us instead. Lucky them!

A week prior, I was asked by Jen O'Malley Dillon and Patrick Gaspard to fly to Virginia to staff Caroline Kennedy. She had agreed to do a few events to help Obama in the final days, and the campaign decided to send her to Virginia, where we were making a big push. I was honored to be asked, not that I could say no. I had never met Caroline Kennedy, the daughter of John F. Kennedy and an important surrogate for Obama on the campaign trail. Her endorsement along with that of her uncle, Massachusetts senator Ted Kennedy, and his son, Representative Patrick Kennedy from Rhode Island, had surprised a lot of politicos and given the relatively unknown candidate a big push in the primaries, bestowing on him the highly sought-after Kennedy mantle. It was especially poignant in retrospect, given that Ted Kennedy, a towering presence in the Senate for close to fifty years was diagnosed four months later with an aggressive brain tumor.

Endorsements from politicians and newspapers are surprisingly crucial to many voters. Busy with their own lives, careers, and families, many Americans do not follow politics with the avidity of the media and the political class, particularly in the early months of a campaign. But they assume the media and other politicians do. Thus an endorsement gives the insecure voter a stamp of approval on a candidate. This was particularly valuable for someone like Obama, who was a groundbreaking figure because of his race. If "they"—the newspapers, the other pols, someone like Caroline Kennedy who is a living link to a glorious political heritage—think Obama is good and can win, then the voter feels free to sign on and cast his ballot for a revolutionary choice. When I first met her, I was surprised by how shy and guarded she was. Despite her extraordinary political pedigree, born to the podium she was not. More Jackie than Jack. But Caroline is highly intelligent and accomplished and I was surprised by how quickly we bonded.

I stayed in Virginia to pitch in any way I could on Election Day in this all-important battleground state. It was only recently that victory had seemed even a remote possibility in this dyed-in-the-wool red state. Virginia hadn't voted Democratic in a presidential race since Lyndon Johnson bested Barry Goldwater in 1964 and before that, in 1948, when Harry Truman had defeated Thomas Dewey. Political observers were more than a little surprised that Virginia had joined other "swing" states, including Colorado, Florida, Missouri, Nevada, New Hampshire, New Mexico, North Carolina, Ohio, and Pennsylvania—states that were in play, meaning they could go either Democratic or Republican heading into Election Day. There are some states that never deviate. California and New York, for instance, *always* go Democratic. Others, like Texas and Oklahoma, *always* go Republican. These battleground states are so important, because it's not the winner of the popular vote that counts in a presidential race. (Al Gore, not George W. Bush, won the popular vote in 2000, and Hillary Clinton, not Donald Trump, won it in 2016.) It is whichever candidate reaches 270 electoral votes.

Both at the rally and traveling around to different Virginia precincts on Election Day, it didn't take a political genius to figure out that things were tilting Obama's way. I had been through enough election cycles by then to have a gut feel for it. I can remember driving through an extremely affluent neighborhood in Northern Virginia and seeing the manicured lawns lined with Obama-Biden signage. Such portents aside, you pretty much know how you're going to do once people start voting and the returns start coming in. The night rarely yields huge surprises, like *Oh, yeah, we won!* (Although eight years later, when Trump won, that's exactly what happened. Except the feeling was *OMIGOD, we lost!*)

But the fact that Obama's victory wasn't a last-second, come-from-behind stunner made winning no less sweet. At eleven o'clock, the networks called the election for Obama. Like our counterparts standing in the cold in Grant Park in Chicago, shown on another TV monitor, we were so shocked, we didn't quite know what to say at first. Then the news hit us. Listening to President-elect Obama's acceptance speech, which he delivered at almost exactly midnight, was a total out-of-body experience for me. I had never felt such a deep sense of accomplishment on a personal level or sense of hope and unabashed joy for the country.

"If there is anyone out there who still doubts that America is a place where all things are possible; who still wonders if the dream of our founders is alive in our time; who still questions the power of our democracy, tonight is your answer," Obama told the crowd, estimated to be around 240,000 strong. "It's the answer that led those who have been told for so long by so many to be cynical and fearful and doubtful about what we can achieve to put their hands on the arc of history and bend it once more toward the hope of a better day," he continued, referring to one of MLK's oft-quoted gems. "It's been a long time coming, but tonight, because of what we did on this day, in this election, at this defining moment, change has come to America."

★ ★ ★

Seventy-seven days later, I woke up at 5:00 a.m. to get to my seat at the inauguration of Barack Hussein Obama. (I wasn't on the dais with the big shots, which, for the first time in US history included all of the living former presidents and their wives—Jimmy and Rosalyn Carter, George H. W. and Barbara Bush, Bill and Hillary Clinton, and George W. and Laura Bush. I was seated in the rows on the lawn below the west front of the US Capitol.) Bundled into puffy winter parkas like a gaggle of Michelin mascots, friends and fellow campaign staffers and I shared hand warmers as we sat in the unusually frigid but sunny winter weather. Yes, we waited for hours along with about 1.8 million other people who stretched all the way back to the Washington Monument—far more than Donald Trump would have in 2017 despite his claims to the contrary—to see President Obama sworn in. Yes, the president appeared to be an inch tall from our distant seats. Yes, the thermometer at noon read twenty-eight degrees—balmy compared to the seven degrees that had given Ronald Reagan little choice but to take his second inauguration, in 1985, indoors—though still cold enough to see your breath and turn your toes into icy nubs. But it was worth every single frozen, faraway moment, even when US Chief Justice John Roberts bungled the repeat-after-me oath of office. Instead of reciting, "I do solemnly swear that I will faithfully execute the Office of President of the United States," as it is written in the US Constitution, Roberts said, "I will execute the Office of President to the United States faithfully..." (President Obama and Justice Roberts held a redo the next day in the White House Map Room.)

Talk about having just one job, Justice Roberts!

Minutes later, standing at the podium giving his inaugural address, the new president stirred me with his words and made me proud of the journey my family had taken. "In reaffirming the greatness of our nation we understand that greatness is never a given," he said. "It must be earned. Our journey has never been one of shortcuts or settling for less. It has not been the path for the fainthearted, for those that prefer leisure over work, or seek only the pleasures of riches and fame. Rather, it has been the risk takers, the doers, the makers of things—some celebrated, but more often men and women obscure in their labor—who have carried us up the long rugged path toward prosperity and freedom.

"For us, they packed up their few worldly possessions and traveled across oceans in search of a new life," he continued. "For us, they toiled in sweatshops, and settled the West, endured the lash of the whip, and plowed the hard earth. For us, they fought and died in places like Concord and Gettysburg, Normandy, and Khe Sahn. Time and again these men and women struggled and sacrificed and worked till their hands were raw so that we might live a better life. They saw America as bigger than the sum of our individual ambitions, greater than all the differences of birth or wealth or faction.

"This is the journey we continue today."

Because I had a job on PIC—the Presidential Inauguration Committee—I had been able to snag tickets to an inaugural ball for Mummy and my brother Chris, who had driven down from Long Island. (My father and sister both had to stay home to work.) My campaign colleagues were flabbergasted when they saw my jaw-droppingly gorgeous, "cut" brother. Six foot two and a gym rat since high school, he now works as a personal trainer.

While Barack Obama was now officially the forty-fourth president of the United States, our work for the Presidential Inauguration Committee was not done. I spent that evening jumping from one inaugural ball to another, staffing them and making sure supporters and elected officials were taken care of.

Some people are serial campaigners, and when one campaign ends, they have an almost addictive need to move as quickly as possible to the next campaign—and the next after that. They might follow up a presidential with a gubernatorial campaign in a place like New Jersey or Virginia, where the state races take place in off-cycle election years. Then they'll work on a midterm race before heading back to the next presidential. The work is hard, but for those at the top, it can be lucrative and psychologically rewarding. There's an old saying that a rolling stone gathers no moss, and this is true for perennial campaigners, too. When you're always on the road, you are either enjoying the single life, or you have a spouse at home willing to raise the kids, make sure the electric bill is paid, and handle all of the adult responsibilities.

For other people, the big payoff for investing nineteen-hour days and sleepless nights on borrowed couches to help bring the candidate across the finish line is a plum job in the administration. For someone who had worked on a successful presidential campaign, this often means a job first on the transition committee or the inaugural committee. That's what I wanted. Not just to help Obama get elected but to support him as he governed.

Luckily for me, in the impossibly tiny world of politics, I got a call right after the campaign from Patrick Gaspard, the brother of my longtime friend Kathleen Gaspard, whom I had first met back in my New York City Council days when I was working for James Gennaro and she was a scheduler for Bill de Blasio. Patrick, as national political director, had been my boss during the campaign—although in a funny coincidence, he was hired after I was and basically inherited me. At the start of his career, he worked for Jesse Jackson's 1988 presidential run, followed by my Columbia mentor Mayor David Dinkins's successful race in 1989. Patrick had had a meteoric rise through the NYC political ranks before moving back into the national arena. He was also best friends with Andy Grossman, who had hired me at Walmart Watch.

The Gaspard family fascinated me. Patrice Lumumba, prime

minister of the Democratic Republic of Congo, had encouraged those of the African diaspora to move there when the country gained its independence in 1960. Among those who answered the call were Patrick and Kathleen's Haitian parents. They were part of Haiti's French-speaking intelligentsia. His father was a lawyer, one of the professions my own parents deeply admired. Born in Kinshasa in 1967, Patrick was three when the Gaspard family moved back to America to New York City, where he grew up.

Patrick, who was associate personnel director of Obama's transition team, was then appointed assistant to the president and director of the Office of Political Affairs in the Obama administration. In his second term, Obama appointed Patrick the US ambassador to South Africa. From there, he became president of the philanthropist George Soros's Open Society Foundation, which supports democratic ideals and human rights around the world. But before all that, Patrick and Jen offered me a coveted job on the Presidential Inauguration Committee, working on African American outreach. I did not like the idea of being pigeonholed—which happens not just in politics but across different industries—but I still jumped on the offer. I knew enough to know that you don't say no to an extraordinary opportunity like that.

Sure enough, a few weeks later, I got another call from Patrick. "I want you to come work for me in the political affairs office at the White House," he said, "but Jen O'Malley Dillon is also looking for White House liaisons for each cabinet-level agency. If that's what you'd rather do, get in touch with her."

The job Patrick offered me was to work as a political liaison (Regional Political Director) advancing the administration's political agenda at the state level and relay what was happening on the ground back to the White House. Jen was looking for people to help put various political appointments selected by the new Obama administration in place at different cabinet agencies such the Commerce Department, the Energy Department, and the Department of Education.

I called Jen. After being on the campaign trail for almost two years, I wanted to slow down a bit—and I wanted a break from being a political director, the job I had done for both the Edwards and Obama campaigns. The liaison gig also paid $120,000—a hefty $48,000 more than the political job.

That is how it came to be that at 8:00 a.m. on Wednesday, January 21, 2009, Obama's first full day as president, I stood in the doorway of the secretary's capacious suite at 200 Constitution Avenue Northwest, twelve blocks from the White House, staring at the glorious purple orchid in full bloom—about two and a half feet of floral splendor—that sat before me.

Outgoing Labor Secretary Elaine Chao—a George W. Bush appointee and the wife of then US Senate minority leader Mitch McConnell, a powerful, conservative Republican from Kentucky—had left the plant and a personal note on the desk for the incoming labor secretary, Hilda Solis, an energetic go-getter then in her early fifties, who would be the first Latina to hold a cabinet secretary post. My favorite part of Solis's backstory is that her parents had met in citizenship class. But she had not had a fairy-tale life after this meet-cute. One of seven children who grew up in Los Angeles, she, like me, had raised her younger siblings and was the first person in her family to graduate from college—this after her high school guidance counselor had tried to dissuade her from attending college at all.

Chao's term had ended at 12:01 p.m. the previous day when Obama had taken the oath of office and become the forty-fourth president of the United States. (Elaine Chao is now Trump's secretary of transportation.)

Besides me, the orchid, and the unopened note, there was a single other human being in the secretary's suite that morning—a very sweet, middle-aged African American administrative assistant. A mother hen who had been there for decades, she had

literally seen hundreds of people come and go during her time
at the department.

Still, I knew she was super pumped to see a young black
woman show up as the White House liaison with the Labor
Department. Her smile was warm and welcoming and her help
invaluable. Because she was a career civil servant—in this case,
part of the permanent workforce at the Labor Department—
over the coming months, she helped me maneuver through the
bureaucratic labyrinth that is the federal government no matter
who sits in the Oval Office. The Labor Department alone had
17,000 employees and a budget of $53 billion. She also pointed
me toward the building's cafeteria, where I ate lunch pretty much
every day. (I am being diplomatic when I say the sad, wilted sal-
ads and the oversteamed veggies left a lot to be desired.) I had
neither an office nor a working computer. Just a new badge and
a mandate. There were about a hundred political appointees at
Labor to "onboard" as Human Resources puts it.

The first problem? Solis, a California Congresswoman from
East Los Angeles and the San Gabriel Valley, wouldn't be confirmed as the twenty-fifth secretary of labor until late February
after a bruising fight with Republican senators representing big
business interests.

But there was someone in charge somewhere in the building.
The Bush administration holdover, a man at least two decades
older than thirty-two-year-old me. (Government rules require
that a previous administration employee remain to assist with
the transition.) But I could tell from our first meeting that he
was as eager to depart as I was excited to arrive. He was friendly
enough, but he didn't go out of his way to share his institutional
knowledge. I had to rely on the secretary's administrative assistant for that. It would be a few days until I was able to onboard
other political appointees.

For that first day at work, I had put on my trusted blue-striped
pantsuit, one of about four pantsuits that had seen a lot of action

during the campaign. I'd hoisted my leather handbag and slipped on my blue pumps, which added about two inches to my five-foot-two-inch frame. A tip for would-be politico operatives: whether you are knocking on doors looking for votes, meeting a state assembly person, or standing in the back of a room during a local town meeting—always dress not for yourself but for the candidate you represent. Me, I would wear jeans, turtlenecks, and a backpack 24/7 if I could. But here at the Labor Department as the White House liaison, I had to look like a professional—a grown-up, you might say.

I did, however, have something special: a tailored pink cotton dress shirt that my then girlfriend had bought at Brooks Brothers as a gift. The pink matched the thin stripes on my pantsuit.

Sure, I was nervous standing in the labor secretary's empty suite. But all of the White House liaisons had gone through training to learn how to bring political appointees into their agency. You have career staffers from all of these agencies but some agencies have hundreds of political appointees—about four thousand in the federal government. (Trump has filled only a fraction.) That was my job. You learn about the intricacies of agencies and then specifically about *your* agency. You get tons of résumés and slates of possible hires from the White House, and have to figure out who to place where, from the highest level—chief of staff and assistant secretaries—all the way down to assistants. I worked closely with the Office of Presidential Personnel (PPO). It's like that kids' matching game where you turn over a square with a picture of a daisy on it and you have to remember where the other square with the same daisy picture is. Except it didn't feel like a game at all. I bore the weight of finding the unconfirmed secretary good people to work for her. It felt like a heavy responsibility. A real adult job.

Five weeks went by before Solis was finally confirmed on February 24. She was set to arrive the next day, and we were excited. Except there was a problem. The orchid left by Elaine

Chao was now brown and dead. Maybe we watered it too much, maybe not enough. Maybe it got lonely. Maybe it needed shade, maybe sun.

Pandemonium.

Someone—not me—had to find a local floral shop to scan the shelf for a replacement orchid as close as possible to the original one.

Solis never knew.

Usually after the White House liaison brings people in and helps the cabinet secretary get confirmed, their job evolves into another post at that agency. But after three months of working at the US Labor Department I found that I missed the seat-of-the-pants aspect of political affairs. A phone call to Patrick Gaspard and a couple of weeks later, I was at my new desk in the Eisenhower Executive Office Building. I was more financially stretched, but happy.

Part of my move to the White House was also personal. There was a big difference between working at the Department of Labor and in the EEOB. I hate to say it, but agency work can be meh! It was like working on Pluto—a dark and distant planet far from the heat and glory of the White House.

The Frances Perkins Building was named for the first female cabinet member. Perkins served as the US secretary of labor under President Franklin Roosevelt from 1933 to 1945. No mere figurehead, she was the force behind the establishment of the Social Security Act. But her namesake building, completed in 1975, is another story. Whether or not the design was intentional I can't say, but it is generally agreed upon that it looks like a file cabinet. That's exactly how it felt, too. A throwback. Everything seemed dark, brown, industrial. The carpet was worn, the file cabinets metal, and it had the unmistakable odor of old papers and dust. There was nothing appealing about it.

Plus, although I had lived in DC when I worked for Walmart

Watch, it was a very lonely place for me. In 2009, it was still very much a one-company town—that "company" being the federal government—and I had never made a lot of friends there. Usually, you befriend the people you work with. Funnily enough, I was *very* popular—people who wanted a job couldn't email or call me enough! But as the White House liaison at the Labor Department, I wasn't working with the people I hired. I was reading their résumés, getting their paperwork in order, making sure they had the right badge to get into their building, reporting back to the PPO, moving on. It was not the ideal situation for an introvert. I had to constantly be "on." Plus, my family and friends were in New York. So was my girlfriend at the time. Every Saturday morning, I would find myself on the New Jersey Turnpike heading north. So there was little chance of feeling rooted in Washington. My choice of neighborhood didn't help. I lived in a drafty, dim, $800-a-month basement apartment in what was then a not-desirable part of town.

Being in the political affairs office gave me instant colleagues. I was able to reconnect with all my pals from the campaign.

One thing my new job required was an FBI security clearance. Let's face it. I was a nerd. I never drank, smoked pot, or tried any harder drugs, and I hadn't piled much debt on top of my student loans, which is another thing I knew the agents look for. They want to make sure you're not a good candidate for blackmail. I was fairly confident that I was clean, but I knew people who were very worried. Campaign people worked and played hard!

The way a background check works is that you give FBI agents three names as references. The agents then get in touch with those people and ask them for other names they should contact. They could talk to ten people for all you know. FBI agents went to every place I had lived to ask my neighbors about me. That included my shady apartment complex in Columbia, South Carolina, where I was so transient—and intentionally stayed so far beneath the radar—that most people didn't have a clue who I was.

I didn't have to wait for the check to be completed—it can take months. But I was still relieved when I passed.

The one stipulation I had going in was that I didn't want to work as a political director in the South again. Been there, done that. Instead, I became the Northeast political director, representing twelve New England and mid-Atlantic states like Massachusetts and New Jersey. The time is mostly one long sleep-deprived, adrenaline-fueled, super exciting blur. There was never a moment that I didn't feel proud to be representing President Obama. Think about that. Not a single nanosecond. Incredible. I don't think that staffers working for most other presidents can make that boast.

Sometimes the public persona does not match the private one, as in the case of John Edwards. But sometimes—more rarely—it did. One of these people was the president himself. Another was Vice President Joe Biden. One-on-one in personal conversation, he is as friendly and talkative as he appears. I learned that when I flew Air Force Two with him.

Pardon my name-dropping and aircraft boasting. I admit, flying on Air Force One and Air Force Two crank up the "amazing level" to at least a twelve. You take a van to Andrews Air Force Base in suburban Washington, DC, and there it is on the tarmac: the iconic plane with the elegant light blue exterior that Jackie Kennedy commissioned back in the early sixties.

I feel almost sick when I hear Donald Trump wants to have it repainted red, white, and blue.

Air Force Two is a bit smaller but also has "UNITED STATES OF AMERICA" painted in capital letters on the outside. I laughed when aviation buffs pointed out that Harry Truman was flown on a plane called "Sacred Cow." (The moniker came from its high security and special status.)

On Air Force One, I never saw the presidential bedroom, the

always-ready medical operating room, the treadmill, or any of the mysterious military gear that it reportedly contains. Apparently, Air Force One can repel a nuclear bomb, a ballistic missile, and incoming fighter jets. Not to mention refuel midair with another plane. Nor was I allowed on the flight deck, where the pilots and crew sit.

But at least I wasn't corralled in the very back of the plane with the press corps who sit in rows of typical airline seats. My seat was a white leather captain's chair in the plane's midsection for presidential staff. You always know where to sit since the super-efficient air force attendants put a place card with your name on the designated seat. The food is also fresh and delicious—and I'm a picky vegetarian. This isn't some sad budget airline.

The first time I flew on Air Force Two was primary night for Jon Corzine's gubernatorial reelection race in 2009. He would win that night but go on to lose when he faced Republican nominee—and future Trump supporter—Chris Christie of Bridgegate fame in November. After the rally, Biden came aboard and sat in the seat right next to me. It was pretty surreal. There I was, this Haitian American kid, a black gay woman whose mother is a home health care aide and whose father drives a taxi. He was charming and funny. He talked about his progressive record and his work with women, with African Americans, with the LGBTQ+ community. You could tell he was really proud. I was pleasantly surprised and pleased. Let's face it—he didn't have to talk to me. He could have been on the phone. But he asked me questions about myself and listened with genuine interest. He really came across as the sweet, kind "Uncle Joe" you read about. I ended up traveling so much with Biden and his staff that his Secret Service detail gave me an official pin that allowed me access to the vice president.

As part of my job, I kept a close eye on the election that followed Ted Kennedy's death in August 2009, less than a year into Obama's first term. This was a staggering personal loss for the

Democratic Party. Ted Kennedy had represented the state of Massachusetts in the Senate for forty-six years, and progressives worshipped him as a champion of education and health care. Heading into the special election to fill his seat, on January 19, 2010, no one expected that his death could possibly be compounded by a second, crushing blow—the loss by Democratic attorney general Martha Coakley to a Republican in an overwhelmingly Democratic state. Brown's election would be the first time a Republican represented Massachusetts in the US Senate since 1972.

As the White House's Northeast political director, Massachusetts was part of my territory. I was paying close attention to the race that pitted Martha Coakley against an obscure Republican state senator named Scott Brown. Sitting at my desk in the EEOB on a seasonably chilly day in early December, I liked what I saw. Internal polling reports showed Coakley leading Brown by twenty points. Then, inexplicably, her campaign went dark—no events; no voter outreach—for two to three weeks around the holidays. I couldn't even get Coakley's people on the phone. They committed a cardinal political sin—taking voters for granted. Scott Brown saw an opening and kicked into high gear. Driving a black GMC pickup truck with a patchwork of stickers on the rear window, he scoured the state, shaking hands and hugging babies. He understood that in politics, visibility is more than half the battle. And Brown's optics were pretty fantastic. Strikingly handsome, he had military experience and had modeled professionally, winning *Cosmopolitan* magazine's America's Sexiest Man contest in 1982. He used the $1000 fee for posing as a nude centerfold to help pay for law school.

Looking back at the election now, it reminds me of the fable about the tortoise and the hare. The hare gets overconfident and takes time out to nap—and wrap a few Christmas presents— while the tortoise plods slowly and surely across the finish line.

Coakley also made some cringe-worthy blunders. She suggested that it was ludicrous for her to stand in the cold outside the Red Sox's iconic Fenway Park and shake hands with voters. During a radio show, she incorrectly described one of the team's star pitchers as a Yankee fan.

During a debate, Brown also scored a powerful zinger of his own. The moderator asked him: "Are you willing…to say…I'm going to sit in Teddy Kennedy's seat, and I'm gonna be the person who's going to block [health care] for another fifteen years?"

"Well, with all due respect," Brown answered, "it's not the Kennedys' seat, and it's not the Democrats' seat. It's the people's seat."

Ouch. Coming about a week before the election, the punch was hard for the Coakley campaign to shake off.

On election night I was in Boston, in Coakley's war room. I knew that the evening wasn't going well. A lot of Democratic voters that should have shown up stayed home. So I expected what came next: Brown beat Coakley 52 percent to 47 percent, imperiling the passage of Barack Obama's Affordable Care Act (ACA), which was gasping for air in Congress—and that Kennedy had done so much to push forward.

But the ACA did pass and was signed into law by President Obama on March 23, 2010. This was a signature achievement of the administration. Although it was unpopular and misunderstood in its early years, the ACA and the protections it provides Americans with preexisting conditions has become a powerful rallying position for Democrats. Keeping the ACA and protecting it from a Republican repeal is one of the reasons the Democrats won so many seats in the 2018 elections.

When I wasn't traveling, one of my favorite extracurricular jobs while I worked at the White House was giving tours of the West Wing. I always laugh when I remember binge-watching the TV show with the same name when I worked for John Edwards in Chapel Hill and Columbia, South Carolina. News flash—the actual West Wing is so much smaller in real life than the fictional lair of TV's President Josiah Bartlet and his scheming staff! Back then, as I lay on my sad, half-inflated blow-up bed, I could never imagine that someday I would be able to guide people through the Roosevelt Room with its amazing portraits of Rough Rider Theodore Roosevelt on horseback and of his cousin Franklin Delano Roosevelt, creator of the New Deal. Or peek into the bright, sunny Oval Office with its paintings of Lincoln and Washington. One stop that was off-limits: the Situation Room—which I always thought was underground, but isn't—the scene of so many tense historical moments like the Cuban Missile Crisis. It was there that Obama and his staff watched the mission to capture Osama bin Laden in May 2011.

But a few months before that momentous day for the country, the political affairs staff had been called to a rare meeting in the Situation Room. Soon the president walked in, to our complete surprise. The Democrats had been walloped in the 2010 midterm elections, and we were all downcast. He told us we had done a good job and thanked us for our work. But the big news that day was his announcement that he was disbanding our office. Obama had already declared that he was running for reelection in 2012, and the duties of the political affairs unit were being absorbed by the campaign office. Patrick Gaspard became executive director of the Democratic National Committee in January 2011. The first political appointee to arrive at the Department of Labor the day after Obama's inauguration, now I literally was the last person left in our large corner suite. Alyssa Mastromonaco, the White House deputy chief of staff in charge of operations, emailed me one day asking, in effect, "Are you still here? We need to get you out of here." That March, just after I flipped off the lights and pulled the door shut behind me, I went to the Oval Office for the customary "exit photo" with the president. Obama put an arm around my back. Gripping my shoulder, he said, "Thank you for your service. You go out there to Chicago, and you make it happen! Go do your best!"

I moved back to Chicago to help make sure the president would get four more years in the White House.

CHAPTER EIGHT

Not All Roads Lead to Washington, DC

While there are only 535 seats in Congress, there are more than half a million political positions in America, according to Amanda Litman in her book *Run for Something*. This means that Washington represents less than 0.1 percent of what's out there. Just as there are many ways to be in the world, consequently there are many ways to hone your political skills besides working for an elected official or campaigning.

And not all roads lead to Washington, DC.

This info just might be the most important advice I can give you. If you want to take a more active role in the political process—in addition to voting, of course—you should know that there are thousands of jobs and volunteer positions available to you. And almost none of them involve pulling up your roots, loading the van, and driving to Washington, to your state capital, or even to your county seat. A famous Massachusetts

Democratic congressman—Tip O'Neill, who led the House of Representatives back when Republican Ronald Reagan was president in the 1980s—quipped that all politics are local. Really local. School boards, town councils, your local library. Granted, O'Neill didn't make that statement in the age of Donald Trump, when *everything* seems to be about him and his presidency. Most of the off-year elections in 2017 and certainly the 2018 midterms were, in one way or another, a referendum on Trump's policies—on health care, immigration, climate breakdown, the environment—and on his chronic lying, media bashing, and the fact that he runs the White House as if he's still the star of a reality-TV show.

But despite Trump's distractions, the point that you don't have to work in politics per se to influence policy and to do good work remains 100 percent true. And especially today, many of these jobs are not set in some generic-looking office park off an interstate exit ramp but in your own living room.

After I stopped working for President Obama, I went back to my New York City roots, working on Bill Thompson's bid to become the Democratic candidate in the 2013 New York City mayoral election. I had known and respected Thompson, who had been in NYC politics for decades and had been twice elected to be New York City comptroller, the city's chief financial officer, in charge of a $66 million operating budget. I strongly believed that he had the experience and leadership qualities to be a good mayor. But on primary day, Thompson came in a close second behind Bill de Blasio.

What helped clinch the primary election for de Blasio was the thirty-second TV spot that featured a black teenager sporting a big afro. Staring directly in the camera, the teen says, "I want to tell you a little bit about Bill de Blasio." Not until the end do viewers realize who he is. "Bill de Blasio will be a mayor for every New Yorker, no matter where they live or what they look like, and I'd say that even if he weren't my dad," said Dante de

Blasio. As analysts noted at the time, the commercial made clear that de Blasio was making a break with policies associated with then mayor Michael Bloomberg. Most important, he gave voice to the anger many black voters felt toward Bloomberg's stop-and-frisk police policy targeting young men of color. Thompson, though black, fell short in harnessing that.

After the primary, I pivoted to becoming Letisha "Tish" James's campaign manager after her public advocate successful runoff campaign. A longtime member of the city council, the charismatic James has an astonishing ability to connect with voters. Fortunately this skill made up for James's utter dislike of asking for money from donors. I had to literally force her into the chair and dial the phone numbers for her to perform this vital, if unpleasant, aspect of campaigning. She is now doing good work as the attorney general of New York State.

Then I jumped to something different, putting my political experience to work for a cause, as I had in my Walmart Watch days, instead of a candidate. I joined the ACLU—the American Civil Liberties Union—another job based in New York City. The ACLU is an amazing organization with chapters around the country. The ACLU was founded after World War I, when so-called "radical" Americans—mainly Italian and Eastern European immigrants—were being arrested and deported without warrants during the Palmer Raids. Named after US Attorney General A. Mitchell Palmer, these raids occurred during the first "Red Scare" in American history. The hysteria was triggered by the rise of communism, the Russian Revolution, and anarchism. Today the ACLU has 1.75 million members and employs a staff of three hundred lawyers. The organization is best known for its work in court, defending challenges to people's right to free speech.

I was working as campaign manager on an innovative program launched by the ACLU called the Reproductive Freedom Initiative. This new initiative wanted to focus on a woman's right to choose whether to bear a child. We advocated to let women control their own bodies. In so many conservative states, we were seeing attacks on this fundamental freedom coming from state legislatures. Rather than just trying to fight these bills in court, we were searching for additional creative techniques and tools to mobilize the resistance. We were employing online ads and digital outreach. Although I was raised in the Roman Catholic faith, which opposes abortion, and I attended parochial schools, I have always felt strongly that no one—not a church, not the government, not a man—has the right to compel a woman to bear a child she does not want and, often, cannot afford. I frequently reflect on the ripe irony that celibate male priests who live in comfortable rectories with housekeepers set themselves up as moral authorities able to opine on such an intensely personal decision for women. My mother and father feel very differently so abortion is not a topic we discuss.

It gave me a thrill to remember that Associate Supreme Court Justice Ruth Bader Ginsburg—"the Notorious RBG"—had also been involved with the ACLU. In 1972, she cofounded the organization's Women's Rights Project. She envisioned that men and women would "create new traditions by their actions, if artificial barriers are removed, and avenues of opportunity held open to them." The ACLU Women's Rights Project was founded to remove these barriers and open these opportunities. As cofounder Ginsburg stated, "Women's rights are an essential part of the overall human rights agenda, trained on the equal dignity and ability to live in freedom all people should enjoy."

In 2014, I also returned to the SIPA program at Columbia University, where I had earned my master's in public administration in 2003. Columbia and SIPA have a special place in my heart. I will never forget how I imagined the steps beneath me turning yellow like in my absolute favorite movie from childhood, *The Wiz*. I think the film resonated with me because it was one of the first times I had seen an all-black cast. And in

2008, a friend gave me tickets to the show *Wicked*, which became one of my favorite Broadway shows. I would play the
soundtrack nonstop in my car while driving around Chicago
working on the Obama campaign.

Back then, when I was a penniless—and yes, anxious and often
overwhelmed—grad student scurrying from class to class with
a massive black book bag on my shoulder, I couldn't imagine
that someday I would be in charge of my own class at Columbia. With the encouragement of my longtime mentor Professor
Ester Fuchs, every Thursday night from January through April,
from 6:10 p.m. to 8:00 p.m., I now teach a graduate class called
Campaign Management.

I adore teaching. Forgive the cliché, but it truly feels that
when I interact with my students, I am shaping a better
world. While I'm helping to train the next wave of campaign
managers/staffers/consultants, I find I lose track of time. I look
up at the beginning of class and then I am off. My students
have to remind me when eight o'clock rolls around. It is such
an immersive, rewarding experience!

I make a point of being on time and polite to my students.
However, I have to establish early on that I am the one running
the show. This can be a struggle for someone who is confronting
much taller students, sometimes from foreign countries, who are
not familiar with female instructors or the importance of being
in one's seat at exactly 6:10 p.m. Sometimes, I do chuckle at myself on the inside when I have to play the heavy with students,
laying down the law on when they must hand in their papers
and projects. I surprise myself with how strict I am!

Because I assume some of you readers are in high school or
getting your associate degree at a community college or enrolled
in a college program, I would like to offer a few tips from the
other side of the lectern. These are things that I wish someone
had shared with me when I was a student. It wasn't always clear

to me how to advance myself because my parents didn't know to offer this kind of advice.

Get to class early. Obvious but priceless. You need to be seated and ready to take notes. Everyone has a slow subway sometime, but repeatedly skulking into the room with a guilty expression after the start of class makes you very memorable to the teacher. And not in a good way.

I hate to say it…but sitting in the front of the class is far better than choosing that cozy last row. Yeah, I know. No one wants to be seen as Suzie or Sammy Suckup, but in college and grad school, you are paying hard-earned money to be taught. Making the transition from mandatory high school to voluntary higher education isn't just a physical change, it's a mental switch. Making a good impression on your teacher is crucial. To get ahead, you need letters of recommendation and mentor opportunities.

Sit up straight and look at the professor. Think about this from the teacher's point of view. It's not easy for a teacher to lecture to a sea of blank, sometimes yawning faces. The occasional nod goes a long way and reassures the teacher that they are not boring the class into a coma.

Turn off your phone and put it away. I'm as addicted as anyone to my phone, but it is vital that you focus on what the teacher and the other students are saying. I know it is convenient to take notes on your phone but don't. Better to tape the lecture and write down pen-and-paper notes. Research proves that you remember things more if you physically write down information rather than typing it.

Okay, end of sermon.

I try not to be the kind of professor who made my eyes glaze over—the one who stands at the front of the classroom and drones on. My students tell me they like hearing anecdotes from my Obama campaign days, but I know the danger of telling too many back-in-my-day stories.

We do, however, start with the history of campaigning, looking back as far as the ancient Chinese military general Sun Tzu's *The Art of War*. This fifth-century BC classic offers lessons on how to get the upper hand over your enemy, whether that enemy is on the battlefield, in the boardroom, or vying to be the next city council member of your hometown. I also invite in almost every week at least one guest speaker—professionals currently working in politics—to give their what's-happening-in-the-trenches perspective.

But I want the class to have more learning and less teaching, so early on, I break my students into groups and give them a project that forces them to think creatively about how to plan a campaign. What makes teaching this topic tricky is that campaign tactics are constantly evolving. All other things being equal, the winning campaign is usually the one that uses innovative technology most effectively to get voters more fired up and connected to your candidate. When Abraham Lincoln ran for president in 1860, he gave exactly one—ONE!—campaign speech. Then, when reporters subsequently asked him what he thought about X or Y issue, he would say, "Read my campaign speech." A hundred years later, in 1960, when John F. Kennedy and Richard M. Nixon held the first ever televised presidential debate, viewers believed that Kennedy, who came across as young, tanned, and relaxed—i.e., TV ready—beat Nixon, who was sweaty and had a five o'clock shadow, hands down. Radio listeners who heard their voices without the visuals, on the other hand, thought the candidates had tied or even that Nixon had won. Fast-forward again to Barack Obama's 2008 campaign, which took advantage of Americans' growing comfort with social media to advertise and organize for the first time. Today's version: Alexandria Ocasio-Cortez, a new member of Congress from New York now known to millions as AOC, and Beto O'Rourke, who challenged Republican Ted Cruz for his Senate seat in Texas in 2018 (and, as I write, is a Democratic candidate for president in 2020), are naturals at Instagram—they are so cleverly skilled at making their followers feel a part of their lives that their example is pushing other candidates to up their game. Or perish.

Similarly, it used to be that the best use of a candidate's time was to plant her or him at a subway station entrance or another high-traffic public spot, and have them shake the hand of every single passerby. Now the name of the game is targeting. This means researching and strategizing about which voters are likely to be in your camp and then devoting time, money, and energy to touching these people as authentically and as often as possible.

And as much as I hate to admit it, Donald Trump displays a showman's canny skill with his Twitter feed, uniting his followers and hijacking the political agenda. But of course it is only a matter of time before someone and something new—for both good and bad—comes along and the preferred platform changes.

Another element of campaigning we discuss in my SIPA class in detail is GOTV—Get Out the Vote. This step of getting bodies to the polls is crucial. You can reach the public all you want, but if they don't actually vote, especially at a time when an election can be won or lost on a minuscule margin, your efforts mean nothing. In the 2018 gubernatorial race in Florida, Democrat Andrew Gillum lost to Republican Ron DeSantis by less than 34,000 votes, or 1 percent. In the 2016 battle for the White House between Donald Trump and Hillary Clinton, a bit more than 77,000 votes in three states decided who won the electoral college, and hence, the nationwide election.

Here's a question I have asked on my midterm exam that might be fun to answer: *The Art of War* and another book called *Campaign Craft: The Strategies, Tactics, and Art of Political Campaign Management*, by Michael John Burton, William J. Miller, and Daniel M. Shea, suggest that campaign management is all about the art, while pollsters use survey data to reveal the science of the industry. In your opinion, is running a campaign more art or science?

As I tell my students, "Don't say BOTH. Pick one. Sure, you can say that there are elements of each, but pick one side to land on at the end of the day."

Of course, I know the answer is both. But that's my professorial privilege.

I have found that one way to keep your spirit refreshed is to alternate between always being the expert—be it as a teacher or a seasoned veteran in your chosen profession—and being a newbie or even a student. Why is this important? Sharing your knowledge is like draining down your smartphone battery, while learning from other people and incorporating new skills is like recharging your battery. When you learn, you absorb energy and also push yourself in new directions. I fell into following that advice, even before knowing it.

In 2010 when I was in the White House, I worked on a video campaign called It Gets Better started by gay rights activist and sex advice columnist Dan Savage and his husband, Terry Miller, that featured gay men and women telling their coming-out stories to try to prevent teenagers who were LGBTQ+, or who were thought to be, from committing suicide after they were bullied. One video featured President Obama along with several gay White House staffers. "We've got to dispel this myth that bullying is just a normal rite of passage; that it's some inevitable part of growing up," the president says. "It's not... To every young person out there, you need to know that if you're in trouble, there are caring adults who can help. I don't know what it's like to be picked on for being gay. But I do know what it's like to grow up feeling that sometimes you don't belong. It's tough... There is a whole world waiting for you, filled with possibilities. There are people out there who love you and care about you just the way you are. And so, if you ever feel like because of bullying, because of what people are saying, that you're getting down on yourself, you've got to make sure to reach out to people you trust."

With the guidance of Brian Bond, White House deputy director of the Office of Public Engagement, I helped to produce the White House It Gets Better video. "When I was five years old, I knew I was different," I say, standing in front of the north entrance to the White House, with its white columns behind me. "I felt being different was my fault. The shame and the embarrassment kept me from talking to my family for years." Toward the end of the video, I come on again. "Be true to yourself, because it *does* get better," I say. The experience had a lasting effect on me.

My total airtime was twelve seconds, but after he saw it, a White House friend, Jeffrey, told me, "Karine, you need to do TV."

Remember how incredibly, painfully shy I was growing up? It still dogged me as an adult. When I worked in the White House Office of Political Affairs, besides our meetings with Patrick Gaspard, we used to have regular check-in meetings with Jim Messina, President Obama's deputy chief of staff. I was always so nervous talking in front of a group of people that I would stumble during my what's-going-on-in-the-Northeast update. TV is one thing I can say had never, not even once, crossed my mind!

The video was the first thing I had ever done on camera. It was a revelation. I thought I would find it terrifying but, in fact, I was totally at ease. Speaking to a camera was far less intimidating than speaking to a group of people. It was like a one-on-one conversation. Except the camera couldn't answer back!

But the fact that Jeffrey saw something in me I didn't recognize had made me start thinking.

So how do you get started in TV? You don't just knock on CNN's door. Producers have to make sure you look good on TV. My longtime friend and now associate professor at Fordham University Christina Greer, who is a regular guest on NY1, a twenty-four-hour cable news channel that focuses on the five boroughs of New York City, connected me to a producer at the TV station. This was in 2014 around the midterms. Obama was president. I went on air a handful of nerve-racking times as a political consultant, as someone who had done presidential campaigns. I was scared and sweaty, and it took me time to build up confidence. But because of that, I had some clips to share with other TV producers and bookers. I thought I was getting somewhere.

Then came my election eve debut on MSNBC. It was a complete and utter disaster.

Christina, who was also a regular guest on MSNBC's prime-time shows, connected me with *All In with Chris Hayes*. I was on with Jess McIntosh from EMILY's List, a political action committee that supports Democratic women running for political office. Chris Hayes asked me a question; I answered it, and then THE ULTIMATE EMBARRASSMENT. Hayes said, in effect, "That's not what we're talking about."

After that, I was so down on myself. It was on at 8:00 p.m.—I mean, you could not get any more prime-time than that—and I had made a fool of myself in front of the entire world. That's how I felt. That in my mind every naysayer who ever told me I wasn't smart enough or that I couldn't do something—going back to the nun who made me learn penmanship and the high school guidance counselor who told me to become a nurse instead of a doctor—I had just proved them all right. "Ha!" I heard them say. "We told you. You can't even do a four-minute interview."

Was this disaster all in my imagination? No. I could tell by the arctic chill after the segment that I had embarrassed myself. There was no response to my follow-up thank-you emails. I don't blame Chris and his staff. I had been truly awful. And in truth, if I hadn't been so dreadful, I might have coasted along doing mediocre TV appearances rather than bearing down to improve. Failing doesn't mean losing, it means trying harder!

Not everything goes smoothly 100 percent of the time. Nor should it. That's the whole point of trying something new! But here's what I want to tell you so you can do it, too. There was something inside me that gave me courage.

During this same period, I was also taking on new challenges in my personal life.

I have never been one of those women who desperately wanted to have children. I had already earned my mom cred babysitting for my little sister and brother. I had gotten a view of what parenthood really entails. The dirty diapers, the screaming, the throwing-themselves-down-on-the-supermarket-floor temper tantrums, the out-all-night, curfew-smashing teen years.

And, of course, there was an unfortunate episode back in my childhood when I left my little sister in Lincoln Park when we lived in Hempstead while I went off with my friends. I still wince when I remember what a truly terrible thing I had done and how lucky it was that there were no tragic consequences.

That is Edwine's tip-top favorite anecdote about me, brought out every single Christmas! It is as much a staple at every family gathering as Mummy's *tchaka* (Haitian-style stew).

My lack of interest in having children is not connected to my being gay. I know a lot of lesbians who hear their biological clocks ticking as loudly as any straight woman. I have many friends— gay and straight—who have frozen their eggs with the expectation that if necessary, they will become single moms and raise their children on their own.

But this biological imperative passed me by. I adore my siblings' boys. I know it saddened my mummy and my papi when I would state right up front, "I don't plan to have kids." Never have I looked at a pregnant woman on the subway or down an office corridor and thought wistfully, *I wish that were me.*

Kids were never part of my life plan.

Then I met Suzanne.

As would befit a journalist and a political operative, we met at the 2012 Democratic National Convention in Charlotte, North Carolina. Suzanne was at the DNC to cover and anchor her show on CNN. This was the convention that renominated Barack Obama for a second term as president. It was an exciting, well-run operation, and the positive vibe would continue through November and victory.

Suzanne is a beautiful woman with striking cheekbones and a dazzling smile. She is older than I am. We met at a donor party being held in a nightclub. I know it's a cliché, but the truth is, I spotted her across a crowded dance floor. No, it's not like our eyes locked and we walked off together into the sunset. But eventually, I did make my way across the room and introduce myself. Where I would say I was met with mild interest—a Fourth of July sparkler, not fireworks! But there wasn't much of a chance for anything to develop at the time, with Suzanne living in Atlanta and covering the presidential campaign and me living first in Los Angeles as a consultant and then in New York as a senior advisor on a campaign. We emailed only a couple of times after meeting in Charlotte. Our first date was the week after the election. I was in Atlanta visiting my nephew and I let Suzanne know I was in town. We grabbed a quick drink at a stylish bistro down the street from her house. Suzanne was wearing jeans and black suede wedge boots. The leather lace on one of her boots was loose. I stopped, knelt down, and retied it. "Oh!" she said, surprised. Then she hopped into her gray Mercedes convertible and sped off.

Standing on the curb, I thought, *This one is different. This one matters.*

I had definitely dated before, but it was hard for someone to catch my attention. Not that I was selfish, but I was self-involved. You had to jump onto me to get me to notice. In other relationships, they had chased me, but in this relationship, I chased Suzanne. Maybe that's why we're together.

Suzanne is warm, brilliant, grounded, funny—and supportive of me. (Just as an example, she was incredibly helpful after my Chris Hayes episode. She would ask me questions and record me on her phone and then I would play it back, again and again, just like a baseball pitcher trying to improve his fastball to figure out what I could do better.)

I also adored her family. At the time, they were struggling with her mom's diagnosis of amyotrophic lateral sclerosis, known by its acronym, ALS, which causes a weakening of the muscles and, ultimately, the nerves that control breathing. You might remember the Ice Bucket Challenge in the summer of 2014, when professional athletes, celebrities, you name it, dumped buckets of ice on one another to raise money and awareness of the disease. In the United States, about five thousand people are diagnosed with ALS every year, and they typically survive about three to five years.

A long-distance relationship can be tough, but we somehow made it work for the first year. During that time, I was living in New York. Suzanne was flying up from Atlanta to see her mom outside Baltimore, Maryland, as much as she possibly could. We spent almost every weekend together, either in Maryland or Atlanta. Having felt so displaced in Columbia, South Carolina, I was surprised by how at-home I felt in Atlanta. There was a large and highly visible black LBGTQ+ community there. Suzanne and I spent a lot of time running outdoors and playing tourist.

Finally, in early 2014, Suzanne and I both moved to Washington, DC. That was the only way she could hope to successfully juggle working, being in a committed relationship, and taking care of aging parents—an intricate feat required of many of us.

But there was one more ball Suzanne wanted to throw up into the air. She wanted to become a mother. She made that crystal clear to me from the beginning. And to my amazement, the idea suddenly seemed very appealing. For the first time, I could see myself forming a family of my own with this woman. To be clear, Soleil's adoption process started very early on in our relationship. So Suzanne began the process on her own as I provided loving and emotional support. As I write this book, I am now excitedly going through the process of adopting Soleil.

Like many couples, we tried out our parenting skills on a dog first. We had never talked about getting a dog until my cell phone rang one night. Suzanne, attending an ALS fundraiser in Wisconsin, was on the line, describing a puppy—a yellow Labrador—she wanted to bid on. Hours later, I got a text: Here's a pic of our new dog! Mardi—short for *Mardi Gras*, to reflect our French names and Suzanne's New Orleans heritage—is a lovable creature with an insatiable need for love and an equally insatiable desire to chase tennis balls hour after hour. When Mardi arrived about ten days later, I called Suzanne into the living room, where I was playing soft toss with her. "I'm pretty sure she's not a yellow Lab," I said. "I think she might be a golden retriever!" We couldn't stop laughing! But, of course, like most things, it's the substance and not the label that matters—even when you're talking about a seventy-five-pound dog who likes to put her head on top of your feet.

By the way, I was dead right about the breed.

And then we got another addition to our family. Soleil was born in the spring. Knowing that she was on the way, we embarked on a grueling twelve-house-a-day search for a new home. We needed to be situated equally between Suzanne's parents in the Baltimore suburbs and the CNN studio on Capitol Hill in Washington, DC, where Suzanne worked. Our perseverance paid off when we found a beautiful brick house on a cul-de-sac in a Maryland suburb known for its good public schools. It had enough room for us and a backyard for Mardi.

We had been living there only a month when the adoption agency called with unexpected news: our soon-to-be baby girl, whom Suzanne was adopting in California, was coming early!

I was based in Washington, working for the ACLU from our new living room. I was in the organization's offices in New York City for a meeting—which I had to cancel. (Suzanne was at work in Washington, DC.) After the purchase of a last-minute, $1,500 one-way plane ticket and a cab ride, I was flying across the country to where Suzanne and I would meet up at the airport and drive together to the hospital! When we left with Soleil to come home, we had nothing but our healthy, gorgeous newborn and the starter kit containing formula and diapers that the hospital handed us, accompanied by a cheery "Good luck!" Of course, we had to rent a car seat and figure out how to correctly put Soleil in it before we could go one inch from the hospital entrance!

Nor had we settled on a name. As with Mardi, we knew we wanted something French but waited until we saw her before we decided. We instantly agreed that this radiant child should be Soleil—French for *sun*.

Like all new parents, we were utterly exhausted in those early months. The crying, the worry, the sense that your entire life is being controlled by someone who can't speak and weighs less than ten pounds and yet wields total control over everyone and everything in the house. Even Mardi would hide under the bed when Soleil started screaming.

One person who was not put off by these squalls? President Obama. Among our most treasured possessions are photos of the president carrying our daughter around at various White House events. There's the 2014 holiday party with infant Soleil in a red velvet party frock and white tights. Another is from June 2015 with Soleil wearing a blue-and-white sundress admiring White House floral arrangements with the leader of the free world. One of my all-time favorite videos is of Soleil, at twenty-two months, crying at the Easter Egg Roll on the South Lawn. It was hot, and she was overwhelmed. The commander-in-chief plucks her up and calms her down.

But, of course, as besotted parents, Suzanne and I found it entirely logical that President Obama also found himself enchanted with our little girl.

CHAPTER NINE

And the Winner Is...DONALD TRUMP

Like a lot of people, I fear I will go to my grave struggling with PTSD from Tuesday, November 8, 2016.

It's a night I wish I could forget, but know I never can.

That fateful day had begun with an 8:00 a.m. Acela train ride. After giving the sleeping Soleil a quick kiss, I had left our house in suburban Maryland and driven down Route 270 in the predawn darkness to Washington, DC's magnificent white marble Union Station, which stands just down the hill from the US Capitol building with its shining dome. I boarded my Amtrak train and started going through Twitter and the news sites. Despite the horrible, divisive rhetoric and outright lies told by Donald Trump, I believed—like most people and the media—that Hillary Rodham Clinton would be elected the forty-fifth president of the United States that night. Nothing I was reading—not the

New York Times, not the *Washington Post*, not the networks, not the polls—nothing—suggested that Trump could win.

There was no question: Trump was unfit to be president. With her passion for policy and her decades of experience, HRC would undoubtedly have been a very effective president. She had succeeded as secretary of state. Certainly better than the current occupant of 1600 Pennsylvania Avenue.

Being an old campaign hand, though, I couldn't shake a pervasive sense of unease, even dread. HRC hadn't captured the nation's heart and mind the way I had witnessed Barack Obama do firsthand in 2008 and again in 2012. Her support felt mushy, tepid, ambivalent in a way that Obama's had never felt. I had started the 2016 presidential election cycle working for Martin O'Malley. Perhaps he could have won the 2016 Democratic primary and then both our lives—as well as that of the nation—would be very different today. When the *New York Times* announced that O'Malley had hired me as his presidential campaign's national political director, I admit, I was thrilled. My bursting-with-pride papi kept that clipping on the front seat of his taxi till it disintegrated.

I admired a lot of things O'Malley had done as a successful, popular, two-term governor of the true-blue state of Maryland. He championed same-sex marriage, passed a gun control bill, and helped the children of undocumented immigrants gain in-state college tuition. A white politician, he had been elected mayor of Baltimore, a primarily black city, for two terms by wide margins. The man was progressive, intelligent, good-looking. Hell, even his relative youth—fifty-two—made him stand out compared to Bernie Sanders, Hillary Clinton, and Donald Trump. It was true he was unknown to voters nationally, and that certainly included the people of Iowa and New Hampshire. On the other hand, O'Malley wasn't burdened with the decades of scandal, fatigue, and baggage that Hillary Clinton hauled. The stars appeared aligned for O'Malley and me.

Sometimes people look for the shiny object. In 2015 Hillary Clinton was the shiny object. By choosing O'Malley, I was deliberately facing away from that, as enticing as it was. I think Suzanne would have been very supportive if I had worked for HRC, but I wanted our relationship to continue to flourish. Moving to Brooklyn where HRC's campaign had its headquarters was out of the question, what with Suzanne's own journalism career in DC and her aging parents who needed help to cope with the tremendous burden of her mom's ALS. Most important, if I were commuting from Brooklyn to Washington, DC, I would have missed so much, each tiny new milestone that baby Soleil was marking. I knew from past experience: a presidential campaign means you work twelve- to fifteen-hour days, seven days a week. I would not have been coming home on weekends from New York City.

Martin O'Malley's campaign was appealing, in part because it was so geographically desirable. His campaign headquarters were in Baltimore, just forty-five minutes away from the suburban Maryland house that I share with Suzanne and Soleil. My relationship with Soleil—who had just turned one—therefore wouldn't suffer. I thought O'Malley had a future, and still do. His campaign felt like an exciting start-up. I liked him. He sang in an Irish rock band. Obsessed with the Constitution and American history, he knew everything about the 1812 war with England. (Our national anthem, "The Star-Spangled Banner," was written in 1814 by Francis Scott Key as the British Royal Navy bombarded Fort McHenry in O'Malley's city of Baltimore.)

I joined the campaign in early spring. Then Freddie Gray happened. On April 12, 2015, the cops arrested Gray—a twenty-five-year-old black Baltimore man. Put inside a police van and taken for a "rough ride," Gray was found forty-five minutes later unconscious and not breathing, his spinal cord nearly severed. After a seven-day coma, Gray died on April 19. His death and the citizen video of his arrest, which showed him screaming in pain, prompted peaceful protests as well as destructive riots.

O'Malley really loved Baltimore, but many activists blamed his zero-tolerance policing while he was mayor from 1999 to 2007. They believe it created a deep, festering tension between the police and the community. The police were encouraged to be very aggressive.

Everything blew up when we were at Netroots Nation in Phoenix, Arizona, an important convention for progressives. Both Bernie Sanders and O'Malley were heckled, and activist Tia Oso took the stage to confront O'Malley.

O'Malley responded with "Black lives matter, white lives matter, all lives matter." He just didn't get the structural racism that was killing black people. Trayvon Martin. Eric Garner. Michael Brown. Sandra Bland.

To hear the candidate you're working for totally miss the mark is awful. That was tough for me to deal with personally since I face racism every day. I believe in the Black Lives Matter (BLM) movement. It was tough for him, too. To O'Malley's credit, we sat down with activists and protestors, who explained that BLM was about black men being murdered and no one seeming to care.

By the end, I think O'Malley understood what BLM is about. But make no mistake, there are definitely going to be moments on every campaign when your candidate will disappoint and bewilder you.

The campaign lasted for nine months, but O'Malley had little name recognition or traction. O'Malley dropped out immediately after the February 1, 2016, Democratic Iowa caucus. My political crystal ball failed to predict that a snow-haired, socialist grandpa in his midseventies from the second-whitest state in the union— tiny Vermont, population 620,000—would fire up Americans across the nation, particularly young people, with a passion no one had witnessed since Barack Obama in 2008.

My bad.

HRC won—barely, with 49.9 percent. Bernie Sanders came in second with 49.6—the closest race in the state's Democratic caucus's history. O'Malley, with less than 1 percent, really didn't place. It was over. And when it's over, it's over.

"Tonight, I have to tell you that I am suspending this presidential bid," he said in a speech. "But I am not ending this fight. Our country is worth saving, the American dream is worth saving, and this planet is worth saving. So as we march forward to the fall, let us all resolve together that the love, the generosity, the compassion, and the commitment of this campaign will continue to point our country forward."

I was in Des Moines, freezing and dead broke. A massive blizzard was threatening. I narrowly got out—otherwise I would have been stuck in Iowa for days. We (campaign managers and the deputy campaign managers) had not gotten paid from the O'Malley campaign for the last four or five months. This non-payment is not unusual with a faltering candidate. They paid for our flights and hotels but that's about it. No salary, no benefits. I had taken a major, major risk working for O'Malley. Suzanne had to maintain the finances of our household. We had a child, and we had babysitters. But joining the O'Malley campaign helped me in a big way, because it led me to MoveOn. More details on that later in this chapter.

Also, I started doing TV more often. I was still smarting a little bit from my disastrous Chris Hayes segment. But now, because I could say I was a former deputy campaign manager on an official presidential campaign, it gave me the mantle of expertise that I needed to step into the TV world with both feet.

Right after O'Malley had dropped out, I was doing a C-SPAN interview on cable TV. It was the biggest one I had done, at an hour long. There's a fifteen-minute interview with the host and then forty-five minutes of taking questions from people calling in. The questions are all over the place, so you really have to be on your toes. One comment I later saw on social media was "I can't believe that she was working on a presidential campaign and she has a one-year-old!"

People can be so incredibly judgmental. And now social media platforms like Twitter, Instagram, and Facebook give them a way to broadcast their opinions. Opinions, by the way, that they would probably never express to my face. Mothers are judged if they stay at home with their children, and they are judged if they go to work. I thank my lucky stars every night that Suzanne and I have a relationship based on equality and respect. We truly share the experience of rearing Soleil. The partner who earns less money doesn't have to do more of the grunt work. I have seen this dynamic in many couples I know. Including my own parents.

I also returned to NY1. I would regularly get in my cream-colored MINI Cooper Clubman and drive up to New York City to get in as much TV practice as I could. And then one day I walked into the green room to an unmistakable voice. "Oh, look at this, the prodigal daughter is back!" There sat my old boss Anthony Weiner, legs akimbo, knee jiggling, skinny as ever, a smirk on his mobile face. This was before he was caught sexting with a minor. He sat there like he owned the room. No longer a congressman or a mayoral candidate, Weiner was, appropriately, a regular panelist on the show *Wise Guys*.

In 2016, I also started doing Fox TV. Fox was easy to do because they needed Democratic guests so badly and most would not go near them. A friend I worked with on the Obama campaign really helped me. She knew all these producers, including the ones on Fox. She had moved to California but before she left, she gave me an Excel document with lists of all of the TV shows, their producers, and, most crucially, their emails.

Invaluable!

I took the clips of my appearances on C-SPAN and NY1 and started emailing the producers. I wrote a two-liner about myself.

A guy at Fox turned out to be really helpful as well, connecting me with someone at the Washington, DC, bureau. The funny thing about appearing on Fox was that, to calm myself down before an appearance, I would remember that whether I bombed or triumphed, it didn't matter, because no one I knew—i.e., no self-respecting Democrat—would ever be watching. And certain aspects proved to be different from MSNBC and CNN. At Fox, they applied the foundation with a trowel and went so heavy on the mascara that I practically had to separate my eyelashes with a toothpick. I always felt like I was in a beauty pageant. But they wouldn't touch my hair. I'm sure it's because they had no idea what to do with it. Meanwhile, all around me, they would be madly blow-drying, teasing, and spraying the other contestants'—I mean pundits'—hair like they had fallen back a few decades to the 1950s. But the weirdest part was how some Republican would be ranting and raving at me on camera. Then in the green room afterward, they would say how crazy candidate Trump was. I realized that some people were willing to say *anything* just to get on TV.

That made appearing on TV much easier. I learned how to arrive at the studio armed with an arsenal of facts. And after I learned to debate Fox guests who didn't seem to be grounded in reality for not using facts in their arguments, I could stand my ground with anyone. I got really good, so good that Bill O'Reilly asked me to be on his show. I drew the line there and refused. A girl has got to have standards.

Then I heard from a weekend producer at MSNBC who had seen me on Fox. I started making appearances on MSNBC. Which I enjoyed a lot more than Fox. Thus, little by little, I would do more. What really propelled me was when I appeared on MSNBC's *The Last Word with Lawrence O'Donnell*. The show had this special "War Room" segment, where experts from the campaign world would focus not on punditry but talk about 2016 campaign strategy.

As a result, I started doing that regularly—either once a week or every other Thursday—to talk about the upcoming election. This was during the spring of 2016. Anytime I did *The Last Word with Lawrence O'Donnell*, I had to be in New York City. One night, I was sitting in the green room, and Joy Reid saw me. She was so enthusiastic. "I see you on *O'Donnell* all the time," she said, "and you're great! I want you on my show."

It amazes me how one thing can lead to another.

I loved appearing on Joy's show. She's such a smart, informed, lively talent, able to equally engage White House officials as well as the ordinary person washing the dishes in their suburban kitchen. Born in Brooklyn to a DRC Congolese father and a mother from British Guinea, she has a degree from Harvard and three children. She is also an Obama campaign alum. I started to do her show regularly throughout 2016. Then CNN saw me. The first show I did was with Erin Burnett. Then I started appearing on Anderson Cooper's show. During the 2016 presidential campaign, CNN tended toward larger and louder panels. The network definitely goes for the glam. Make no mistake, how you look matters on television. A lot. CNN also likes makeup on its guests but you don't feel like you're actually auditioning to be a beauty queen. MSNBC takes the lightest touch but they have plenty of deft makeup artists. Today, I make my cable home at MSNBC as a political analyst.

One of the reasons MSNBC wanted me is my role with MoveOn.org. They wanted to highlight the voice of a committed progressive from an important organization on the left. Let me explain how I landed the MoveOn job. It was the kind of old-fashioned networking every unemployed politico has to perform.

Here's how it goes.

The primary is over, the election has passed, and your candidate didn't win. Maybe they lost by an inch, maybe they lost by a mile. Maybe it was a horrible upset that means your dreams of being that smart young staffer with the going-places career is on ice for the time being. Whether it was one vote or three million votes, it doesn't matter. Win or lose, that credit card bill needs to be paid, and you can't negotiate with the grocery store for food, no matter what President Trump believes. Bottom line: you, Mr. or Ms. Politico, need a new job.

So I started doing "the coffee rounds." This is when I start sending out friendly emails to contacts, friends of friends, former mentors, colleagues, former professors—whomever—asking if they want to meet for a quick coffee.

Of course, since I don't drink coffee, it's chai tea with soy or coconut milk for me.

Everybody in Washington, DC, does the coffee rounds. That's probably why there is a Starbucks or an independent coffee shop on every single street corner, with every last table taken as people "meet for coffee" and ask for job leads in late November. Is it fun begging people for half an hour of their time? In a very short word: no. And a lot of people are too busy or distracted and just don't get back to you. Don't take that personally. It's life. Fortunately, since everybody has done "the coffee rounds" at some point in their career, some people try to be nice about it. If the person can't meet for coffee, just ask for ten minutes in their office or ten minutes on the phone to pick their brains about job leads.

I probably don't have to tell you this, but...don't be the kind of person who "sucks up" to bosses but "kicks down" to subordinates. Life is too short and, honestly, you will get a bad reputation. Because you know what they say: you see the same folks on the way down as you saw on the way up! I know one eminent Washington, DC, fixture who screams so often at her female subordinates while they use the toilet that most of the women flee to the bathroom on the floor below.

Anyhow, I met with one of MoveOn's executive directors, Ilya Sheyman, at the Starbucks on Pennsylvania Avenue near the EEOB. He was hurrying to fly out that night to San Francisco. I had met Ilya while working on the O'Malley campaign. We clicked, and a few short weeks later I started out as consultant for three months with him. Then MoveOn renewed my contract, and eventually I came on staff. It is an amazing organization, and I am so lucky to have landed there.

MoveOn.org began in 1998, when two tech entrepreneurs created an online petition about Bill Clinton's impeachment and emailed it to their friends. Like many Americans, they were enraged by how much attention the impeachment was taking up. It went viral.

Soon their petition to "Censure President Clinton and Move On to Pressing Issues Facing the Nation" had hundreds of thousands of signatures. (Note where the MoveOn name comes from!) For the first time in history, an online petition broke into and helped transform the national conversation. It revealed how the internet could be harnessed to power a true progressive revolution, linking concerned people remotely.

Here is our official history and position: "In the years that followed, MoveOn pioneered the field of online organizing, innovating a vast array of tactics that are now commonplace in advocacy and elections and shifting power toward real people and away from Washington insiders and special interests. MoveOn campaigners were the first to use the internet to run virtual phone banks, to crowdsource TV ad production, and to take online organizing offline, using the internet to mobilize activists to knock on doors and attend events. We proved that individual Americans could pool lots of small contributions to make a big impact by raising hundreds of millions of dollars for progressive causes and candidates.

"Together, in collaboration with allies, we have grown the progressive movement and demonstrated that ordinary people's voices can make a difference—that collectively, we possess extraordinary people power. MoveOn members have played crucial roles in persuading the Democratic Party to oppose and eventually end America's war in Iraq, in helping Democrats retake Congress in 2006 with our influential 'Caught Red Handed' campaign, in securing the Democratic nomination for President Obama in 2008 with a pivotal endorsement before the Super Tuesday primaries, and in passing health care reform in 2010.

"More recently, we've surfaced student loans as a potent national issue, catalyzed the fight to expose and push back against the Republican War on Women, helped elevate the leadership of Senators Bernie Sanders and Elizabeth Warren and other progressives fighting economic inequality, mobilized more than half a million people to help take down the Confederate flag from the South Carolina state capitol grounds, led a massive grassroots mobilization to secure President Obama's diplomatic agreement with Iran and prevent a costly and unnecessary war of choice." Furthermore: "Since the 2016 election, we have formed a pillar of the Resistance to Trump." Since its inception, MoveOn's members have played pivotal roles in resisting the administration's policies, including the repeal of the ACA and its family separation and child detention policies.

I am super proud to be the voice and face of this fantastic, progressive organization. Plus, it is a truly innovative organization with a "virtual office" approach; i.e., I don't have an endless commute to a downtown office. Instead, we all work remotely, connected by computer, phone, and video. It is so much more ecologically beneficial, not to mention eliminating the wear and tear on everyone's nerves that commuting creates. I beg bosses to consider the virtual office—there are so many benefits to your employees not to mention the planet. Plus, the organization that advocated for Obamacare provides excellent health and dental benefits as well as vacation time. They walk the walk.

Our core values are "equality, sustainability, justice, and love."

My main role at MoveOn is to get our voice heard. This usually means appearing on television or speaking at rallies. For a long time I was scared, scared, scared. Now I love it. Seriously. We're in such a fight. I think, *Yeah, I have this platform so I'm going to use it. I'm going to say what I have to say.* I speak for others, which inspires me.

Here is how I prepare for a TV spot. The producer sends me via email or text the topic to be discussed on the show ahead of time. They also tell me with whom I'll be appearing—you know, the other guests. Particularly when I was appearing on Fox, I would do extensive research on the other guests as well as the host so I would be ready to counter their arguments. I think that's why I was so successful. Once I joined MoveOn, I would communicate with our comms staff before an appearance to clarify what precisely is MoveOn's messaging on a particular topic. No surprise, I do an extensive amount of reading on the subject to be discussed.

The secret to being successful on TV? Know your material cold. I find preparing in advance is an important way to stay calm and appear confident on camera. You never want to be at a meeting or on camera with your mouth hanging open. Then bring your own personal experience to the topic. That makes the subject come alive to the viewer. Stories are what move people today, not statistics. Because I am a child of Haitian American immigrants and am a naturalized American citizen, I have a unique perspective to share on, say, immigration.

Finally, it is important to forget that millions of people might be watching you on TV. You really need to simply see being on TV as having a spirited conversation with your fellow guests. Otherwise, you can freeze up and become tongue-tied.

I admit it was pretty strange, if rather flattering, when people began to recognize me from my television appearances. Inevitably, this happens when I am racing through an airport with like five minutes to get through security or picking up my dry cleaning when I am wearing my sweats after a long, hot run. Just the most awkward moments you can imagine.

Although MoveOn started as an online organization, we also have a lot of nonvirtual events like rallies. I have found it sometimes harder to overcome my shyness and self-consciousness when speaking in front of a crowd than a cable TV camera. Speaking to a camera, no one's looking at you, so you just speak your mind. But with a live crowd, people can get up and leave. They can look at you as if they think you are crazy or like "I really love what she's saying." It's very different. More feedback, good and bad!

In my humble opinion, it's harder speaking to a crowd of people. No question. But wherever I am, I remind myself that I am representing people who don't have a voice in our society. Rather than seeing my speaking gigs as a burden I fear, I frame them as a privilege I should appreciate.

Let me return to Election Day 2016. Yes, *that* long day's journey into night. To keep my nerves steady as the jolting train headed north to Manhattan, I kept repeating to myself: Americans elected Obama twice; they are not going to vote for a racist, bankrupt birther who boasts about assaulting women.

Sigh.

I was going to New York City, because I was scheduled to appear on a number of cable shows to present MoveOn's progressive perspective as well as to offer some observations as a former Obama politico. I was charmed to learn that women were leaving their "I voted" stickers on the famous women's rights activist Susan B. Anthony's grave in Rochester, New York. As the mother of a young daughter, I did think it would be awesome for a woman to be president. At two years old, my daughter had known only a black president and I thought how wonderful it would be for her to now know a woman president.

Only on Election Day did I begin to truly sense, "Oh, this is real." Yes, I know, it felt like the two previous years had been consumed with Trump but, suddenly, the threat of his winning got very serious.

I expected to offer commentary when needed, particularly in the later hours on MSNBC after the election had been called, we all assumed, for HRC. I was taking down notes to formulate what I would be saying. I wanted to make sure that I was up-to-date with the latest news. I took the network-provided car service from the train station in Manhattan and made a stop at Mark Halperin and John Heilemann's show, *With All Due Respect*, which in 2016 aired on Bloomberg TV. After that, I headed over to MSNBC.

The network corridors were buzzing with Election Day excitement. In newsrooms around the country, there is no question: Election Day is the single biggest regularly scheduled event. And this election was unique. This was the final day of a two-year presidential circus that had consumed the country, if not the world. We all assumed, and I certainly hoped, that after tonight, the chants of "lock her up" and "Crooked Hillary" would subside.

I greeted the producers and bookers, brewed myself a cup of herbal tea in the green room, and chose a sesame seed bagel from the inevitable tray of sad-looking baked goods that sits in the corner of every green room I have ever visited. At this point, I was a rapt viewer of the TV screen overhead in the room. I kept alternating between the polls, Twitter on my phone, and that annoying but inescapable *New York Times* election needle.

At 7:05 p.m., the first state I remembered Donald Trump winning was Kentucky. It made sense since Kentucky was one of the few states that had a 7:00 p.m. (EST) poll-closing time. Kentucky, a state won by Bill Clinton twice in 1992 and 1996, moved to the Republican column in every presidential election thereafter. I stared at the television and thought, "Wow, Donald Trump actually just won eight electoral votes. This is going to be a long night." Then I heard Vermont was called for HRC and Trump took Indiana. While these outcomes were expected, to hear Donald Trump winning states was nauseating at best.

Things began to get dicey at 10:39 p.m. when Ohio was called for Trump. In 2012, the election had been called for Obama around 11:15 p.m. I began to feel my stomach tighten. Although I hadn't had much to eat other than the bagel and some cold cheese pizza, I had no appetite. I noticed that other people—staffers, interns, the on-air talent—had a certain wary look in their eyes.

None knew where this election was heading.

At 10:53 p.m., Florida was called for Trump, closely followed by North Carolina at 11:14 p.m. Suddenly, the unthinkable was happening. None of the commentators or newscasters were leaving their on-camera spots so I remained in the green room, glued to the TV.

When Pennsylvania was called for Trump at 1:35 a.m., I texted Suzanne. I felt a cold chill go down my spine as I thought about the country our sweet two-year-old would be growing up in—a little black girl with two moms. This was scary stuff.

By 2:30 a.m. when Wisconsin's ten electoral votes went to Trump, we all gasped as reality set in. Trump had been elected president even though three million more Americans had voted for his opponent. My friend Joy Reid was talking about how she wanted to move to London with her teenage children—that she didn't feel safe living here in the United States.

"We need you here more than we've ever needed you before," I remember saying to her that night. I didn't feel like crying, I felt like fighting back. The network put me in a car service. I was staying at the same hotel in Harlem where I always stayed when I went to New York City to do TV. I took solace in the familiarity, and the larger-than-life Harriet Tubman statue at the intersection of Frederick Douglass Boulevard, St. Nicholas Avenue, and 122nd Street, installed a few years after I left SIPA.

It reminded me that the country had overcome bigger problems than Donald Trump.

I returned from the hotel after a short power nap to give TV commentary in the wee hours of that desperate morning. At 3:45 a.m.—MSNBC; 4:00 a.m.—NBC *Early Today*; 5:35 a.m.—CNN. In my memory it's all a blur to me. Trump had blown through the supposedly impregnable blue wall of the traditional Midwest states to win the electoral college and take the presidency. *Now what?* asked a shaken nation and terrified world.

Between appearances on different shows that day, I called my mummy. To my surprise, she had paid rapt attention to the presidential election. That whole fall, she kept calling, begging me, "You have to keep Trump from winning!" Being a long-time New Yorker exposed to Trump's endless tabloid headlines over the decades, Mummy knew he was a blowhard, reality-TV star, not presidential timber. "He's not a good man, Ka!" she wailed into the phone.

My friends in politics were even more devastated than my mother. Some couldn't stop crying for weeks. Others investigated moving to another country. Some went on vacation for months, only returning in time for the Women's March in January. A few confessed to me that they had visited their doctors looking for antianxiety medications and antidepressants. Almost everyone felt that everything they thought they knew about their country had been upended. Even today many of them tell me that they still have to shake themselves, flabbergasted that Trump is actually president. Some tell me that Trump is the first thing they think about in the morning and the last thing at night.

I was shocked on Election Day 2016, but looking back, I am not surprised. We have a divided country. And there really were "secret Trump" voters who said one thing to pollsters, then pulled the lever for Trump in the voting booth. Now Democrats have to go back to the drawing board. Obama was a once-in-a-generation politician who was able to put together a coalition. We need to reassess. We can't lie down in despair, because now the fight begins.

Trump's election turned me into an engaged ball of energy. I didn't take a vacation for over eighteen months. I was on fire resisting Trump's agenda to divide us.

A particularly empowered moment came the day after Trump's inauguration. I was part of the broadcasting coverage of the Women's March in Washington, DC, appearing on various shows. The day before, I was part of PBS *NewsHour*'s special inauguration coverage, which had been depressing at best with Donald Trump talking about "American carnage." I don't usually agree with former president George W. Bush on any topic, but I, too, found Donald Trump's inauguration speech to be "some weird shit." I felt sad as I reflected on Obama's two joyous and hopeful inaugurations. And now this dark, scary occasion. That day, I felt truly down.

But twenty-four hours later, my spirits were lifted as I saw the crowds of women pouring out of Union Station in their bright pink hats heading to the National Mall. I felt truly hopeful. Men were there. Women were there. There were children in strollers, babies wrapped up and snuggled on their parents' chests. There were old women with white hair and teenagers with hair every hue of the rainbow. The posters and placards were by turns funny, sassy, outrageous, and moving.

I did television all day, and what struck me was how unexpected this turnout was. Yes, there had been a march planned, but this explosion of millions of women taking to the streets— no one predicted that. There were marches all over the world. Literally. People showed up in Antarctica.

It was a gray winter day with intermittent sun, but the marchers looked happy and determined. It was so crowded; lots of people couldn't hear the speakers or even move. Talk about a recipe for claustrophobia. Seeing those waves of women filled me with hope for our country. I later learned that every single state in the union was represented at the march. I spoke to a woman from Long Island who told me that January 21, 2017, was the first day she had felt happy since the night of November 8, 2016.

I knew *exactly* how she felt.

There have been terrible days since the Women's March. Charlottesville and the tragic murder of a beautiful young woman named Heather Heyer by a neo-Nazi deliberately driving his car into a crowd. The fear of nuclear annihilation during the days when Trump ranted about "fire and fury" being directed against North Korea. The attacks on health care protections, only averted at the last minute by one vote from Senator John McCain. The tax giveaway to corporations and the billionaire class. The list seems endless: the transgender military ban; the Brett Kavanaugh hearings, and the powerful, moving testimony from Dr. Christine Blasey Ford about how a drunken Kavanaugh attacked her in high school; the withdrawal from the Paris Agreement on climate change; Trump's attacks on the Department of Justice; the brutal killing and dismemberment of the *Washington Post*'s Jamal Khashoggi; the Helsinki press conference when Russian president Vladimir Putin literally dog-walked the American president as Trump sided with Putin, a former KGB agent, against his own intelligence people.

The apathy and cowardice of the Republicans in the House and the Senate giving the president free rein to destroy the traditions and norms that have maintained our republic for more than 230 years.

And yes, I took it very personally when Donald Trump referred to the beautiful country of my hardworking, honest parents—Haiti—as a "shithole."

But of all the moments, it is the separation of children at the US-Mexico border that affected me most. That one struck home with me. I can still remember my horror when I heard the audio tape of those children crying out for their mamis and papis. I kept thinking how I would have responded if, at age five when

I accompanied my parents on a flight from Paris, I was ripped from their arms by uniformed men speaking a language I did not understand. (When I arrived in the United States, I spoke only French.)

I envisioned how terrified I would have been, how desperate, how lonely, how confused. Then to be put in a steel cage with other children, to sleep on a cement floor, to rock myself to sleep under an aluminum heat blanket? I can tell you: I would have been permanently damaged and scarred by being taken away from my parents at that age.

I needed to go to the border and see what it was like for these children. I needed to bear witness to this injustice. Randi Weingarten, president of the American Federation of Teachers, gave me an opportunity.

I flew to El Paso, Texas, after a layover in Dallas, where I realized that the women really do have "big hair." El Paso, a flat city in West Texas right on the Rio Grande River, was not at all what I expected. It wasn't violent or chaotic. Many people cross back and forth to Juárez, the large Mexican city right across from El Paso. But it was hot—ninety-three degrees in June.

Weingarten brought together a diverse group of educators and civil, human rights, and faith leaders to protest and bear witness to the family separation policies and indefinite internment. I felt as if I had been called to offer up my platform and I did on behalf of MoveOn. We would go to the border and protest these inhumane actions taken by the Trump administration. We wanted to lend our voices to others. Like the people fleeing from violence, danger, gangs, and hunger in Central America, my parents had fled the brutal dictatorship of the Duvalier family and the grinding poverty of Haiti.

The day started off with a rally and press conference held outside the United States District Courthouse in El Paso, which is the place where family separation begins. Following the rally and press conference, we boarded a yellow bus and traveled to the Tornillo tent city, a detention facility, to deliver books, clothing, and others supplies to the children being held at the detention camp facility. We were not allowed into the detention center. We instead held a prayer vigil led by the interfaith clergy who traveled with us. I was able to meet and interview Dolores Huerta, an iconic labor leader and civil rights activist who had worked closely with Cesar Chavez to found the United Farm Workers. "Stop these inhumane policies," Huerta said. "We need legal counsel...so that we don't have three-year-old children—babies—trying to represent themselves in court."

Because I was broadcasting from El Paso, I was able to share what I was seeing and what I was hearing on the border about family separations. I felt I was making a real difference. I had been so inspired by Jacob Soboroff, who, along with Chris Hayes, both of MSNBC, has done so much to bring this story to the attention of the public. I was proud to do my part.

I felt that I brought a lot to the discussion. I was an immigrant, a person of color, and a mom. I was haunted by the idea that I lived in a country where government workers were willing to separate children from their parents and put them in cages. I kept thinking of how Suzanne and I would feel if our sweet, innocent, cherished Soleil, age four, was ripped from our arms. My heart literally breaks as I write these words. The idea that the Trump administration has lost track of these children and their parents is a blot on humanity that will live on long after Trump and his cronies have left office.

If there was ever American "carnage," this was it.

CHAPTER TEN

What I'm Fighting for—and How We Can Win

May 6, 2016. That's the day I felt my family dodged a bullet. Soleil, who was not yet two, was at daycare when my phone started to blow up. There was an active shooter at the shopping mall adjacent to the daycare facility. The emails from the head administrator were to let parents know that the center, with its brightly colored circular rugs and different stations for creative play, was on lockdown. It took a moment before I realized Soleil was safe. It was only by pure coincidence—blind luck—that my partner, Suzanne, and I had moved our daughter to a different, closer daycare. We were still on the email list that went out to parents whose children attended the daycare.

But it hardly mattered that Soleil was now several miles away from these unfolding events. My heart was pounding as though I had just competed in an 800-meter race—and taken first place. I could see the teachers' faces—all of them young women of color—and imagine their terrible fear as they raced at top speed to gather up the infants and toddlers in their care hoping, praying, that if they followed their well-rehearsed drills, they could keep these precious beings and themselves safe. All while projecting confidence and good cheer to their tiny, innocent charges that *everything was okay!*

I thought of Suzanne's and my friends and acquaintances— the mothers and fathers of these children. The police tell you not to come, the school tells you not to come, the administrators tell you not to come, but I had zero doubt that they were at that moment hurtling to the daycare center, panicked beyond all imagination, to see if their babies were safe.

The next email I got gave the all clear: the kids were fine. The teachers were fine. The gunman had been subdued—a mentally ill man with a history of public disturbances.

But I couldn't help myself. I put aside the exams I was grading for my Columbia students, postponed the grooming appointment I was going to make for our dog, Mardi, and sidestepped the whites I had planned to presoak in OxiClean before washing. I grabbed my car keys and ran to my car, only just remembering to slam the front door so Mardi didn't get loose.

I had to see Soleil, even though it was the middle of the afternoon and she usually stayed at daycare for another three hours.

I cradled Soleil's little head and buried my nose in her soft curls, a barrette in my eye. She was nonplussed by my unexpected appearance, more interested in a pink unicorn covered in glitter than in me as I worked hard to quiet the boiling cauldron of bright red rage I felt—mingled with overwhelming relief.

Even the 2012 slaughter of twenty elementary school children— all of them six or seven years old—and six adults at Sandy Hook Elementary School in Newtown, Connecticut, didn't change the gun laws in America. It was the worst day of Obama's presidency and according to his wife, Michelle, the only time he asked her to come to the Oval Office unexpectedly. "When I walked into the

Oval Office, Barack and I embraced silently," Michelle Obama wrote in *Becoming*. "There was nothing to say. No words."

Nothing has changed since that terrible day—December 14, 2012. Every single day, there's a new headline about innocent people taken from this earth because the National Rifle Association (NRA) owns senators and congress members.

You almost get used to it. But we can't allow that.

The gun maniacs definitely are not complacent. In fact, mass shootings sometimes lead to a spike in gun sales. This tends to happen when the Democrats—aka gun-safety folks—are in charge of national politics. I saw a CNN Money headline dating back to his presidency that read "Is Barack Obama the Best Gun Salesman in History?" There was no such fear on Valentine's Day in 2018 after the Parkland, Florida, shooting at Marjory Stoneman Douglas High School in which seventeen people died. With Republicans leading both the executive and legislative branches of the federal government, there was not a chance that a national restriction on gun sales would be passed by Congress and signed by the president. Meeting with Parkland survivors, Trump called not for fewer guns but *more*. He suggested fighting fire with fire— arming teachers in the classroom.

Of the 251,000 gun-related deaths worldwide in 2016, half occurred in just six countries. Because of NRA money pouring into Republican coffers, the United States ranked number two, just behind Brazil in number of fatalities. (Recently, two groups asked the Federal Election Commission to investigate whether Trump's 2016 campaign illegally coordinated its advertising strategy with the NRA. The gun lobby donated over $30 million to the Trump campaign, triple what it donated to Mitt Romney's presidential race four years earlier. There is also the mysterious connection between a red-headed Russian woman named Maria Butina and her connections to top NRA officials and Republicans.)

Thanks to the ready availability of firearms, more than twenty thousand people kill themselves with a gun each year. One statistic stuns me every time I see it. While it's the fatalities that grab the headlines, an estimated 100,000 Americans survive a gunshot injury every year. Many of these survivors are permanently disabled. It's hard to measure the cost—financially, emotionally—to themselves, their families, and society.

The trauma can persist. A year after the Parkland shooting, two teenagers who were students at Marjory Stoneman Douglas High School took their own lives. Survivor's guilt might have played a role, according to one of the suicide victims' families. The father of a Sandy Hook Elementary School shooting victim took his life more than six years later.

There is another, rarely mentioned consequence: the all-pervasive fear. I have a friend who, when she drops her teenagers off at middle school and high school every morning, utters a silent prayer that what happened at Marjory Stoneman Douglas High School will not happen to them that day. That the kids won't have to crouch under their desks in silence as they have practiced during countless active-shooter drills to keep from being the target of a real shooter. My friend struggles every day with this sense of dread. As do the children. For several weeks after the Parkland shooting, her twelve-year-old would come home from school talking about which teachers she thought would "take a bullet for students." This is NOT normal. Do we as a society have any idea of the emotional damage we may be inflicting on these vulnerable young psyches?

This same friend sent her son to camp in rural Vermont, thrilled that he could immerse himself in nature. For a month, he would be away from not just technology but all modern conveniences, including running water and wristwatches. Her reverie was smashed when her cell phone rang one afternoon in early July. It was the camp director calling to say that a man with an AR-15–style rifle had entered the camp and had become belligerent when he was asked to leave. The campers and counselors, some of whom were whittling or reading while others were up the mountain on a hike, had to be immediately evacuated. They were sequestered at another camp for nearly two weeks while the gunman remained at large before being caught. Many parents picked up their sons and brought them home. The remainder vainly tried to recapture the esprit de corps they had enjoyed before. "So much for Max getting away from it all," she told me, sighing. "But thank God everyone was okay. It could have been so, so, so much worse."

But saying prayers and seeing the bright side are not enough.

I'm fighting against the absolute insanity of how we approach guns in our country.

There are so many ideals I'm fighting for as well.

Because I am a dark-skinned Haitian American child of the working class. Because my parents are immigrants from a beautiful country derided by Donald Trump. I believe in justice and equality. I believe that the growing economic inequality between the 1 percent and everyone else is an existential threat to the survival of a country I love deeply. I know racism is alive and well and growing. I think health care is a human right, not a lottery that people play. It enrages me when I see folks having to raise money for their kids' cancer treatments on Kickstarter or GoFundMe. Although I have worked every day of my life at either a full-time or part-time job since I turned nineteen, I have gone without health insurance for years at a stretch because I just couldn't afford it. I always think of the first black woman elected to Congress in 1968, Shirley Chisholm, and her quote about health care: "We have never seen health as a right. It has been conceived as a privilege, available only to those who can afford it. This is the real reason the American health care system is in such a scandalous state."

And in so many ways, I am fighting for my family.

The 2008 Great Recession isn't something that happened

to other people. It happened to Mummy, who lost a house in Hempstead, Long Island, to a predatory tax lien.

Gone.

This was the modest, all-paid-for redbrick Colonial that my mother and father had worked years to buy—and that Mummy, who is in her sixties, planned to use for her retirement. She has worked two to three jobs a week—years of sixty-hour weeks— caring for senior citizens. Papi, now in his seventies, has driven a taxi for four decades, getting up at 4:00 a.m. so he can be in line early to pick up the first international travelers at JFK Airport. It's an exhausting life of waiting, driving, and hoping for good tips. Now Uber, Lyft, and Via are decimating his income.

For ten years—since the Great Recession in 2008—Mummy was underwater on the second house my parents bought in a better school district, in Wheatley Heights, after I left for the city and Columbia. She was a victim of a system that preys on people who don't understand how it works. The house finally sold in a short sale while I was writing this chapter.

Suzanne, Soleil, and I would be thrilled to have Mummy join us in Maryland, but living on the crust of a daughter's charity in a basement bedroom, far away from her friends and her church, is a hard place for a proud, self-sufficient woman to end up. I managed to save up enough money to buy her a small condo in Freeport, Long Island, New York, thirty minutes closer to the city than Wheatley Heights. The tremendous relief she said she felt after shouldering the financial strain for so long made my efforts to scrimp worth it. "I can't believe this is mine, and I don't have to worry about how to pay for it," she told my brother Chris when he drove her to see her new place.

So I'm not just thinking about the next ten, twenty, thirty, or forty years of my life, paying off my grad school loans and saving money for Soleil to go to college, I'm also thinking about the next decades, God willing, of Mummy's life. I am sandwiched between generations, as so many people are. I also feel guilty, because I used to go to meetings with Mummy to translate and read over documents before she signed them. But when I left for grad school, I started living my own life like an American daughter and stopped paying attention. I thought she had the situation in hand and then bad things started happening that I didn't know about and my mother couldn't understand. Do I blame my mother? Absolutely not. I blame a financial system that uses incomprehensible jargon and shady gimmicks to lure hardworking people into unsustainable money traps: mortgages with interest rates that no one tells you will one day skyrocket without warning, credit cards with massive hidden fees and interest charges. One of my heroes is Senator Elizabeth Warren of Massachusetts, who has dedicated her career to protecting the American consumer from the corporate predators who, in search of vast profits, are hollowing out the middle class and the working class. How utterly typical of Trump's attack on the 99 percent have been his efforts to destroy the Consumer Financial Protection Bureau established by Obama. "People feel like the system is rigged against them," says Warren. "And here's the painful part: they're right. The system is rigged."

I know in my heart that guilt about my mother losing her life savings and rental property is a useless emotion. The better thing to do is to channel it into action.

Most of all, I am fighting for Soleil to have her best chance in life. A real opportunity to grow up in a gun-free environment. A real opportunity to get a good college education that won't bankrupt her. Or us. A real opportunity to live a healthy, happy life without being impacted by racism or sexism. A real opportunity to fulfill her unique promise in this world. A real opportunity to live in a world that is not being decimated by climate breakdown or choked to death by pollution or poisoned by toxins like mercury and lead.

Today, Soleil is a thriving preschooler with large, expressive eyes, an infectious laugh, and a fixation on unicorns and the color purple. She will wear her Spider-Man pj's one night and her ballerina nightgown the next. She is impressively independent and fearless.

Even at her tender age, I already tell her that I am Haitian American. When she gets a little older, I'll tell her, a smile tugging the corners of my lips, that Haiti was the first country where enslaved people overthrew their colonizers to create the first ever independent country of freed people. I'm going to tell her how that independence, that strength, continues to run through our blood. I'm going to tell her, too, about the tough times my parents faced in Haiti. I'll tell her about how my mom, who lost her own mother, started working young— so, so young—because she was forced to fend for herself when she was still just a child. I'll tell her about how my parents eventually left Haiti, fleeing a dictatorship where their words were censored but their ambitions couldn't be. My daughter will hear about how my mom worked as a home health care aide here in the United States, my dad drove an NYC taxicab, and how they scraped by, never able to take a break, just so that I could catch mine. I'll tell her how that ethos of hard work, grit, and determination runs through our family.

It runs through our country, too.

Whenever I feel overwhelmed by the Trump presidency and Republicans, I think to myself that I am doing my job at MoveOn so that Soleil will have the good life that she, and every child, deserves.

Donald Trump's election in 2016 and the results of the 2018 midterm elections show that Soleil is growing up in a world that can feel truly chaotic and unpredictable. So much so that on the nights when I'm home and not appearing on TV, I even take my smartphone with me on Mardi's last backyard outing of the night so that I don't miss the latest news. It's crazy, but it can sometimes change *that* fast. This, by the way, is a case of doing what I say and not what I do! Because unless you're a news junkie like I am, it is critical to disconnect from technology especially in the last two hours before you go to bed so the blue light does not wreak havoc on your sleep. You need to focus on the people and activities that nurture your soul.

Besides that brief public service announcement (!), I want to take a step back and look at the larger US political trends underlying these minute-by-minute and tweet-by-tweet events. To give you a little context for how they fit in:

In the 1990s, about the same time that I became a naturalized American citizen, Republican and Democratic leaders could sometimes seem almost indistinguishable from one another. Sure, there were differences at the margins. Republicans tend to believe in smaller government except where it suits their purposes such as a larger military, and Democrats tend to believe in a more active government, which usually translates into a larger one. But twenty-five years ago, the leaders of both parties worked hard to cast themselves as moderates—the way, according to Gallup, that 50 percent of Americans identified themselves. The other half of the country was split between people who identified as conservative and those who identified as liberal. In the summer of 1992, Bill Clinton—who was running for president against the Republican incumbent, George H. W. Bush—criticized Jesse Jackson for including the rap artist and black activist Sister Souljah on a political panel. Talking about black gang violence in Los Angeles, she had earlier told the *Washington Post*, "If black people kill black people every day," she said, "why not have a week and kill white people?"

Clinton pointedly distanced his candidacy from the extremes in the Democratic Party, which Jackson represented, and sealed his place as a centrist. In political lore, Clinton's move became known as the "Sister Souljah Moment." As time went on, the Democratic Party moved so far to the center that calling someone a "liberal" became almost an insult.

Fast-forward to 2007. When I signed on with the John Edwards campaign, I didn't think this country was ready for a black president and maybe in hindsight it's true—we ended up first with the anti-government Tea Party movement, which pulled the Republican Party sharply to the right in 2016 with Donald Trump's brand of right-wing, white nationalism, which he launched by questioning Barack Obama's citizenship and his right to be president. (The US Constitution says that in order to run for president, a person must be a resident of the United States for fourteen years, be at least thirty-five years old, and be a "natural born citizen.")

The 2018 midterms show that today, candidates—and voters—on both the left and right have each gone to their respective corners. Vastly different from 1992, a recent Gallup poll found that 51 percent of Democrats now identify as "liberal." An example of an even bigger turn was the defeat of longtime New York congressman Joe Crowley by Alexandria Ocasio-Cortez in the 2018 New York Democratic primary for his seat in the US House of Representatives. At twenty-nine, she is the youngest woman ever elected to Congress. Ocasio-Cortez calls herself a "radical." She used her first weeks in Washington to highlight wealth inequality, among other issues, proposing a 70 percent marginal tax rate on income above the first ten million dollars. "Do we want to live in a city where billionaires have their own personal Uber helipads in the same city and same society as people who are working eighty-hour weeks and can't feed their kids?" she asked on *The Late Show* with Stephen Colbert.

I believe that labels are helpful only as signposts of the times. So I try to get away from them and get right to the issues that bring people together. Jon Favreau, Obama's chief speechwriter, put it succinctly in an interview with Axios. People "want ideas that are commensurate with the size of the challenges we're facing." I agree. That's why Medicare for All (a proposal in which all Americans could get health insurance through the government), affordable higher education, and affordable housing are gaining traction. We want policies that help everyone. We can't start leaving people out. Or as the late senator Paul Wellstone, a Democrat from Minnesota who died in a plane crash in 2002, put it, "We all do better when we all do better."

There's a knee-jerk reaction in the country these days that we have to worry about the white working class and appeal to them. But we simultaneously need to worry about blacks, Latinos—everyone. We need to be both inclusive and multi-racial. As I mentioned earlier in the book, when I was growing up, there were not white issues and Haitian American issues. My parents shared the same concerns as the parents of my white schoolmates on Long Island. When you're talking about afford-able housing, for example, it should not matter what color you are or where you're from.

While Republicans are increasingly stuck as the party of angry, older white men—they're not doing anything to reach out to other groups of people—I'm thrilled to see that the Dem-ocrats, who have been known as a "big tent party" for a long time, are moving the tent poles farther out to accommodate more and more people. This was evident in the 2018 midterm elections, when people who had never governed before raised their hands, and said, in effect, "I want to be part of making laws and making change." For example, the most Democratic women—ever—were elected to the House of Representatives in 2018. AOC has gotten a ton of press, but there were also two Native American women, Sharice Davids from Kansas and Deb Haaland from New Mexico, who were elected. Two Muslim women, Ilhan Abdullahi Omar from Minnesota and Rashida Tlaib from Michigan, were elected. For the first time in this country, if you're a Native American or a Muslim woman, you have representation now. You have someone who looks like you in the Capitol. And there are other gains. Jahana Hayes became the first black congresswoman from Connecticut. Ayanna Press-ley became the first black congresswoman from Massachusetts.

Joe Neguse, a first generation Eritrean American, became the first black representative in Congress from Colorado. We again have a woman Speaker of the House.

No one could have predicted such an enormous groundswell after Trump was elected in 2016. But the deep and urgent need to counter his divisive rhetoric and policies—in which his fellow Republicans have been complicit—is guiding the Democratic narrative and setting the path for the years ahead. This is important for women of all ages. It's important for young women. It's important for people of color. It's important for people of diverse religious faiths. It's important for Native Americans, who were the first people here and tend to be forgotten. This is huge!

When you say you want to go to Congress and you want to be part of change, you're also saying that you're not giving up on this country. You're saying, "We can be better than this." Many people are disenchanted with America, but these fresh new faces have signed on to write legislation that can really make America all it can be.

Going forward in the upcoming 2020 presidential primary, Democrats will have the biggest—and certainly the most diverse— field of candidates in modern American history. But we cannot just leave the fate of the country to these men and women who are entering the race. We are the ones that will decide the Democratic Party's future. We are the ones who have to pitch in and help the Democratic Party win in local, state, and national elections.

Winning elections requires the mobilized support of an activist base—the sort of base we're seeing so energized right now across the country. Where I work, at MoveOn, our millions of members form a big part of the Democratic Party's base. As we listen carefully to our members, we learn about their priorities and what motivates them. And it's not centrism or incrementalism. It's a bold progressive vision for our future. These people are not motivated by their wallets or pocketbooks. They are motivated by a sense of fairness.

There has never been a greater need for action than now. Donald Trump, Mike Pence, and the Republican Party are tearing down the safeguards for vulnerable people like my mummy and your mom, my papi and your dad, my Soleil and your child that President Obama and the Democratic Party put in place. Affordable health care. Laws against the predatory mortgages that triggered the 2008 recession. Protection for consumers against usurious credit card and payday loans. Donald Trump and the Republican Party are rolling back decades-old protections of clean air and clean water.

As Nancy Pelosi, the Speaker of the House of Representatives, says, "Organize, don't agonize!"

That is our challenge. Let's go make it happen!

★ ★ ★ ★ ★

RESOURCES

Political Basics and the Media Maze

When we say "politics," what do we really mean? Are we talking about government, political campaigns, issues like climate change, the democratic process, the left wing, the right wing, the news, people protesting, people voting? In short, yes, all of it. Politics is everything, and everything is political. And to be politically active, you need to be informed. So let's step back here and look at two aspects of politics that I believe are essential for progressives to pay particularly close attention to: voting rights and the media.

Let's start with voting. Personally, I believe there is a concerted effort among conservatives to corrupt the political system—something we witnessed in the 2018 absentee ballot scandal in the Ninth Congressional District of North Carolina. The outright fraud required new primaries and a new general election in 2019.

Bluntly, red states—i.e., Republican states—actively discourage people of color and young people from voting. It is crucial for the survival of our country that every eligible person registers to vote and votes in every election. I believe there is also a strong desire to keep American students—particularly students of color and from marginalized communities—ignorant of their rights. And ignorant of how their government works. I don't think it's a coincidence that the reddest, most conservative states like Mississippi, Alabama, Louisiana, and Oklahoma also have among the poorest educational outcomes in the nation.

To vote is, of course, to cast a ballot on Election Day. You, the voter, make a decision to vote for one of the candidates. But unfortunately, it's not quite that simple, because every state is not the same when it comes to voting. So I'll explain by using my home in Maryland as an example. In Maryland, you can register to vote online and in person anytime, and when you do, you can choose your party affiliation (if you choose to). I am a registered Democrat in the state. You may be asked if you want to register to vote when changing your address, applying for or renewing a driver's license, or registering to obtain health insurance through the Maryland Health Exchange.

In order to vote in Maryland—and in every state—you must be a US citizen. If you were born in the United States, you will have a birth certificate and are eligible to vote automatically. I can vote because I am a naturalized US citizen; i.e., although born in Martinique, I took the US citizenship test and passed. To register to vote in Maryland, you need to live in the state and be at least sixteen years old. (You have to be eighteen to actually vote but you can register early when you get your learner's permit.) You can't vote if you have been convicted of buying or selling votes, have been disqualified to vote by a court due to mental incompetency, or are currently incarcerated for a felony conviction. Once you are released from prison, you can vote, but you need to reregister to do so.

But like I said, different states have different laws. Vermont and Maine allow people to vote independent of their criminal record. In fact, in those states, voting is even allowed from prison. In the 2018 midterm election, Florida voters approved an amendment to the state constitution to give people with felony records who have completed their sentence the right to register to vote in Florida for the first time. (People convicted of murder or felony sexual offenses are not eligible.) Focused on race-neutral reforms and alternatives to incarceration, The Sentencing Project estimated that in 2016 nearly 1.5 million Floridians had completed felony sentences but could not vote— approximately 9.6 percent of the voting-age population. According to the group, the decision by Florida voters has put pressure on Kentucky and Iowa to change their laws. There are currently only three states—Kentucky, Iowa, and Virginia—that permanently disallow people with felony convictions to vote, barring intervention by that state's governor.

The way I see it, this push to restore voting rights to former felons puts the rest of us on notice, highlighting the extreme importance of voting. If you are not registered, put that at the very top of your to-do list. I'm serious. The easiest way to register is to Google "how to vote in your state," then follow the directions. Make sure you are on an official government website. Look for the .gov at the end of the web address. A Google search can lead you to a privately-owned website, as I discovered while writing this chapter!

A little primer on voter suppression: in a nutshell, it's any attempt to discourage or stop people who can legally vote from doing so. Sounds like a crazy idea in the world's leading democracy, doesn't it? But in every election across the United States, a range of tactics are used to make it difficult to vote. These include things like shutting down polling sites in some districts, or making the ones that are open have long lines that turn people off from voting. Or requiring voters to produce unnecessary documents that they might not have on hand when they show up to vote. Or even physically scaring people away from voting. That last one is, thankfully, illegal, but the other two measures I mention are perfectly legal in some states. In fact, they are backed by laws usually created by Republican legislatures who want to make it more inconvenient for some people—read: those from minority communities who tend to support Democrats—to vote. Many of these tactics have been struck down in courts, but others persist. They are often justified by claims that they counteract voter fraud—that is, people voting illegally—which has not been found to be a problem in this country. Our bigger problem is voter turnout, which in the United States is embarrassingly low. Only 61.4 percent of eligible voters cast ballots in the 2016 election. Where were the other 38.6 percent? We need laws to encourage, not *discourage*, more people from voting.

In Maryland, if you are a first-time voter, they may ask for voter identification. This means a Maryland driver's license or ID card; a student, employee, or military ID card; a US passport; or a current utility statement, bank account, or paycheck showing your name and address. These last documents should be dated within three months of Election Day.

But what works in Maryland may not work in Tennessee or Georgia or New Mexico or Nevada! Be alert, be prepared with your identification papers and forms, and be ready to fight like hell for your right as a citizen to participate in our democracy.

Bottom line: all the outrage on Twitter, all the angry Facebook posts, all the podcasts, all the anger about billionaires not paying taxes mean squat if you don't vote. In my opinion, Election Day should be a national holiday and early voting should be encouraged. But the fact that it is not is no excuse. You must become a voter to make your voice heard. And there is a downside to not registering to vote if you have even the slightest glimmer of political ambition. Meg Whitman, the former CEO of eBay, first registered to vote at age forty-six and only registered as a Republican in 2008. This omission became an issue during her unsuccessful 2010 run for governor of California, in which she spent an estimated $144 million of her own money, losing to Jerry Brown. Former Hewlett-Packard Company CEO Carly Fiorina, who also ran in 2010 as a Republican in California to become a US senator—and in 2016 as a Republican candidate for president—was lambasted in the press when it turned out that she, too, had a sporadic voting record at best. (Fiorina voted in six of fourteen elections in California since 2000. During the previous decade, she had lived in New Jersey *but never voted!*) If you ever want to run for office, make sure you are registered to vote and then establish a record of voting in every primary election, every general election, every midterm election, and every special election. Simply showing up to cast a vote for president every four years is not enough. (People who do vote but only sporadically are called "intermittent" or "low-frequency" voters.)

You know who are "high-frequency" voters? People who are over sixty-five! They stand ready every single election to defend their Medicare and Social Security benefits. Remember, their priorities may not include affordable college, stopping an environmental apocalypse, or keeping the ACA around.

As President Barack Obama pointed out at a 2018 rally for Stacey Abrams, a Democrat who ran a history-making campaign for governor in Georgia: "When words stop meaning anything, when people can just make stuff up and there's no consequences, democracy can't work. The only guardian of truth is you. You and your vote."

When you register to vote, you will need to make a decision about whether to join a political party. Today, the two major parties are the Democrats and the Republicans. (There are also third parties such as the Green Party, which nominated Jill Stein as its presidential candidate in 2016, and the Libertarian Party, which nominated Gary Johnson.) It is also possible to register as an independent, which means you are not identified with any political party. As of April 2019, Gallup found that 26 percent of Americans identified as Democrat, 27 percent identified as Republican, and 44 percent as independent. Vermont senator Bernie Sanders and Maine senator Angus King are both independents who caucus with the Democrats.

As you might suspect, I am not a Republican. I believe the Republican Party opposes economic equality and social justice. I think it is becoming a negative force in our society, and has caused far more problems than it has solved. Made up increasingly of older white men, it represents the interests of the very rich in America—people like the billionaire Koch brothers, Walmart's Walton family, and big corporations. It is also a party of climate change deniers and white nationalists. Republicans in Congress are eager to strip people of health care, be it Medicare (for people sixty-five and older), Medicaid (for low-income and disabled Americans), or the Affordable Care Act (ACA). Sometimes called Obamacare, the ACA allows people who don't get health insurance through their jobs to buy it from private insurance companies. Depending on your household income level, you can often get subsidies that make health insurance downright cheap.

Today, the Republican Party led by Donald Trump and Mike Pence is working to destroy the ACA. And to allow insurance companies to exclude coverage for preexisting conditions like heart disease, cancer, diabetes, depression—even acne. I suppose if you are independently wealthy and selfishly believe that all of life's blessings are reserved only for you and your family, then it makes sense to be a Republican. Let the little people die by the side of the road.

The alternative is the Democratic Party. Okay, it's far from perfect. But the Democratic Party has been a champion of regular working folks. Look at the New Deal during the 1930s, when America was trapped in the Great Depression and people were homeless and starving. Twelve thousand people lost their jobs every day, and the average family income plummeted 40 percent from $2,300 in 1929 to $1,500 in 1933. One detail that floored me: so many people in New York were starving that the African nation Cameroon sent $3.77 ($69.36 in today's dollars) in aid. It was the Democratic president Franklin Delano Roosevelt whose administration worked to put downtrodden Americans back to work. It was the Democrats who passed the Civil Rights Act in the 1960s, which helped African Americans and women to gain their rights. It was the Democrats who passed the legislation that created Social Security, Medicaid, Medicare, and the Affordable Care Act.

I remember reading Senator George McGovern's book *What It Means to Be a Democrat* when it first came out in 2011. McGovern, who ran unsuccessfully for the presidency in 1972 against Nixon, beautifully captured what I believe today: "Being a Democrat means having compassion for others. It means putting government to work to help the people who need it." He wrote forcefully about the need for good health care, an effective and affordable education system, the importance of keeping all neighborhoods safe and protecting the environment. He also urged us to stand up for all our fellow human beings—especially those "who have been kept down."

That is a good start!

THE MEDIA MAZE

When I was a little girl, I can remember my papi reading the *New York Daily News* and my mummy turning on the nightly news—first the local broadcast, then the national one—in our kitchen on Long Island as she cooked. In my civics classes in high school, we would read glossy news magazines like *Time, Newsweek,* and *U.S. News & World Report,* and heft the massive Sunday editions of the *New York Times.* A confession: I never liked the way the black ink would smear on my fingers after reading the newspaper. But I still have a book of clippings—now yellow and fragile—that I assembled from articles about the events I ran at Kellenberg.

Things have changed in terms of journalism and how the media covers politics today. I imagine there are young people reading this who have never read a print newspaper of any kind! It's not just a guess. A 2018 survey by the Pew Research Center has found that the physical newspaper is the preferred method of reading the news for just 7 percent of Americans. Even among the subgroup of people who prefer reading to watching or listening to the news, 63 percent turn to the web versus 17 percent who turn to newspapers. I know that the advent of the web and the birth of free classified websites like Craigslist carved away the advertising base of traditional print newspapers and news magazines. Before the internet and the invention of the twenty-four-hour news cycle, subscribers couldn't wait for their news-weekly of choice to land in the mailbox. Carefully reported and painstakingly fact-checked, they offered both a recap of the previous week's top events but also often broke new ground on what to focus on going forward. But these days, *Newsweek* and *U.S. News & World Report*—once mighty titans of journalism that shaped the opinions of millions upon millions of Americans and whose cover stories could form the national narrative—now exist only as websites. *Time* magazine, once the glory of the massive Time-Life publishing empire, is a shadow of itself and a whisper in terms of national clout.

Newspapers are no longer flush with grocery and department store ads or thick with job and apartment classifieds. (In the past, the Sunday *Los Angeles Times* was so heavy, newspaper carriers supposedly had to make sure it didn't crush small dogs as they flung the paper out of their car windows onto subscribers' lawns!) This means that they've been forced to downsize significantly, laying off hundreds of thousands of journalists in recent years. According to an article from the British newspaper the *Guardian*, newspaper jobs have declined catastrophically, from nearly 458,000 in 1990 to about 183,000 in 2016, a fall of almost 60 percent.

The world of traditional network TV no longer exists, either. Three nightly newscasts hosted by three powerful anchors no longer set the national agenda. Cable news has exploded, and viewers have a much wider selection to watch. This includes Fox News, which these days I call "State TV." The conservative network sets the agenda for the Trump administration and is devoted to disseminating misinformation and terrorizing senior citizens with tales of imaginary caravans filled with Islamic terrorists coming up from Honduras and Guatemala. It's instructive and fun sometimes to flip between Fox News and MSNBC or CNN—or even NBC, CBS, and ABC—and see the differences in what these outlets consider news and how they cover it. Sometimes what one outlet treats as a national emergency—the "caravan" of migrants making its way to the US border is a good example—others hardly cover at all.

One of the more important subjects not being taught in enough classrooms? Journalistic literacy. People simply read things on the web—Facebook, Twitter, websites—and assume the information is true. Gullible voters were told on Facebook, for example, that Pope Francis had endorsed Donald Trump for US president. Not! In the 2016 presidential election, the Russian government spread false news all over the web, particularly on Facebook and Twitter. With the rapidity and destruction of a raging, uncontrollable wildfire, misinformation spreads across the web, leaving destruction and despair in its wake. Think of all the crazy stories out there like Pizzagate and President Obama not being born in the United States. (Pizzagate was a false conspiracy tale that claimed a Comet Ping Pong pizza parlor in Washington, DC, was the site of a secret underground human trafficking/child sex abuse ring, involving senior members of the Clinton campaign. Things got serious when a North Carolina man drove up with his guns to "self-investigate" and shot off his AR-15–style rifle inside the restaurant. He was sentenced to four years in prison. Thank God he didn't kill or injure the staff and customers. More recently, a fire was set at Comet. A twenty-two-year-old California man was charged with arson.)

Bottom line: you need to be very careful in what you read and, more important, what you believe. Always vet the publication or source of what you are reading. (People over the age of sixty-five are particularly prone to believing and sharing false news. Hello, birthers like Donald Trump.) Some websites are set up to mimic legitimate news sources when, in reality, they are pushing a right-wing agenda. Other websites simply lure you deeper and deeper into stupidity. Seriously. I can't be the only person who has found themselves flicking through celebrity slideshows? This clickbait stuff is powerful, addictive...

And a total waste of time and brain cells.

But even with this healthy note of caution about what is legit and what isn't, if you are interested in politics, this is a golden age of choice. Thanks to the web, you can immerse yourself in what is going on around the world, in Washington, DC, at your own state capitol, and on the streets of your hometown. The internet is home to fantastic progressive organizations like my own MoveOn.org and Indivisible. Founded by four Hill staffers in 2016, Indivisible provides a citizens' guide to resisting the Trump agenda. You can find organizations to join, politicians to support, and causes to embrace. Below is a sampling of methods I employ to stay informed and engaged.

No question, Twitter is an incredible tool for following the news as it is made in real time. And, of course, to see people's responses to the news. I am on Twitter all the time and I warn you: it can be very addictive. Taking a break from Twitter—a mental health day or week here and there—is a good self-care habit to cultivate. (When I go on vacation with Suzanne and Soleil, we really try to practice good social media hygiene—i.e., putting limits on our use of Twitter. We want to set a good example for our daughter, who will, at some point, have her own phone...off in the far, far future!) It is also vitally important that you read the whole article rather than just the headline before you retweet something. Everyone wants to be fun and memorable on Twitter but remember that colleges, universities, and employers now review your tweets before admittance or an offer of a job. And they often monitor your tweets afterward as well.

Here are some of the important journalists I follow on Twitter:

Daniel Dale
@ddale8
Former Washington, DC, correspondent for the Canadian newspaper the *Toronto Star* and reporter for CNN. He has "made it [his] mission to fact-check every word Donald Trump utters as president." Dale is smart and relentless.

Mike DeBonis
@mikedebonis
Covers Congress for the *Washington Post*.

Eric Bradner
@ericbradner
National political reporter for CNN.

Heidi Przybyla
@HeidiNBC
NBC national political reporter.

Yashar Ali
@yashar
Contributor to *New York Magazine* and HuffPo.

Pete Williams
@PeteWilliamsNBC
NBC justice correspondent.

Ashley Parker
@AshleyRParker
White House reporter for the *Washington Post*.

Jonathan Lemire
@JonLemire
White House reporter for the Associated Press (AP). (Based in

more than one hundred countries, the AP provides news coverage to newspapers, websites, outlets, and TV stations around the world.)

Judd Legum
@JuddLegum
Writes the newsletter *Popular Information*.

Josh Dawsey
@jdawsey1
White House reporter for the *Washington Post*.

Jonathan Swan
@jonathanvswan
Reporter for Axios. Known for having deep sources within the Trump administration.

Jim Acosta
@Acosta
CNN's chief White House correspondent.

Eli Stokols
@EliStokols
White House correspondent for the *Los Angeles Times* and an MSNBC political analyst.

Kyle Griffin
@kylegriffin1
Producer for Lawrence O'Donnell's *The Last Word* on MSNBC.

Manu Raju
@mkraju
CNN senior congressional correspondent.

Yamiche Alcindor
@Yamiche
PBS NewsHour White House correspondent. (Born in Miami, Florida, she is a Haitian American like me.)

Katy Tur
@KatyTurNBC
MSNBC anchor. Tur's book, *Unbelievable*, about her time covering the 2016 Donald Trump presidential campaign, is an amazing read and offers an extraordinary view of Trump and his base.

Jennifer Epstein
@jeneps
White House reporter for Bloomberg.

Jesse Rodriguez
@JesseRodriguez
Director of Booking for MSNBC.

Jennifer Bendery
@jbendery
Senior politics reporter for HuffPo.

Robert Costa
@costareports
National political reporter for the *Washington Post*. Moderator of *Washington Week*. Political analyst for NBC and MSNBC.

Zeke Miller
@ZekeJMiller
White House reporter for the Associated Press.

Kasie Hunt
@Kasie
NBC Capitol Hill correspondent; host of *Kasie DC*.

Jake Sherman
@JakeSherman
Coauthor of online newsletter *Politico Playbook*. Coauthor of *The Hill to Die On: The Battle for Congress and the Future of Trump's America*.

Maggie Haberman
@maggieNYT
White House correspondent for the *New York Times*; CNN analyst.

Philip Rucker
@PhilipRucker
White House bureau chief at the *Washington Post*; political analyst for NBC and MSNBC.

Dave Weigel
@daveweigel
Covers politics for the *Washington Post*.

Jeff Zeleny
@jeffzeleny
CNN senior White House correspondent.

Brian Stelter
@brianstelter
Anchor of *Reliable Sources* and CNN's chief media correspondent.

Sam Stein
@samstein
The Daily Beast and MSNBC contributor.

Jonathan Martin
@jmartNYT
National political correspondent for the *New York Times*.

Jake Tapper
@jaketapper
CNN anchor of *The Lead with Jake Tapper* and *State of the Union*. Author of several books and a novel.

Jamil Smith
@JamilSmith
Senior writer at *Rolling Stone*.

Dave Wasserman
@Redistrict
US house editor of the nonpartisan *Cook Political Report*; NBC News contributor. (*Nonpartisan* means that the publication favors neither Democrats nor Republicans.)

Joy Reid
@JoyAnnReid
Host of MSNBC's *AM Joy* and author of *Fracture: Barack Obama, the Clintons, and the Racial Divide* and *We Are the Change We Seek: The Speeches of Barack Obama*. She is also a dear friend.

David Axelrod
@davidaxelrod
Director of the University of Chicago Institute of Politics; senior political commentator, CNN; and the political strategist who helped guide Obama to victory. His book, *Believer*, about his forty years in politics, is invaluable.

Lawrence O'Donnell
@Lawrence
Host of MSNBC's *The Last Word*.

Chris Hayes
@chrislhayes
Host of MSNBC's *All In with Chris Hayes*.

Rachel Maddow
@maddow
Host of MSNBC's *The Rachel Maddow Show.*

Nicolle Wallace
@NicolleDWallace
Host of MSNBC's *Deadline: White House.* A former staffer for President George W. Bush and Senator John McCain, Wallace is a former Republican who brings a fresh, bracing perspective and enormous insight to the Trump administration. She is also a lovely human being!

Alex Burns
@alexburnsNYT
New York Times national political correspondent.

Eugene Scott
@Eugene_Scott
Washington Post political reporter.

Jason Johnson
@DrJasonJohnson
Politics editor for *The Root.*

Darren Sands
@darrensands
Politics reporter for BuzzFeed News.

Errin Whack
@emarvelous
Associated Press national reporter.

Maria Hinojosa
@Maria_Hinojosa
Anchor for *Latino USA.*

Michael Schmidt
@nytmike
New York Times reporter.

Shawna Thomas
@Shawna
Vice News DC bureau chief.

Alexi McCammond
@alexi
Axios reporter.

Geoff Bennett
@GeoffRBennett
NBC News White House correspondent.

Stephanie Ruhle
@SRuhle
MSNBC Live anchor.

Ali Velshi
@AliVelshi
MSNBC Live anchor.

Mariana Atencio
@marianatencio
MSNBC correspondent.

Jacob Soboroff
@jacobsoboroff
MSNBC correspondent.

Nia-Malika Henderson
@niaCNN
CNN senior political reporter.

Juana Summers
@jmsummers
AP national political reporter.

Suzanne Malveaux
@SuzanneMalveaux
CNN national political correspondent and anchor.

April Ryan
@AprilDRyan
White House correspondent and Washington bureau chief, American Urban Radio Networks.

GENERAL UPDATES

So the alarm goes off and another day dawns. Because Suzanne reports very early to CNN each morning—i.e., like 3:30 a.m.—I am in charge of getting Soleil off to daycare. It is a good thing I also like to get up at daybreak! After the hustle and bustle of getting our daughter dressed and fed, packing her lunch, finding her missing stuffed toy of the week, and dropping her off with a quick kiss at daycare, I drive back home listening to NPR.

I am really lucky that I work from home for MoveOn.org. I turn on MSNBC or CNN and scan various websites so I am fully up-to-date in terms of what is happening in the news. Let's face it: it is practically a full-time job to keep track of Trump's demented tweets.

Here are the sites and online newsletters I check constantly:

- Politico.com: *Politico* also has a magazine and a newspaper.
- Axios.com: The name means *worthy* in Greek. Crisp, short, well-reported news items.
- *The Daily 202*: This is a must-read from the *Washington Post*.
- The Beat DC: This website focuses on "the intersection of politics, policy, and people of color."

- Yahoo News: This provides a general news roundup as well as Michael Isikoff's investigative reporting.
- The *New York Times*: One of the most storied newspapers in the world.
- The *Washington Post*: For my money, the one indispensable publication you must read if you are interested in American politics. It is often written in a more lively and accessible manner than the *New York Times*.

A personal note: It is very important for you, the citizen, to actively support good journalism and the people who create it. And when I say *support*, I mean financially. You should buy a monthly subscription to a newspaper app. It's not right that people read the news but don't consider buying a subscription. I have a subscription to the *New York Times* that is billed automatically at $14.99 a month and a basic subscription to the *Washington Post* at $9.99. I believe there are often specials and deals for students. Really, this is serious. A free press is crucial to our democracy.

Or as Alexandria Ocasio-Cortez—aka AOC—tweeted in January 2018: Healthy democracy *requires* high-quality journalism. W/o a wide range of independent outlets & the revenue to sustain them, our democracy will continue to crumble.

- The *Wall Street Journal*: Owned by the Australian media billionaire Rupert Murdoch, the man who gave us Fox News. Ugh. His newspaper is the must-read for the financial crowd. Its opinion page skews very hard to the right. Read it so you know what the enemy is up to. When the *WSJ* criticizes Donald Trump, take notice.
- CNN.com: Founded in 1980 by Ted Turner, CNN was the first television channel to offer twenty-four-hour news coverage. I'm not sure there is a hotel room in the world where some edition of CNN isn't playing.

Another word to the wise: it is important to read and watch both news stories and commentary. News stories answer the traditional "who, what, when, where, and why" questions. Commentary—often categorized as opinion, editorial, op-ed—presents an explanation and analysis of what happened. It is important to absorb both. For example, both the *Washington Post* and the *New York Times* feature liberal and conservative writers. With the *New York Times*, these would be Michelle Goldberg—progressive—and Bret Stephens—conservative. With the *Washington Post*, the liberal writer would be E.J. Dionne Jr. and the conservative would be Marc Thiessen.

Because I am an MSNBC political analyst, I do watch a lot of television. Here are my thoughts about who to watch on television today. Or on your phone, your tablet, or your computer.

First, I recommend any and all of the following programs on MSNBC:

The Rachel Maddow Show: Maddow has a devoted and huge following. For many viewers, her ability to break down an issue or a news event in her opening is jaw-droppingly amazing. She also puts the day's news into historical context. Highly recommended. (Also of interest: Maddow's podcast about Spiro Agnew, called *Bag Man*. Turns out, corruption didn't start with Donald Trump. Forty-five years ago, envelopes of cash were being dropped off in the White House for Vice President Spiro Agnew, the former governor of Maryland who was Richard Nixon's running mate.)

The Last Word with Lawrence O'Donnell: Airs every night after Rachel. I love the first ten minutes of his monologues. I always learn something new.

Deadline: White House: With her effervescent laugh, keen questions, and experience working for President George W. Bush and Senator John McCain, former Republican Nicolle Wallace brings a fresh perspective on the Trump White House and just how abnormally it behaves.

AM Joy: My weekends *always* include *AM Joy.* Joy Reid is whip smart and her feisty commentary provides some of the best political insights around.

All In with Chris Hayes: Chris Hayes is a lively rising star in political coverage. Hayes is also an author. His books include *A Colony in a Nation*, about our unequal criminal justice system.

Hardball: Hosted by the voluble veteran Chris Matthews. He knows his stuff and gets terrific guests.

Velshi & Ruhle: Hosted by Ali Velshi and Stephanie Ruhle—they make a great team. Worth watching for an in-depth understanding of the economy and how that ties into politics.

Live with Katy Tur: For an astute take on the mind-set of Donald Trump and his supporters. Tur followed his 2016 campaign for more than a year and was a constant target of Trump's.

Morning Joe: A must-watch morning show that virtually everyone in politics, government, and the media starts their days with. Host Joe Scarborough is a former Republican congressman from Florida who is married to cohost Mika Brzezinski, a TV journalist who is the daughter of President Jimmy Carter's national security advisor, Zbigniew Brzezinski.

MTP Daily: Hosted by Chuck Todd, who is my favorite person to watch during election season. MTP stands for *Meet the Press*, which is a long-running Sunday morning show that Chuck also hosts.

Shows to watch on other networks:

The Lead with Jake Tapper, **CNN:** Anchor Jake Tapper provides a deep dive into national politics and the big issues of the day. Tapper also hosts the Sunday show *State of the Union.*

Washington Week, **PBS:** Hosted by the *Washington Post*'s Robert Costa. On the air since 1967, this roundtable show featuring journalists presenting a roundup of the news out of Washington, DC, is a refreshing change from the partisan wrangling you see on some of the other political shows.

PBS NewsHour, **PBS:** Straight news with no bells and whistles. Broadcast seven nights a week, this daily evening news program is known for its in-depth reporting. Hosted by Judy Woodruff, the program grew out of its coverage of the United States Senate Watergate hearing in 1973.

(The Watergate scandal would lead to President Richard Nixon announcing on August 8, 1974, that he would resign as president of the United States. His vice president Gerald Ford succeeded him.)

Die-hard political junkies have long tuned in Sunday mornings for their most satisfying fix. That's when a few of the best political talk shows air, including:

State of the Union, **CNN:** Hosted by CNN's chief Washington correspondent, Jake Tapper.

This Week, **ABC:** Hosted by former Clinton White House staffer George Stephanopoulos.

Face the Nation, **CBS:** Hosted by Margaret Brennan, former White House correspondent.

Meet the Press, **NBC:** Hosted by the tireless Chuck Todd.

For commentary, especially around the Trump presidency, I pay special attention to these people who appear regularly on the major news networks:

Norm Eisen: Senior fellow at the Brookings Institution, a Washington, DC, think tank and research center, who served as Obama's "Ethics Czar" from 2009–2011 and US ambassador to the Czech Republic 2011–2014.

Joyce Vance: A former Obama-appointed US attorney for the Northern District of Alabama from 2009 to 2017 who gives terrific commentary about the legal system.

Shaun King: A civil rights activist and writer who covers the Black Lives Matter movement. In 2018 he relaunched the *North Star*, the publication that the famous abolitionist Frederick Douglass founded in 1847.

Timothy O'Brien: Executive editor of *Bloomberg Opinion* and the author of *TrumpNation: The Art of Being the Donald*.

Natasha Bertrand: National security correspondent for *Politico*.

Jamil Smith: A journalist who covers just about everything involving politics and culture. He's currently a senior writer at *Rolling Stone* magazine, but has also worked in TV journalism for years, including as a producer on *The Rachel Maddow Show*.

Ari Berman: Journalist who wrote *Give Us the Ballot: The Modern Struggle for Voting Rights in America* (2015)—a must-read for anyone interested in defending their right to vote.

Michael D'Antonio: Pulitzer Prize–winning journalist and CNN commentator who wrote a biography of Donald Trump in 2015 titled *Never Enough* and a book about the Obama presidency in 2017.

Shannon Watts: Founder of Moms Demand Action, a group of American mothers fighting for gun regulations and public safety.

Sherrilyn Ifill: A law professor and president of the NAACP Legal Defense Fund. She is the cousin of one of my heroes, the late Gwen Ifill, who hosted *PBS NewsHour.*

Malcolm Nance: A former navy officer who comments on US intelligence and terrorism. Published two excellent books: *Defeating ISIS: Who They Are, How They Fight, What They Believe* and *The Plot to Hack America.*

Maya Wiley: A civil rights lawyer and activist who formerly served as board chair of the NYC Civilian Complaint Review Board that oversees policing in New York.

Jill Wine-Banks: A lawyer who served as one of the prosecutors during the Watergate scandal of the early 1970s that brought down President Nixon. She has a lot to offer in terms of commenting on Special Counsel Robert Mueller's investigation into the Trump campaign's ties to Russia.

TV SHOWS

The past couple decades have witnessed some excellent political television—both comedies and dramas. Here are a few of my favorite shows:

The West Wing **(1999–2006):** Portrays the White House of a fictional Democratic president. I watched this show religiously when I was working for John Edwards.

Veep **(2012–2019):** Pure political satire with the hilarious Julia Louis-Dreyfus as the vice president and then, in later seasons, president.

House of Cards **(2013–2018):** Political drama/thriller. Dark and addictive. Gives you a sinister view into Washington politics.

The Thick of It **(2005–2012):** Brilliant British comedy series that parodies the UK government. It was created by Armando Iannucci, the same writer who later created *Veep*.

The Simpsons—**"Don't Blame Me. I Voted for Kodos" episode (1996):** I know, *The Simpsons*? This episode is a clever parody of the 1996 presidential election between then president Bill Clinton and Republican nominee Bob Dole. The title of the episode has served as a perennial metaphor for our divided political system.

MOVIES

And of course, there are plenty of movies—both classic and contemporary—that depict the behind-the-scenes intrigues of American political life. Here are a few notable ones:

***Mr. Smith Goes to Washington* (1939):** A very old movie that still feels relevant. Jimmy Stewart plays a freshman US senator who attempts to fight corrupt politics in Washington.

***The Manchurian Candidate* (1962):** Truly a must-see Cold War classic about an American Korean War veteran (played by Frank Sinatra) who is brainwashed by the Communists and then gets involved in an international conspiracy to take over the US government. The movie was remade and updated in 2004, starring Denzel Washington.

***The Candidate* (1972):** Another film that feels particularly appropriate these days. Robert Redford plays a decent guy who is dragged into the dirt of politics when he agrees to run as a Senate candidate in California.

The American President (1995): Who doesn't love a political romance? This now-classic film features Michael Douglas as the widowed president who falls in love with an environmental lobbyist played by Annette Bening.

In the Loop (2009): This is the film spin-off of the British TV series *The Thick of It*. Very funny political satire that portrays the British and American political machinations around the 2003 invasion of Iraq. *The Sopranos* star James Gandolfini plays an American general.

Game Change (2012): Dramatizes Republican presidential candidate John McCain's decision to select Alaska governor Sarah Palin to be his running mate in 2008. Palin, who was woefully ignorant of history as well as current events, domestic and foreign, would in turn pave the way for Donald Trump's pugnacious populism. (The HBO movie is based on the book of the same name written by John Heilemann and Mark Halperin.)

The War Room (1993): A go-to political documentary for young politicos. This documentary film gives an inside look at Bill Clinton's 1992 presidential election.

Race (1998): An insightful movie about interracial campaigns in mid-1990s in Los Angeles. The film examines two candidates (played by a talented multiracial cast) running for an open city council seat that becomes enveloped in violence and mudslinging.

Street Fight (2005): Another must-see political documentary. A thrilling film that chronicles the 2002 mayoral race in Newark, New Jersey. The film introduces a young attorney and challenger (now US senator and Democratic presidential candidate Cory Booker) who takes on the powerful political machine of the sixteen-year incumbent, James Sharpe.

Election **(1999):** A Reese Witherspoon movie that is really good for political science. A comedy that follows a high school election and the dark side of politics.

The Special Relationship **(2010):** A really good movie about President Bill Clinton's over-twenty-year relationship with British Prime Minister Tony Blair. The film primarily focuses on elections and internal relationships.

Mitt **(2014):** It's difficult to find documentaries on candidates that lost. This Netflix documentary shows the impact of campaigns on people at the presidential level by chronicling Mitt Romney's presidential bid from Christmas 2006 to his 2012 concession speech to President Barack Obama.

BOOKS

Just as the Trump administration has reinvigorated print and TV journalism, so has it fueled an incredible explosion in terms of book publishing. Here are just a few of the insightful books about politics and Trump that have appeared in the last few years.

Fear: Trump in the White House by Bob Woodward. Boy, this one left me shaken. Written by the famous *Washington Post* journalist who, along with Carl Bernstein, broke open the Watergate scandal, Bob Woodward really fleshes out how inept and unprepared the Trump administration is, particularly in terms of handling any sort of crisis. Woodward has covered eight presidents—from Nixon through Obama.

Everything Trump Touches Dies by Rick Wilson. Hard to believe in these perilous times, but this book had me screaming with laughter. Rick Wilson is a scorched-earth conservative and Republican operative. He is also a die-hard Never Trumper who believes that Trump is destroying the Republican Party Wilson has loved and served for decades. Wickedly funny and observant, Wilson is worth reading.

Hacks: The Inside Story of the Break-Ins and Breakdowns That Put Donald Trump in the White House by Donna Brazile. Bighearted, opinionated, colorful, Donna Brazile is a national treasure. Long a leader in Democratic politics, the New Orleans–reared Brazile headed up Al Gore's unsuccessful 2000 campaign for the presidency, making history as the first woman to take on that role. Brazile also served as chairperson of the Democratic National Committee. You've probably seen Brazile on TV—she's the dazzling black politico with the colorful hair. This book reveals the terrifying run-up to the 2016 election when the DNC computer systems were hacked by the Russians. Riveting about how presidential campaigns really work.

The Politician: An Insider's Account of John Edwards's Pursuit of the Presidency and the Scandal that Brought Him Down by Andrew Young. There's an undeniable dark side to politics. I'm not just talking about "dialing for dollars," which every pol has to do—i.e., cold-call friends, family, and yeah, strangers, to ask for money. No, this tell-all by a close aide to former North Carolina senator and vice presidential candidate John Edwards is more Shakespearean tragedy.

Seriously.

Young ends up selling his credibility and his self-respect in service to electing a politician he increasingly realizes has massive flaws. But the chance to advance—sheer ambition—is irresistible until it all ends in disaster, shame, and a *National Enquirer* front-page scandal.

Believer: My Forty Years in Politics by David Axelrod. This is a much more inspiring book about politics, believe me! Obama's strategist shares his life story, starting with the moment his family's housekeeper popped Axelrod—age five—on top of a mail-box in New York City in 1960 so the child could see John F. Kennedy campaigning for president. Axelrod fell in love with the political life right there. He would go on to work as a po-litical reporter in Chicago, then switch to being a political con-sultant. He has worked with luminaries such as Illinois senator Paul Simon—famous for his liberal values and bow ties—and Massachusetts's first African American governor, Deval Patrick. Most famously, Axelrod helped guide the career of his fellow Chicagoan Barack Obama, culminating in Obama's two terms as president of the United States.

Believer is excellent in the way it explains how important tell-ing a coherent story to voters has become as well as the signifi-cant role government plays in helping people. It is also a portrait of the deep friendship between Obama and Axelrod.

Of particular note: Axelrod captures the deep toll his politi-cal career took on his wife and his children, one of whom has severe epilepsy.

The Shadow President: The Truth about Mike Pence by Michael D'Antonio and Peter Eisner. This well-researched and detailed book probes the man behind the genial political face of the vice president. Pence is ruthlessly ambitious.

Finding My Voice: My Journey to the West Wing and the Path Forward by Valerie Jarrett. In *Finding My Voice* Valerie Jarrett tells a story that is unique to her fascinating life and, in some ways, a universal American tale. As she overcame racism and sexism she leveraged her advantages on behalf of others. Set in places as varied as Chicago, Tehran, and the White House, this book will take you on a journey that you'll never forget.

Lead from the Outside: How to Build Your Future and Make Real Change by Stacey Abrams. A national political leader, author, serial entrepreneur and nonprofit CEO, Abrams served in the Georgia House of Representatives for eleven years and as minority leader for seven years. In 2018 Abrams was the nominee for governor of Georgia, becoming the first black woman to become the gubernatorial nominee for a major party in the United States. This book serves as a guide for women, people of color, millennials, members of the working class, and members of the LGBTQ+ community on how to garner power to make real change. Abrams leans in on her impressive career, sharing with readers how to use their skills and experience to lead from the outside.

And finally, I urge everyone to reacquaint themselves with the famous English author George Orwell, who has in these strange times made quite a comeback in classrooms and book groups. Orwell wrote *Animal Farm* (1945)—a political fable about how the brutal ruler of the USSR, Joseph Stalin, betrayed the 1917 Russian Revolution. He also wrote *1984* (1949). Set in a totalitarian future, the novel introduced famous phrases such as *Big Brother is watching you*, *newspeak*, and *doublethink*. Even now—*especially* now—Orwell gives us insight into what is at stake when our democracy is under attack.

ACKNOWLEDGMENTS

I am grateful to Peter Joseph, my editor at Hanover Square Press, for believing in this project and taking a chance on a new author. I would also like to thank Natalie Hallak for her many editorial insights. The team at Hanover Square Press could not have been more encouraging and professional. I am truly lucky to have Erin Craig, Shara Alexander, Lynette Kim, and Tracy Wilson helping me, as well as Lydia Carey, with her research skills.

Michael D'Antonio, a gifted journalist and good friend, has been my guide throughout the publishing process.

My friends have been an incredible source of support. They include Ellyce Anapolsky, JP Austin, Maggie Austin, Ken Bennett, Tyclie Blunt and family, Brian Bond, Wally Brewster, Khephra Burns, Dexter Clarke, Monique Dorsainvil, Yodit Girma, Christina Greer, Mohammed Hadi, Lillian Harris, Katie Ingebretson, Sam Jean, Jeffrey Lerner, Luis Miranda, Ellen Qualls, Oscar Ramirez, the Ringgold family, Stacey Samuel, Bob Satawake, Paul Simon, Terrance Stroud, Susan L. Taylor, and Laurel Wright George.

I would also like to thank Anderson Cooper, Chris Hayes, Lawrence O'Donnell, Joy Reid, Jake Tapper, Nicolle Wallace, and Judy Woodruff, as well as Stacey Abrams, David Axelrod, Michelle Cumbo, Edwidge Danticat, EJ Dionne, Lynda Hamilton, James Holmes, Stephanie Kotuby, Valerie Jarrett, Sara Just, Minyon Moore, and Stacey Samuel. A big MoveOn shout-out to Anna Galland, Ilya Sheyman, and Nick Berning.

Many people have graciously opened doors for me. Among them: Carol Banks, Jennifer O'Malley Dillon, former New York City mayor N. David Dinkins, Ester Fuchs, Patrick Gaspard, Veronica King, Dale Mann, David Medina, Sarah Meyland, Charol Shakeshaft, Basil Smikle, and Leslie Voltaire.

I can never fully express my gratitude and love for my parents, Elaine Antoine and Jean Christopher Jean-Pierre, Sr.; my siblings, Edwine Jean-Pierre and Jean Christopher Jean-Pierre, Jr.; and my extended family, including Vonnette Angerville and Frantzy Pierre, as well as the Malveaux family. I especially want to thank my mother for having the courage and generosity to share her story in this book.

Most of all, I want to say that every word of this book was written with love for my partner, Suzanne Malveaux, and our daughter, Soleil Malveaux Jean-Pierre. You are my life.

INDEX